Mediation and Children's Reading

Studies in Text and Print Culture

General Editor: Sandro Jung, Shanghai University of Finance and Economics

This series focuses on up-to-date, text-specific, and text-theoretical approaches to the literature and culture of Britain, Europe, and America from the fifteenth to the mid-nineteenth centuries. It publishes innovative scholarship that promotes an understanding of literature as closely related to, and informed by, other discursive forms, especially the multifarious visual cultures of a given time.

Advisory Board:

Anne Marie Hagen, *Mediation and Children's Reading: Relationships, Intervention, and Organization from the Eighteenth-Century to the Present*

Michael Wood and Sandro Jung, *Anglo-German Dramatic and Poetic Encounters: Perspectives on Exchange in the Sattelzeit*

Sandro Jung, *James Thomson's* The Seasons, *Print Culture, and Visual Interpretation, 1730–1842*

Betsy Bowden, *The Wife of Bath in Afterlife: Ballads to Blake*

Michael Edson, *Annotation in Eighteenth-Century Poetry*

Sandro Jung, *The Publishing and Marketing of Illustrated Literature in Scotland, 1760–1825*

Herbet Gottfried, *Erie Railway Tourist, 1854–1886: Transporting Visual Culture*

Sandro Jung and Kwinten Van De Walle, *The Genres of Thomson's The Seasons*

Mediation and Children's Reading

Relationships, Intervention, and Organization from the Eighteenth Century to the Present

Edited by
Anne Marie Hagen

LEHIGH UNIVERSITY PRESS

Bethlehem

Published by Lehigh University Press
Copublished by The Rowman & Littlefield Publishing Group, Inc.
4501 Forbes Boulevard, Suite 200, Lanham, Maryland 20706
www.rowman.com

86-90 Paul Street, London EC2A 4NE, United Kingdom

British Library Cataloguing in Publication Information Available

Library of Congress Cataloging-in-Publication Data Available

ISBN 9781611463262 (cloth: alk. paper) |
ISBN 9781611463279 (electronic)

♾™ The paper used in this publication meets the minimum requirements of American
National Standard for Information Sciences—Permanence of Paper for Printed Library
Materials, ANSI/NISO Z39.48-1992.

Contents

Introduction

Mediation: An Interdisciplinary Approach to Studying Reading

Anne Marie Hagen

"Books are founders of families as well as men," the author and critic Anne Mozley proclaimed in 1870, arguing that childhood reading lays the foundation for the child's future.[1] Published in *Blackwood's Edinburgh Magazine*, her essay "On Fiction as an Educator" contains typical arguments about the cognitive, emotional, and educational benefits of childhood reading as well as the cultural value of internalizing an appreciation for books. By the late nineteenth century, the Romantic image of the "primitive" child close to nature had merged with evolutionary theories and established the narrative of the child reader on a developmental trajectory from a primitive reader into a discerning, accomplished reader who had attained culture and knowledge.[2] Still, for all the benefits of reading, misgivings circulate about the power of texts to negatively affect readers.

"If good [books] be not provided, evil will be only too easily found, and it is absolutely necessary to raise the taste so as to lead to a voluntary avoidance of the profane and disgusting," Mozley's contemporary, the British children's book author Charlotte Mary Yonge, warned.[3] In the eighteenth and nineteenth centuries apprehensions about the reading habits of children and adolescent men and women proliferated; the how, where, why, and what so-called impressionable categories of readers read were of great societal concern. Those most at risk were those thought to be unsophisticated and inexperienced readers without the ability to separate fiction and reality and prone to read to excess: the working classes, female readers, and the young.

With the rise of mass publishing and the emergence of national education systems, which increased general literacy, such concerns spread. The medical profession's reservations about the possible damage to the health of female readers are well documented; prominent physicians argued that academic reading could affect a girl's fertility and thus her ability to fulfill her most

1

important societal function as a future wife and mother.[4] However, a strand of the gendered moral narrative of reading dangers also affected young male readers, who it was thought could become politically anarchized, criminal, or sexually deviant.[5] Concerned professionals investigated whether formal education caused "overpressure" or strain on young brains and nervous systems, particularly in girls and working-class children.[6] Children's reading was thus implicated in the specters of physical, moral, and social degeneration in the debates on the future of the nation at the turn of the twentieth century.[7]

Nor are such tensions wholly confined to the past. Historically, the emergence of any new media or textualities and associated changing reading patterns have triggered concern about what these changes entail for children and reading as well as for the idea of the child/childhood.[8] In the twenty-first century, rapidly evolving digital technologies and modalities of reading have prompted a resurgence of questions in the media and in child and literacy research about the effects and goals of reading.[9] As much is still unknown about the effects of digital modes of reading on the comprehension, memory, brain physiology, and reading habits of the individual, there is a possibility that "the effects on society are profound," as a leading reading researcher Maryanne Wolf cautions.[10] Sensationally worded headlines in newspapers and magazines, such as "This is your child's brain on reading," are not uncommon.[11] Even though the article quoted here presents reading as valuable, the phrases used in a bid for the reader's attention echo those ominous warnings which compared reading to vices with detrimental effects on the consumer.[12] And similar to the hopes and ambitions associated with childhood reading in the past, present-day discourses on young people's reading also emphasize that reading has the power to transform lives.[13] A Google search for "children's reading" will return as the top results sites and organizations dedicated to improving literacy and children's lives through literacy.[14] Not only does reading offer children the highly prized cultural capital that comes from being knowledgeable about book culture, but it gives them the required foundation for educational success, and it provides them with training in citizenship, these sites suggest.[15]

Of course, children's books have arguably always sought to educate in one way or another. Even as "instruction with delight" became the norm for writing for children from the middle of the eighteenth century, didacticism in the form of literacy skills, factual knowledge, and moral, social, and religious instruction has remained central to the idea of children's book.[16] Present-day narratives of liberation, civilization, and democratization such as those briefly referenced here suggest that the instrumentalism characterizing eighteenth- and nineteenth-century views of children's reading arguably remains central to ideas about young readers today. Today, as it has done in the past, public discourse on reading registers misgivings and expectations that reveal the strong cultural values underpinning ideas of young people as readers, the cultural significance of reading, and the book as object. The persistence and strength of such beliefs and values underscore the necessity of theorizing reading experiences, as researchers such as Robert Darnton and Leah Price advise, to tease out the cultural work that reading is considered to perform.[17]

This collection of essays is about these ideas and ideals about reading and its effects: it pursues them in books for children, research about child readers, and in accounts of childhood reading. In case studies of Anglo-American reading from the eighteenth century to the present, the contributors explore how childhood reading is and has been shaped by ideas of childhood reading as both a keystone skill with intrinsic value and the potential to improve society and the life of individuals as well as a source of potential problems. These essays further cohere in exploring a central methodological question: How do these historically consistent and seemingly contradictory views about the value of reading affect scholars' approach to the study of reading? The essays are also aligned in seeing reading as a form of "mediation." They approach reading as a site of interaction that involves texts in a material format, individuals as well as wider institutional networks: childhood reading is an arena where values are consciously and unconsciously transmitted.

While inevitably a collection cannot present an exhaustive picture, this volume broadens the disciplinary range of voices and methodologies in the discussion of children's reading as a mediated activity: it brings together experts in literature, education studies, graphic communication and design, social policy, and library and information science and explores how research across the humanities and social sciences can be in dialogue with each other and with related professional fields outside academia.[18] The volume's interdisciplinary approach supports the position of reading research which sees reading as inherently cross-disciplinary and argues that "a single perspective is inadequate" for studying it because reading, at a minimum, concerns the interaction of readers and artifacts (born from complex production and distribution processes); acts of reading are also embedded in social contexts.[19] The single theoretical term "mediation" resonates across disciplinary boundaries while highlighting conventions and discourses that are particular to a field or a discipline. Focusing on reading as a form of "mediation" thus captures the complexity of reading, and it functions as a theoretical hub for the discussions in these essays.

MEDIATION AS RESPONSE TO METHODOLOGICAL ISSUES

As we have already seen, the study of children's reading entails unique complexities, and in this volume, we strategically invoke the concept of mediation as means of acknowledging and reckoning with such challenges. Histories of children's and young adult literature have stressed the need to employ a framework that looks beyond the book itself to incorporate not only readers and their sociocultural positions but also the institutional settings in which these literatures are studied.[20] In this sense, mediation is a helpful concept as Joan Shelley Rubin succinctly explains, "rejecting the view that a printed artefact is simply the embodiment of an author's words, the term [mediation] denotes the multitude of factors affecting the text's transmission."[21] As critics like Rubin and others have recommended, mediation offers an approach that moves between the content of texts and their materiality, while also considering the experiences of individual readers and the broader social and cultural circumstances that shape the practice of reading.

Mediation proves to be an inextricable part of reading, for as Paul Ricoeur famously observed, reading is a meeting between "the world of the text" and "the world of the reader."[22] This premise, that literature is intrinsically a social phenomenon which cannot be separated from human society or history, informs the discipline book history.[23] In his elaboration of Ricoeur's observation, Roger Chartier characterizes reading as an activity in which the meaning of texts "depends upon the forms through which they are received and appropriated by their readers, or listeners."[24] Chartier further argues that reading "is not just an abstract operation of intellect," but "an engagement of the body, an inscription in space, a relation of oneself and others."[25] Reading, then, in addition to being a cognitive and affective hermeneutic operation in which the reader interacts with a material text that has been produced and distributed, is an embodied practice that is historically, culturally, and geographically specific; reading, after all, always takes place somewhere.

Consequently, mediation is a concept that encourages focus on the relational elements of reading: its social and material conditions and settings; the cultural and political values it conveys; and its textual and material forms. In their influential introduction to book history, David Finkelstein and Alistair McCleery identify mediation as a "crucial concept underpinning contemporary interpretations of what is . . . print culture" due to its capacity to accommodate the many aspects of the reading process.[26] They demonstrate the necessity of historicizing the reading experience, echoing Roger Chartier's argument that textual meaning is dependent on the forms in which the text reaches the reader, and that this meaning is further affected by the "specific dispositions" that apply to readers in the particular contexts in which reading takes place.[27] In this wide formulation, mediation is print culture itself; it is "the nexus of practices creating and sustaining the ideological, psychological, political and economic power of the printed word for a given social group."[28]

Mediation is thus useful for investigating reading and print culture in general. It is, moreover, a productive concept for the study of children's reading specifically, as it allows interrogation of a set of contradictions that are characteristic of this field of study. At the most foundational level, we see a concern that the child's encounter with a text is necessarily facilitated in some way or hyper-mediated. To illustrate this concern, let us return to Anne Mozley, who in her essay argues that the book that has the greatest impact on a child's imagination—to the extent that he or she will fondly recall this book as an adult—is the one which finds its way to the child's hands "by a sort of chance, through no authority or intervention," and which the child reader sequesters himself or herself to read to prevent being interrupted by any of the adults likely to interfere and spoil the fun: "neither nurse, nor governess, nor mamma herself."[29] Mozley's description of this (middle-class, as suggested by the list of adults) reading scenario illustrates the cultural value placed on not only literacy, but on becoming a reader and finding enjoyment in books; reading is here figured as a formative experience on the path to independence and obtaining the cultural capital associated with literature.[30] Only obliquely does Mozley's idealized picture refer to the fact that children often do not select or procure their own reading material and that their reading time or reading practice is often regulated in some way. Her portrait of the child engrossed in a book of choice exemplifies the enduring romanticized image of the solitary reader, an image masking the reality that reading is a fundamentally social and relational act.

Just as the solitary reader of a single text remains embedded in an interactive network, the acquisition of literacy that prefigures such interactions also attests to the social nature of reading. Reading and literary interpretation are taught skills: the "presuppositions, expectations, and habits of understanding" that the reader brings to a text are formed within a social setting.[31] With this assertion, Paul Armstrong reminds us that the readerly habitus is an underlying factor in each encounter between reader and text, affecting how the reader makes sense of the text. Notably, children become socialized as readers in "two of the most powerful disciplinary institutions [in society]—the family and the school"; as Thomas McLaughlin observes, this socialization encompasses both how we learn to think about reading and how we internalize the physical behavior involved in reading.[32] Adults model reading practices and the cultural values ascribed to this activity. Even the book which the child comes across "by chance" is produced for children by adults with specific goals and ideals in mind. On a larger scale, the curation of children's literature in collections is similarly a result of adult intervention: which works, genres, and authors have survived and been preserved is a matter of chance, personal whims and convictions, institutional policies, and cultural values.[33] What is valued about texts and reading runs as an undercurrent to these processes of collection, transmission, and socialization, but the cultural values and ideals surrounding reading are rarely explicit or explicitly acknowledged.

The term "mediation" accentuates this contrast between romanticized ideal and reality and making this term central to analyses of reading scenarios usefully brings the cultural values and assumptions about reading to the fore.

One further challenge for the study of children's reading concerns the availability of sources of data and how to interpret them, and mediation provides a way of reckoning with the challenge of regarding children's reading as a discrete historical subject worthy of and available for study. In his seminal work on the historical child reader, Matthew Grenby argues that there is a "structural clash" between the fields of book history and children's literature studies because children are not "readers in the sense that book historians usually envisage."[34] This constraint is complex, emphasizing first that the child's access to books is partly managed on behalf of the child reader and does not necessarily reflect the child's preferences. Second, it insists that the image of reading and readers presented in books for children is "particularly prone to propagandising" to encourage children to read; it also follows that accounts of childhood reading must be scrutinized regarding representativeness and accuracy.[35] Third, it questions to what extent the researcher studying children's reading practices can presuppose a reader that interacts with a text and is affected by it in a similar manner to an adult reader.[36]

Within children's literature studies, too, the question of how "the child" can be understood by adults is fraught with tension. Influential works theorizing this question include Jacqueline Rose's *The Case of Peter Pan, or The Impossibility of Children's Fiction* (1985) and Karìn Leznik-Oberstein's *Children's Literature: Criticism and the Fictional Child* (1996), which both posit the unknowability of the child reader and the child in literature, as it is impossible to know "the Other."[37] This collection's use of the term "mediation" to focus our enquiry calls attention to this boundary and the methodological issues it represents. Framing reading as a mediated and relational activity enables interrogation of available sources of data regarding representativeness, accuracy, and assumptions of cultural values of reading. It is also a means of methodologically foregrounding the role of the adult in reading—the researcher, adult facilitators of reading (parents and guardians, teachers, librarians, and others), the collector, as well as the author and others involved in the production of books, not at the expense of the agency of the child reader, but to probe this structural binary.

Additional methodological complexities arise because children's reading is universally prized, especially in societies where "text is ubiquitous and all pervasive," as Shafquat Towheed has expressed it.[38] Reading is an activity so enmeshed in our everyday lives that it has been suggested it defines the very fabric of society.[39] Eva-Maria Simms, for example, compares reading to Edmund Husserl's category "natural attitude," which she paraphrases as "something accepted without question and without opportunity for reflection."[40] How, she asks rhetorically, can anyone obtain the critical distance necessary for studying this topic? The value placed on reading affects readers, those who facilitate reading, and those studying reading, making it difficult to separate one's own experiences and beliefs about reading from reading as a topic of study. Or, building on Husserl's phenomenological perspective, we can say that to study reading, the researcher must acknowledge how their own experiences are related to and implicated in shared attitudes to reading, and work to make explicit the unrecognized theorizing about the world that is present in the natural attitude.[41] Wendy Griswold, in her work on public reading programs, illustrates the difficulty when she points out that "the unchallenged assumption is that reading and talking about reading contribute to social wellbeing," and that these programs are therefore "aggressively promoted" without necessarily being accompanied by documentation to support that conclusion.[42] Griswold sees such undocumented promotions as an expression of the literacy myth, which identifies literacy as a necessary and direct cause of social and individual transformation.[43] If such attitudes apply to reading in general, children's reading is arguably even more strongly affected by aspirations of benefit and transformation, as described earlier. Mediation offers a platform from which to explore assumptions and "natural attitudes" because it enables theorization of multiple positions and experiences and how they interconnect in social and material conditions and settings.

Moreover, because the act of reading is typically either recounted (by the reader) or observed and recounted (by a researcher or facilitator of reading), but not directly available for study, it becomes embedded in discourses on reading, resulting in a related methodological difficulty that, among others, Daniel Allington discusses as the impossibility of unmediated access to reading and Anouk Lang calls "the inevitability of interpretation."[44] Employing the term "mediation" allows us to contend with this inextricability and see it as a productive site of inquiry, as mediation serves to remind us that descriptions of reading are difficult to separate from the values attached to it and are a product of the sociocultural settings in which reading takes place; mediation enables an approach to reading as a topic of study that scrutinizes the accounts and descriptions of reading as constructs. It furthermore takes into consideration how the researcher is also implicated in the transmission of cultural values attached to reading. Accounts of children's reading, as told by readers and others, promoted in books and reading programs, facilitated in publishing, and encapsulated as collections, can thus be rigorously analyzed via the perspective of mediation.

NEW DIRECTIONS: MEDIATIONS
AND CHILDREN'S READING

Adopting "mediation" as our framework enables us to apply a broad definition of "reading" to our enquiries, for the conceptualization of reading as a
relational practice foregrounds questions about textual, visual, and material
strategies as well as social worlds, agency, and intervention. Stressing reading as a complex activity in this way, the collection has not forgotten the
book. Rather, it positions the book as a constructed and social artifact that is
both a mediator of cultural expectations and that contributes to forming these
expectations.[45]

The contributors to this volume employ a range of methodologies and theoretical approaches to investigate children's reading. Their exact subjects vary
in time and place, but center on Anglo-American contexts and Anglophone
reading and, using mediation as the fulcrum, each contribution is informed
by the central questions: How is children's reading shaped by ideas and
values ascribed to this practice? How might we approach the cultural role
of children's reading in a specific historical moment? And how might we
as researchers manage the assumptions and expectations attached to reading
when investigating it?

This book has a broadly chronological trajectory from the eighteenth century to the present which allows the reader interested in diachronic developments to compare instantiations and ideas of reading at different times. The
juxtaposition of historical and present-day scenarios of children's reading
enables the volume's inquiry into cultural assumptions about actual reading
practices.[46] However, while the collection identifies historical continuities as
well as changes in attitudes toward reading, we do not argue that there is a
transhistorical and essentialized "reader," recognizable across space and time.
Emphasizing the historical horizons of *all* reading scenarios benefits the study
of reading more generally because this approach may decrease the influence
of the researcher's own historically produced reading habitus on the analysis,
which is one of the challenges of studying reading, as discussed earlier.[47]

At the same time, the book is organized into four thematic parts that
highlight specific issues surrounding children's reading: sources of historical reading data and methodologies for capturing them; the facilitatory role
of institutions and organizations; materiality and visual strategies in children's books; and reading as an activity affecting the readers' social worlds.
However, there are naturally some overlaps between chapters in the different
sections and the collection can be read against the grain of its formal organization; for example, the social relationships in which reading takes place,
what Elizabeth Long has called "the social infrastructure of reading,"[48] run as
an undercurrent throughout and it is possible to read the essays with this focus

in mind. Similarly, issues of materiality and textuality, how they prompt specific modes of reading and interaction between text and reader, or how these concerns relate to issues of access to reading materials and their preservation are investigative preoccupations shared by the contributors.

Thus, the two essays in part I of this book, "Historical Reading Practices," establish the chronological starting point of the collection and confront issues of the availability of historical reading evidence, traces of the individual child reader in history, and how historical material can be interpreted. Both essays offer new strategies for interpreting well-known accounts and ideas of reading, which is a perennial question for the history or reading.[49]

In chapter 1's case study of eighteenth-century Scottish readers, Elspeth Jajdelska engages with the familiar argument that historically, children's reading was strictly regulated. Jajdelska tests her readers' relative freedom to read and, not least, freedom to *interpret* what they read, against an elaborate framework of socioeconomic and cultural factors. This fine-meshed scheme illustrates how historians can mine personal accounts of reading and thus adds to the available range of methodologies for analyzing a source widely recognized as requiring stringent interpretation.[50] Uncovering historical child readers' means of access to literary culture and independent reflective spaces in different milieus, this chapter further nuances both the image of the child reader and of the monolithic adult mediator that have come under scrutiny in recent years.[51]

In the second chapter, Rebecca Davies analyzes how eighteenth- and early nineteenth-century novelists used the mediating role of maternal educators to debate socially imposed limitations on women's reading. Informed by theories of material culture and intellectual history, Davies argues that by portraying young adult women readers struggling with their suggested reading lists—an educative strategy common within the maternal, domestic system of childhood education—the authors engaged in epistemic practice; they interrogated a conflict between individual understanding and systems of knowledge as mediated spatially and materially through print. Davies shows how the novel genre is particularly suited to exploring this tension between individual and system; another strength of this chapter is its demonstration of how fictional meta-discussions can be mined for ideas of reading and women's voices in settings where women's opportunities for participating in public discourse are socially circumscribed.

Part II of this volume, "Programs and Collections," moves the discussion to organizations and institutions as mediators of reading. This "middle layer," positioned between the societal and individual levels, has the potential to overcome the micro-macro dichotomy of reading research, as Christine Pawley has argued.[52] Both essays in part II share Pawley's interest in "nonmarket" agents of print culture, which are not accentuated in book history models like Robert Darnton's influential communications circuit illustrating a text's transmission from author to reader, but which nevertheless have significant impact by facilitating frameworks and conditions for reading and the study of reading. These agents arguably also influence "the specific dispositions that distinguish communities of readers and traditions of reading," as Roger Chartier formulated it.[53]

To Suzan Alteri, special collections are social constructs telling specific narratives. In chapter 3, she traces the histories of some of the most well-known university library special collections of children's books in the United States to argue that understanding the composition of an archive is a crucial aspect of working with historical sources of reading. Alteri shows how ideas about reading, collecting, academic disciplines, and socioeconomic and cultural factors relating to gender are embedded in the archive and impact what can be studied about reading through the archive. However, as Alteri also argues via these case studies, the archive is not a static entity but changes with interpretation and reinterpretation of its content, and the archives today emerge as "active sites of agency and power" where library professionals have an important function as mediators.[54]

Public reading programs can be, as Danielle Fuller and DeNel Rehberg Sedo have found, "overladen with expectations" regarding the social effects of the program.[55] In chapter 4, Emma Davidson and Tracey Cooper turn these expectations into data, interviewing participants and employees of "Bookbug," a present-day Scottish nationwide program promoting reading. The chapter presents an analysis of the program's success in meeting its objective, which is to remedy the social inequality that stems from disparity in literacy skills and access to books. By assessing a program run by a national charity organization and aimed at families, Davidson and Cooper provide valuable insight into the intersection of the private and the public sphere: while bolstering parental involvement is demonstrated to be important to address inequality related to reading, the role of public services remains key.

The essays in part III, "Textual and Material Strategies," examine visual strategies employed by authors, book designers, and publishers to promote certain ideas of reading and aid the communication of textual messages. The two essays comprising this part focus on the twentieth and twenty-first century, respectively, but literacy and the attendant development of the reader's emotional or ethical register, cognitive skills and knowledge, and the relation of these to the material shaping of the text and the book are not new concerns. Due to their pedagogical potential to help explicate text for less experienced readers, images have long been associated with children's reading. From the 1740s onwards, publishers produced specifically designed children's books that integrated visual and haptic elements—illustrations, movable parts, and books in sizes adapted to small hands—in line with the pedagogical theories of John Locke. Locke wanted to bring the object or concept to which the word refers and the look of the word and the letters representing it into closer contact with each other via the affordances of the book. Material features were used strategically to entertain and cajole children into reading, certainly, but also into learning about the world, and thereby expand children's repertoire of mental images on which abstraction, and consequently reading, relies.[56]

In chapter 5, Sue Walker unfolds how pedagogy intersected with technological developments in graphic design and printing to mediate information in British nonfiction books for children in the mid-twentieth century. At this time, child-centered learning approaches and the idea that individuals learn by relating new information to their horizon of experience had gained momentum and acceptance in educational and governmental circles,[57] and Walker notes that government guidelines for the education sector provided an added impetus for book design in this period. However, the chapter's emphasis is how designers adopted pedagogical ideas about reading and gave them material expressions. Meticulous bibliographic examinations explicate these designer strategies for visual organization of information material and the mediating function of information design strategies that have since become established as norm in publishing for children.

Where Walker examines creator intent, Jennifer Farrar focuses on reception in chapter 6. Farrar presents the findings of an ethnographic study of parents co-reading metafictive post-millennial picturebooks with their children, and her chapter highlights how graphic design can be perceived as a source of potential tension that challenges received ideas about reading, depending on the reader's experiences. The powerful influence parents wield as mediators of children's reading is thrown into sharp relief through Farrar's analysis of how parents respond to these postmodern picturebooks, which demand a different type of reading strategy than readers of their generation may be accustomed to. Through this reader response study, Farrar interrogates the formation and function of family literacy and the individual's "literate habitus" and emphasizes the necessity of increasing the awareness around multiliteracy and its role in helping readers navigate the twenty-first-century media landscape.

The fourth and final part of this collection is called "Texts, Worlds, and Mediation" and examines contemporary expressions of reading as an activity that has the potential to impact readers' social realities. The two chapters in this part reinforce the collection's focus on the cultural value of reading expressed in beliefs about the effects of reading, or how books and reading are credited with "producing a certain kind of individual," as Leah Price has put it.[58] Here, views of literacy, genre, and reading technologies play vital roles in the authors' explorations of how the book mediates in social relationships.

In chapter 7, Evelyn Arizpe examines the distinctive multimodality of post-millennial picturebooks and how certain ideas of reading are both communicated and resisted in print. Books actively contribute to socialization into a literary culture, fashioning the child reader by calling attention to their own materiality.[59] Through a corpus analysis, Arizpe interrogates reasons for the popularity of this motif, which elides digital reading in favor of a marked emphasis on skills associated with reading (the correct handling of material books and behavior in settings associated with reading) and stresses reading as a social activity and "reader" as a desirable social identity in the twenty-first century.

Rounding off the volume, in chapter 8, Fiona McCulloch also discusses concerns about reading technologies, via a contemporary young adult (YA) novel in which the main character battles an insidious social media narrative. McCulloch explores the "traditional" didactic role of YA fiction in this new media landscape as a genre where difficult and provocative topics can be safely explored and used to promote crucial social skills, in this case metaliteracy.[60] Reader reviews in online forums not only provide an indication of the novel's reception among its intended audience but also suggest how reading can act as a pharmakon, a term that refers to something with the capacity to heal as well as damage,[61] substantiating McCulloch's argument that the text's mediating function opens a space for repairing damage that has been inflicted by language upon the reader.

The strength of any case study, as with the studies featured in this volume, lies in its ability to illuminate a topic from different perspectives. Using a variety of methodologies and theoretical approaches, the essays in this collection uncover a diverse range of reading experiences that demonstrate how reading intersects with socioeconomic realities, cultural backgrounds, linguistic abilities, and constructs of gender. For example, in probing historical sources describing reading practices, Davies and Jajdelska uncover the voices of people belonging to marginalized groups, with the familiar caveat that the sources privilege certain readers and types of reading.[62] McCulloch shows how media can limit young persons' lives when inflected with "dominant cultural views" of gender and race, but also how books and digital platforms of reading can harbor spaces of independent agency for young readers from which they can challenge these views, using strategies learned from social reading practices.[63] Regarding contemporary reading studies involving human respondents, Davidson and Cooper and Farrar stress the researcher's ethical responsibility to select appropriate methods of interaction and analysis that fit the needs of individual families and their different socioeconomic, linguistic, and cultural backgrounds. Based on their findings, it is evident that there is a variety of experiences in the public sphere that remain under-analyzed and that when these varied experiences intersect with the uniform messages and programs of public institutions and organizations, tensions as well as opportunities may arise; Alteri's analysis of institutions supports this conclusion. Diverse backgrounds can also enrich reading experiences and reading spaces, as these authors note. This is a vital recognition if the aim is to use books and literacy to bridge social differences.

The essays in this volume stress the importance of studying how reading is a practice that is fundamentally shaped by a myriad of political, cultural, and social factors, and aggregated the essays establish reading as a complex activity which must be interrogated. For example, Alteri's analysis of how gender has shaped children's literature collections and made the study of children's literature both possible and legitimate through programs in education and library studies forms the basis of her argument for a redefinition of the category "book collector," but she also posits that the collections, and children's reading and literature, to a certain degree have remained associated with "applied" rather than properly "academic" disciplines as a result. And in her study of graphic design strategies, Sue Walker explains that the pedagogical force of images and events recognizable from the child's own life stems from the assumption that relatable experiences will spark a child's interest and facilitate learning. But this assumption prompts the question, relatable to whom? In this sense, Walker's essay implicitly exposes why child-centered pedagogies have regularly faced criticism for being based on idealized models of learning that "exclude the child's cultural and institutional biography," failing to take diverse social circumstances into account.[64] Images and design have the potential to subvert established perspectives by teaching children strategies for reading at odds with the utilitarian strategies promoted in schools, as Farrar's study finds, but this potential may face resistance among parents and guardians. And while the established trend of substituting animals for humans in picturebooks does little to portray the experiences of visible minority groups and has come under recent scrutiny as an example of lack of racial diversity in character representation,[65] Arizpe finds that the illustrations minimize other social differences and the mediating authority of adults and the school, emphasizing the agency of the child reader. Even as the essays in this volume highlight a range of reading practices and the relevance of diverse social and cultural experiences for understanding reading as a complex activity, it is important to acknowledge that this collection is defined by a focused geographical and chronological scope. Rather than aiming for a comprehensive exploration of reading and mediation, this volume offers a lens into topics that deserve consideration from other angles, and we hope that the studies presented here spark future research into other relevant issues and approaches.

The contributors to this volume show that they are conscious that mediating factors and circumstances are what to a large extent define reading as an activity imbued with cultural value. Using "mediation" as a connecting node has enabled the contributors to locate reading experiences in a range of sources and has demonstrated the need to display a critical awareness of the structures through which texts have been made available for child readers and for researchers. It is only by acknowledging the assumptions on which our sources of data about reading at least partly rest that we can continue to develop reading as a field of study. In extension of this, the essays assert that we need to be aware of our own position as researchers; we are all affected by the narrative of reading as a particularly valuable activity. Mediation offers a way of contending with this issue. For example, while the source material explored by Jajdelska in this volume gestures toward the transatlantic influence of Scottish reading pedagogies, it would also be valuable to examine transnational perspectives on reading in a mediation framework more broadly to uncover more voices, geographical spheres of influence, and concomitant variations and points of convergence in ideas about the cultural work of reading in a globalized, multilingual, and multicultural world. Translation studies offer an example of this approach by theorizing the process of translation as one of mediation to interrogate the notion of translation being a simple and transparent exchange or direct transfer, seeing it instead as a process of meaning-making entailing intervention in the text and interpretation and re-presentation of its ideas for new audiences and new cultures.[66] A mediation perspective lays bare processes, networks, discourses of power and the role of the translator or other mediators; it makes the implicit explicit. These are transferable lessons for the study of reading, and which this collection has adopted.

This collection also probes how a renewed focus on and celebration of the materiality of the book and the sensory, embodied experience of reading can be understood as a counterpoint to and defense against technological changes in book production, the challenges of digital reading, and the perceived power of digital technologies to disrupt established cultural values attached to reading. Arizpe and Farrar have shown that this is a useful approach to investigating issues relating to class and the mediation of cultural power as well as the agency of the child reader. While materiality is often discussed in terms of media nostalgia, it should not be understood as unequivocally reactionary: Davidson and Cooper's analysis of responses to the gifting component of the Bookbug program suggests that children's pleasure in possessing and interacting with material books can contribute to closing attainment gaps. In other investigations in this volume the text functions as a mediator in a way that is similar to Rita Felski's term "affordance" to indicate that reading is an interaction where "meanings are coconstituted by texts and readers."[67] For example, McCulloch's YA text is a discursive space with permeable qualities, an interface between the reader and the world: in shaping and responding to the text and its paratexts, the author and reader emerge as agents manipulating this interface. Davies highlights the epistemological mediation of knowledge and social norms conveyed by both genre and the material text as ways for nineteenth-century women to participate in public philosophical discourse. Young readers' responses to books appear in many forms in the essays in this volume to illustrate how materiality can be a meaningful aspect of agency.

The accounts of reading experiences analyzed in this volume suggest that we *do* remember a particular book from when we were young, like Anne Mozley asserted in 1870. We remember how the book came into our possession and how interacting with it affected us. The authors in this volume offer a range of useful approaches for locating evidence of these complex and elusive experiences, whether in the past or the present. Similarly, the contributors present innovative strategies for theorizing about the interaction between the reader and the text in ways that acknowledge and interrogate the fact that reading is a relational activity transmitting strong social and cultural values. Setting "mediation" as a connecting node has also demonstrated that it is imperative to ask questions of books, data sets, archives, libraries, and public programs or policies regarding how these are designed, compiled, and organized, because the analyses in these essays have highlighted how assumptions about the effects of reading on the reader permeate every aspect of the investigation of reading. In exploring changing and persistent ideas about the cultural work of reading, the volume offers ways for researchers across academic disciplines to contend with reading as a practice bound up with a plethora of ideas about reading.

NOTES

1. Anne Mozley, "On Fiction as an Educator," in *A Serious Occupation: Literary Criticism by Victorian Women Writers*, ed. Solveig C. Robinson (Peterborough, ON: Broadview Press, 2013), 187–207, 189.

2. Sally Shuttleworth, *The Mind of the Child: Child Development in Literature, Science and Medicine* (Oxford: Oxford University Press, 2010), 4. Frequent expressions of nostalgia for childhood reading captures another side of this narrative, as seen in, for example, J.M. Barrie, "Wrecked on an Island," *National Observer* 11, no. 274 (February 17, 1894): 345.

3. Charlotte Mary Yonge, *What Books to Lend and What to Give* (London: National Society's Depository, 1887).

4. Prominent physicians expounding on the issue include Henry Maudsley and Edward Clarke; see, for example, Crista DeLuzio, *Female Adolescence in American Scientific Thought, 1830–1930* (Baltimore, MD: Johns Hopkins University Press, 2007).

5. François Proulx, *Victims of the Book: Reading and Masculinity in Fin-de-Siècle France* (Toronto, ON: University of Toronto Press, 2019). Patrick Brantlinger, *The Reading Lesson: The Threat of Mass Literacy in Nineteenth-Century British Fiction* (Bloomington, IN: Indiana University Press, 1998), describes the penny dreadful, which was broadly regarded as a potential catalyst for criminal behaviour. See also Kate Flint, *The Woman Reader, 1837–1914* (Oxford: Oxford University Press, 1995).

6. Jacob Middleton, "The Overpressure Epidemic of 1884 and the Culture of Nineteenth-Century Schooling," *History of Education* 33, no. 4 (2004): 419–35.

7. An outline of the debate as it unfolded in the UK in the late nineteenth and early twentieth century can be found in, for example, Hilary Marland, *Health and Girlhood in Britain, 1874–1920* (Basingstoke: Ashgate, 2013). Bronwyn Lowe, *"The Right Thing to Read:" A History of Australian Girl-Readers, 1910–1960* (New York and Abingdon: Routledge, 2018), draws parallels between early twentieth-century expressions of concern for the reader's wellbeing and similar concerns today.

8. Among the scholars who have observed this parallel is Patricia Crain, *Reading Children: Literacy, Property, and the Dilemmas of Childhood in Nineteenth-Century America* (Philadelphia, PA: University of Pennsylvania Press, 2016). Reading modes and practices have been associated with and affected by social and techno-logical transformations at different points in history; see, for example, Anouk Lang, "Introduction: Transforming Reading," in *From Codex to Hypertext. Studies in Print Culture and the History of the Book*, ed. Anouk Lang (Amherst, MA: University of Massachusetts Press, 2012), 1–24; and Shafquat Towheed, "Introduction," in *The History of Reading Vol. 3. Methods, Strategies, Tactics*, eds. Rosalind Crane and Shafquat Towheed (Basingstoke: Palgrave Macmillan, 2011), 1–12.

9. See, for example, Pablo Delgado, Cristina Vargas, Rakefet Ackerman and Ladislao Salmerón, "Don't Throw Away Your Printed Books: A Meta-Analysis on the Effects of Reading Media on Reading Comprehension," *Educational Research Review* 25 (2018): 23–38.

10. Maryanne Wolf, "Skim Reading is the New Normal. The Effect on Society is Profound," *The Guardian*, August 25, 2018, https://www.theguardian.com/commentisfree/2018/aug/25/skim-reading-new-normal-maryanne-wolf.

11. Carina Storrs, "This Is Your Child's Brain on Reading," *CNN*, February 3, 2016, https://edition.cnn.com/2015/08/05/health/parents-reading-to-kids-study/index.html; Open Education Database, "Your Brain on Books: 10 Things that Happen to Our Minds When We Read," https://oedb.org/ilibrarian/your-brain-on-books-10-things-that-happen-to-our-minds-when-we-read/.

12. See, for example, Brantlinger, *The Reading Lesson*, 22–23, for a discussion of reading being compared to vices including smoking.

13. Several works on the history of reading engage with the frequent use of the terms "transformational" and "transformative" to describe reading. See, for example, Bonnie Gunzenhauser, "Introduction," in *Reading in History: New Methodologies from the Anglo-American Tradition*, The History of the Book, no. 6, ed. Bonnie Gunzenhauser (London: Pickering & Chatto, 2010; Abingdon and New York: Routledge, 2016), 2–9.

14. The ranking is naturally partly a result of such companies using different techniques to secure first-page positions.

15. "We know that learning to *read* and *reading* for pleasure transforms *children's* lives," The Children's Reading Company, https://childrensreadingcompany.com/; "Our mission is to encourage and educate families about their important role in raising a reader and preparing their *child* for kindergarten," The Children's Reading Foundation of the Mid-Colombia, read20minutes.com/; "Together we can grow successful *readers*, engaged citizens, and thriving communities," The Children's Reading Connection, https://www.childrensreadingconnection.org/, all sites accessed March 18, 2019.

16. See M.O. Grenby, *The Child Reader, 1700–1840* (Cambridge: Cambridge University Press, 2011), 16–18; 254–66.

17. Robert Darnton, "First Steps toward a History of Reading," *Australian Journal of French Studies* 23 (1986): 5–30, reprinted in *The Kiss of Lamourette: Reflections in Cultural History* (London: Faber & Faber, 1990), 154–187; Leah Price, "Reading: The State of the Discipline," *Book History* 7 (2004): 303–20.

18. The genesis of the present collection is a workshop aimed at developing frameworks which would grow interdisciplinary dialogue on children's and young adults' reading. The workshop "Mediating Children's Reading" formed a part of the 2016 RSE Susan Manning series of workshops at the Institute for Advanced Studies in the Humanities (IASH) at the University of Edinburgh. The editor and contributors would like to thank IASH and the Royal Society of Edinburgh for their generous support, which made that event possible.

19. Shelby A. Wolf, Karen Coats, Patricia Enciso and Christine A. Jenkins, eds., *The Routledge Handbook of Research on Children's and Young Adult Literature* (New York and London: Routledge, 2011), 1. For similar arguments concerning print culture for young readers, see also Anne Lundin, "Introduction," in *Defining Print Culture for Youth*, eds. Anne Lundin and Wayne A. Wiegand (New York: Libraries Unlimited, 2003), xi–xxii. Similar arguments concerning the history of reading more generally are expressed by Lang, "Introduction" and Towheed, "Introduction."

20. Lundin, "Introduction," builds on the framework established in Janice Radway, "*Beyond Mary Bailey* and Old Maid Librarians: Reimagining Readers and Rethinking Reading," *Journal of Education for Library and Information Science* 35, no. 4 (1994): 275–96. Radway figures this print culture as comprising scholarship on the reader (naming reader-response theory and ethnographies of reading as examples), on literacy studies (also a socio-cultural approach to the text), and on the social history of books. A similar rationale is employed by Wolf, Coats, Enciso & Jenkins, eds., *Handbook*.

21. Joan Shelley Rubin, "What Is the History of the History of Books?" *The Journal of American History* 90, no. 2 (2003): 555–75, 562.

22. Paul Ricoeur, *Time and Narrative*, vol. 1 (Chicago, IL: University of Chicago Press, 1990), 79.

23. For an elaboration on this insight in the context of theorizations of the history of the book, see David Finkelstein and Alistair McCleery, eds., *An Introduction to Book History*, 3rd ed. (Abingdon: Routledge, 2013), 25–26.

24. Roger Chartier, "Laborers and Voyagers: From the Text to the Reader," reprinted in *The Book History Reader,* eds. David Finkelstein and Alistair McCleery (London: Routledge, 2002), 87–98, 88.

25. Roger Chartier, *The Order of Books: Readers, Authors and Libraries in Europe between the Fourteenth and Eighteenth Centuries,* trans. Lydia Cochrane (Stanford, CA: Stanford University Press, 1994), 20.

26. Finkelstein and McCleery, eds., *An Introduction,* 25–26.

27. Finkelstein and McCleery, eds., *An Introduction,* 25–26.

28. Rubin, "What Is the History," 562.

29. Mozley, "On Fiction," 189.

30. Anne Mozley's belief in the power of reading and the role of secrecy in developing a child's independent reading was echoed by other, near-contemporary authorities on children. See, for example, Ellen Key, *The Century of the Child* (New York and London: George Putnam and Sons, 1909), 248–49.

31. Paul Armstrong, quoted in Joan Bessman Taylor, "Producing Meaning through Interaction: Book Groups and the Social Context of Reading," in *From Codex to Hypertext,* ed. Anouk Lang, 142–158, 143.

32. Thomas McLaughlin, *Reading and the Body: The Physical Practice of Reading* (New York: Palgrave Macmillan, 2015), 27.

33. Additionally, survival of works is affected by the books' physical condition, which is a particular challenge when it comes to children's books; see Grenby, *The Child Reader.*

34. Grenby, *The Child Reader,* 8.

35. Grenby, *The Child Reader,* 8, 10–12.

36. Grenby, *The Child Reader,* 10.

37. See also Perry Nodelman, *The Hidden Adult: Defining Children's Literature* (Baltimore, MD: Johns Hopkins University Press, 2008).

38. Towheed, "Introduction," 2.

39. At various points in history, it has been claimed that reading defines living in a modern society, often with a view to debating problems with "the modern condition." For example, Harold Griffing and Shepherd Franz wrote in "On the Conditions of Fatigue in Reading" in 1896 that: "The Increasing Part Played by Reading in the Life of Civilized Man is a Striking Characteristic of Modern Culture. In Fact, the Man of Today Might Be Defined as a Reading Animal," *The Psychological Review* 3, no. 5 (1896): 513–30, 513.

40. Eva-Maria Simms, "Questioning the Value of Literacy: A Phenomenology of Speaking and Reading in Children," in *Handbook of Research on Children's and Young Adult Literature,* eds. Wolf, Coats, Enciso and Jenkins (New York and London: Routledge, 2011), 20–31, 21. Similar observations are routinely made, including by Towheed, "Introduction," and Price, "Reading," 303.

41. Edmund Husserl, *Ideas Pertaining to a Pure Phenomenology and to a Phenomenological Philosophy. First Book: General Introduction to a Pure Phenomenology* (The Hague: Springer Netherlands, 1982).

42. Wendy Griswold, *Regionalism and the Reading Class* (Chicago, IL and London: University of Chicago Press, 2008), 59.

43. This is not to suggest that documentation of the social effects of reading does not exist, simply that reading programs take the causation for granted; see also DeNel Rehberg-Sedo and Danielle Fuller, *Reading beyond the Book: The Social Practices of Contemporary Literary Culture* (London and New York: Routledge, 2013). Griswold references Harvey Graff's work; see Harvey Graff, "The Literacy Myth: Literacy, Education and Demography," *Vienna Yearbook of Population Research*, vol. 8 Education and Demography (2010): 17–23.

44. Daniel Allington, "On the Use of Anecdotal Evidence in Reception Study and the History of Reading," in *Reading in History*, ed. Bonnie Gunzenhauser, 11–28; Anouk Lang, "Explicating Explications: Researching Contemporary Reading," in *Reading in History*, ed. Bonnie Gunzenhauser, 119–134, 119.

45. See, for example, Leah Price on the book as mediator or agent in "Reading" and *How to Do Things with Books in Victorian Britain* (Princeton, NJ: Princeton University Press, 2012). Social aspects of interactions with texts have become a preoccupation in a range of theoretical approaches to literature. For example, recent work on affect emphasizes reading as socially embedded in various settings and material and interpretive frames, interpretation thus essentially being understood as an act of mediation; see, Rita Felski, "Introduction," *New Literary History* 45, no. 2 (Spring 2014): v–xi, vi, and Rita Felski, *The Limits of Critique* (Chicago, IL: The University of Chicago Press, 2015).

46. Karin Littau convincingly employs this contrasting method: Karin Littau, *Theories of Reading: Books, Bodies and Bibliomania* (Cambridge: Polity, 2006), 10–12; as does Lowe, *The Right Thing to Read*.

47. As also asserted by Lang, "Introduction," 21. Lang here draws on Bourdieu to argue the need to free ourselves from "the unconscious suppositions that history imposes upon us," and to make these presuppositions visible.

48. Elizabeth Long, "Textual Interpretation as Collective Action," in *The Ethnographies of Reading*, ed. Jonathan Boyarin (Berkeley, CA: University of California Press, 1993), 180–211.

49. This was noted by Robert Darnton as early as 1986; see Darnton, "First Steps."

50. See, for example, Allington, "On the Use of Anecdotal Evidence"; Rosalind Crone, Katie Halsey and Shafquat Towheed, "Examining the Evidence of Reading: Three Examples from the Reading Experience Database, 1450–1945," in *Reading in History*, ed. Bonnie Gunzenhauser, 29–46; Jonathan Rose, *The Intellectual Life of the British Working Classes* (New Haven, CT: Yale University Press, 2001).

51. See Grenby, *The Child Reader*.

52. Christine Pawley, "Beyond Market Models and Resistance: Organizations as a Middle Layer in the History of Reading," *The Library Quarterly* 79, no. 1 (2009): 79–93.

53. Chartier, "Laborers and Voyagers," 48; see also Gunzenhauser, "Introduction," 7, for a similar argument.

54. Terry Cook, "The Archive(s) Is a Foreign Country: Historians, Archivists, and the Changing Archival Landscape," *The American Archivist* 74, no. 2 (Fall/Winter 2011): 600–32, 600; as argued by Christine Pawley, "Beyond Market Models," 86.

55. Fuller and Rehberg Sedo, *Reading beyond the Book*; see also note 43.

56. See Gillian Brown, "The Metamorphic Book: Children's Print Culture in the Eighteenth Century," *Eighteenth-Century Studies* 39, no. 3, New Feminist Work in Epistemology and Aesthetics (Spring 2006): 351–62.

57. Chung & Walsh outline how child-centered pedagogies have been understood and conceptualized in the US education system; as part of this project, the authors describe what "child-centered" denoted in the 1930s-60s, the period examined by Walsh in this collection. See Shunah Chung and Daniel J. Walsh, "Unpacking Child-Centredness: A History of Meanings," *Journal of Curriculum Studies* 32, no. 2 (2000): 215–234.

58. Price, *What We Talk About*, 8.

59. This correlates with a similar tendency, namely the humanization of the book and the book literally speaking up in its own defense in it-narratives in certain historical conditions: see Price, *How to Do Things with Books*.

60. Lee A. Talley, "Young Adult," in *Keywords for Children's Literature*, eds. Philip Nel and Lissa Paul (New York and London: New York University Press, 2011), 228–32, situates this genre within the history of children's literature and didacticism.

61. Jacques Derrida, *Dissemination*, trans. and intro. Barbara Johnson (New York: Continuum, 2004), 125–30.

62. See, for example, Price, "The State of Reading," 313.

63. Referring to reading together or talking about books and reading in a social setting, social reading today is perhaps most often used in reference to interactions on digital platforms. However, "behaviours enabled by social reading sites are in a continuum with historical practices such as epistolary communities, reading unions and reading groups, although their digital nature makes them specific," as Padmini Ray Murray and Claire Squires have argued in Padmini Ray Murray and Claire Squires, "The Digital Communications Circuit," *Book 2.0*, 3, no. 1 (2013): 3–24, 13–14.

64. S. Power, M. Rhys, C. Taylor and S. Waldron, "How Child-Centred Education Favours Some Learners More than Others," *Review of Education* 7, no. 3 (2019): 570–92.

65. As reported in UK media, drawing on analyses by the Centre of Literacy in Primary Education (CLPE). See, for example, BBC, "More Animal Main Characters than Non-White People in Children's Books," *BBC Newsround*, November 20, 2020, https://www.bbc.co.uk/newsround/54900501; Alison Flood, "Children's Books Eight Times as Likely to Feature Animal Main Characters than BAME People," *The Guardian*, November 20, 2020, https://www.theguardian.com/books/2020/nov/11/childrens-books-eight-times-as-likely-to-feature-animal-main-characters-than-bame-people. See also Leslie Bow, "Racial Abstraction and Species Difference: Anthropomorphic Animals in 'Multicultural' Children's Literature," *American Literature* 91, no. 2 (1 June 2019): 323–56.

66. Anthony J. Liddicoat, "Translation as Intercultural Mediation: Setting the Scene," *Perspectives* 24, no. 3 (2016): 347–53.

67. Felski, *The Limits of Critique*, 164–65.

Part I

HISTORICAL READING PRACTICES

Chapter 1

Socioeconomic Status and Varied Freedoms in Eighteenth-Century Childhood Reading

Elspeth Jajdelska

Many children enjoyed the benefits of print in the seventeenth century, whether through oral sharing or independent reading.[1] But the eighteenth century saw some landmark developments in the history of children's reading which impacted both children's freedom to read, in many senses, and how reading was conceived by the mediators, in the sense of gatekeepers (e.g., of libraries) as well as of interpreters (through questioning, oral reading, or shared reading) of the children's reading. As the population rose, both the number of copies of books and the number of new titles overall grew rapidly. As Matthew Grenby, author of the authoritative work on British child readers in the period has shown, this growth supported an increasingly specialized marketplace for books, and even bookshops, for children.[2] From Locke's *Thoughts Concerning Education* (1693) to Rousseau's *Émile* (1762), theories of education emphasized that the child should enjoy learning and that included reading. Consequently, books for children ought to be enjoyable as well as educational. At the same time, rising disposable incomes meant that books, while still expensive, were within the reach of a wider range of families and that children had greater leisure than many of them had had in the past. Taken together, all these developments meant that more children could spend enough time reading in solitude to become competent in fluent, silent reading.[3]

These changes—in population, in the market for print, and in the opportunities for leisure and pedagogy—were part of a broader change in the way that printed texts were *conceptualized* in the period. As Carey McIntosh and others have shown, the eighteenth century was a time when rising consumption of text was altering the role and understanding of speech in public and private life. Family letters, for example, could serve as a way to construct and pass on family identity, alongside oral sources.[4] Rhetoric was changing from the craft of speaking correctly in varied social contexts, to guidance on polite, written composition.[5] Eighteenth-century readers and writers were aware of this changing relationship between speech and writing to varying degrees, as Paula McDowell has shown.[6]

These were changes which people at the time identified. Adam Smith, for example, condemned guides to rhetoric with lists of tropes, memorized by renaissance schoolboys to aid them in spoken performance as "a very silly set of books and not at all instructive."[7] But there were also changes in the relationship between speech and writing in the time which are harder to detect, both then and now. Throughout the seventeenth and eighteenth centuries, there is evidence of a persistent social norm prohibiting social inferiors (typically defined by rank, especially below that of gentleman, as well as by gender and age) from speaking uninvited to their superiors. This was enforced with different degrees of rigor in different contexts throughout this long period, but was remarkably persistent. In 1622, for example, the preacher William Gouge warned that children, along with wives and servants, should wait for "a fit time and just occasion of speech" before speaking to their parents.[8] In 1753, an apothecary by the name of James Nelson published *Essay on the Government of Children* that took a similar view: "children should speak or be silent . . . when bid."[9]

However, there was also a growing list of exceptions to this rule, occasions when superiors were encouraged to condescend to inferiors and hear their speech uninvited.[10] Children, for example, were increasingly encouraged to converse with parents and question them without invitation, specifically in educational settings, reflecting the new emphasis on learning from the child's perspective. Parents, too, were encouraged by educational theorists to question their children about what they had read.[11] Eighteenth-century child readers then had a range of sometimes conflicting ways to situate themselves in relation to the text. For example, they could be evaluating as critics, engaging with adults in interpretation; they could experience the text mediated by an adult oral reader, taking on the voice of the text's narrator and interpreting that through vocal performance; or they could be silent hearers of an authoritative narrator whose voice they must generate internally.

These changes in the norms of spoken decorum were related to a division between the norms of print and those of speech. Seventeenth-century theories of rank discouraged those below the rank of gentleman from interest in genres such as lyric verse or speculative thought, as improper to their station. For example, the seventeenth-century diarist and gentleman Samuel Pepys remarked of a book on trade that though it had "some things good," it was nonetheless "very impertinent"; the obvious explanation for this impertinence is that the author was a fisherman and so policy was not his proper sphere.

Similarly, a preacher in 1699 distinguished between the benefits of arithmetic for lower ranks like tradesmen, to work well in "their respective Callings," but a gentleman's education was suited only to "men of higher Quality," so that they might be useful "either in the Church, or in the State, in the Court or at the Bar."[12] In the eighteenth century, the print market continued to grow in pace with the rising population.[13] This population change, and a move to towns, also created the potential for looser social networks, making change in social norms easier. In combination, these created an environment in which print decorum could increasingly be distinguished from spoken decorum. In 1758, for example, the Exeter merchant George Coade addressed Prime Minister Pitt through his local newspaper, acknowledging the "Decency and Respect" due to "a Gentleman of your exalted station," but at the same time claiming the "Freedom of an *independent Man*" to address Pitt uninvited on the topic of government, traditionally the reserve of the ranks above merchant alone.[14] Eighteenth-century children then, if they could read fluently, had the option of conceiving of themselves as both the equals of their books' narrators and as their inferiors.

This is not to say that eighteenth-century children read either free from constraints, or with the same set of constraints that apply today. Correct oral reading was not an adjunct to silent reading, but an essential accomplishment for children and adults alike.[15] Oral reading was also a check on whether children were correctly interpreting what they read, with correctness at the level of intonation and punctuation having implications for correct meanings at the larger scale. The eighteenth-century elocution movement, popularized through public lectures, sought to move public speaking and oral reading away from sixteenth- and seventeenth-century emphases on heavy rhythms and a "sing-song" tone of changing intonation, toward what they called a "conversational" style. At the same time, however, elocutionists were concerned to control the way texts were read aloud, so that pausing and emphasis were still "correct," that is, as the author intended.[16] Some of this concern for a correct oral style can be seen in this advice from the Edinburgh professor of anatomy, Alexander Monro, to his ten-year-old daughter in 1739:

> A Girl ought to learn to read well, that is easily distinctly with the proper Pauses, and with Tone and Cadency of Voice which the different Subjects require. She then is capable to entertain her Companions.

> Read each Chapter or Section of a Book twice, first for the Sense and then for the Language. Copy such pieces of Books as you think most usefull, and that hit your Taste most, observing carefully to keep every Comma Point or other Pause as it is printed.[17]

Correctness, then, was inextricably linked to interpretation, both at the level of literal "Sense" and at the level of broader meaning, or "language." As Grenby has shown, parents gave children freedom to choose where, when, and how long they read, but kept a careful eye on what they read and how they interpreted it.[18] Grenby's evidence also suggests that there were substantially more child readers among middling and upper middling families than either the rich or the poor.[19] However, he also shows how the interpretations of books by children from prosperous families were not in fact fully autonomous. Adults were involved in the children's reading intensively enough that "Many producers and consumers of children's literature understood that supervision was not merely a monitoring process but was an act of co-authorship," so that "the majority [of children's authors] did understand their work as an ongoing collaboration with the mediating adult."[20] Not all reading was co-interpreted in this way: "There is evidence to show that children read outdoors and in whatever fragments of time were available to them," and that "this was particularly true of working-class children, who often did not benefit from scheduled reading time or dedicated reading spaces."[21] Citing David Vincent's pioneering work on nineteenth-century working-class autobiography, Grenby points out that working-class readers especially were likely to read in the fields when they could.[22]

In what follows, I wish to build on the work of Grenby and Vincent and explore in more depth what "freedom to read" meant for children from different social classes in eighteenth-century Scotland. As well as exploring Grenby's distinction between freedom to choose what, where, and when to read, I consider what freedom to *interpret* reading might mean for different child readers. As Grenby points out, better off and more heavily supervised, child readers could experience reading as a process of co-interpretation with the guiding adult. In that case, the child might be seen as an active participant in reaching an interpretation sanctioned by the adult. However, poorer homes, where mothers in particular were less free to spend time on this kind of supervision, may have offered a level of freedom beyond this, freedom to form interpretations entirely independently. In particular, I consider the case of Scotland, building on Elizabeth Hagglund's study of literacy and education based on autobiographies of Scottish female readers. Hagglund's book chapter is on a smaller scale than Grenby's project, but through analysis of ten eighteenth-century women who left autobiographical writings, she identifies some key distinctions between the reading experiences of girls of different social classes in eighteenth-century Scotland, with a valuable insight into the reading experiences of the poorest in particular. Her findings suggest that although some differences in literacy, access to books, and reading patterns from this time were related to social class, this was not a straightforward story in which poorer girls read less, and less widely, and richer girls read more.

Almost all girls were educated at home, and attitudes and access to books varied within social classes as well as between them, with even the poorest having some kind of access to reading. Family approval or disapproval could be a decisive factor, and again was not necessarily determined by social class alone.

Hagglund's analysis is a pioneering and valuable contribution to our understanding of how categories such as gender and social class affected the experiences of child readers in the period. Her focus is, explicitly, on gender in relation to class in the period, rather than the question of mediation in relation to class, where "mediation" refers to agents who controlled or determined to a greater or lesser extent how the child experienced the text, for example, through oral interpretation, frequency of access, or implicit communication of social or moral attitudes toward a given text. However, Hagglund illuminates and contextualizes source material which offers unique insights into the distinctive, and elusive, experience of readers of the very poorest categories as well as those from prosperous homes. Building on her work, I revisit some of Hagglund's sources to look specifically at the question of freedom to interpret what these readers read. I suggest that where Hagglund identifies limitations on access to learning for girls of all ranks, in at least some of the material she looks at, there is evidence that poor female readers enjoyed *greater* freedom to interpret than readers from homes where parents had more leisure and access to a greater range of texts.[23]

In what follows, I distinguish between three freedoms in relation to children and books in eighteenth-century Scotland: freedom to read alone and therefore to choose the location and speed of reading, freedom to choose what to read, and freedom to interpret what is read. I take each of these in turn and consider how far each was available to children from homes of different socioeconomic status, including laboring class homes where children had varying family roles, and in particular whether they were involved in herding, an occupation which offered extensive periods of unsupervised solitude. Although we can find evidence of laboring class reading throughout Britain at this time, Scotland may offer some extra opportunities for case studies.[24] Levels of reading literacy were high among all levels of society.[25] The cultural centrality of Calvinist religion and an emphasis on active engagement with religious texts by all believers meant that in many contexts, Scots of inferior status engaged with contentious, abstract ideas.[26] Through its emphasis on self-scrutiny, Calvinism may also have encouraged a comparatively high number of lower status Scots to write memoirs, even when these were secular; biography, autobiography, and diary writing were practices that could be shared within families.[27] In what follows I look at a small selection of eighteenth-century Scottish readers from varying backgrounds. My sources include four women whose biographies or autobiographies discuss childhood reading. Three of these (Elizabeth Cairns, Marion Shaw, and Janet Hamilton) came from laboring class families, while the fourth grew up in a home precariously balanced between mercantile and laboring ranks (Elizabeth Hamilton). All four appear in Hagglund's study, discussed earlier. In addition to these autobiographical writings by Scottish women, I look at the memoir of shepherd and author James Hogg. I also consider printed sources that are not autobiographical but contain useful information about children's freedom to read in varied settings. These include the advice to his ten-year-old daughter by Edinburgh professor of anatomy, Alexander Monro (not published until the twentieth century), and the diary of Philip Fithian, tutor to the children of a wealthy Virginia planter. Fithian was a student of the influential Scottish Presbyterian and President of Princeton, John Witherspoon, and remained close to his mentor after completing his studies, following his advice to take the post with the family of Robert Carter III.[28] Witherspoon brought to Princeton eighteenth-century approaches to polite oral reading, setting up a prize for "reading the English language with propriety and grace," distinguishing this skill from oratory, which had its own prize.[29] No diary of this kind by a Scottish teacher survives from the eighteenth century, so Fithian's diary, while apparently remote from Europe, provides valuable insights into a student habituated to the attitudes to reading of an eminent Scotsman, a student who then found those attitudes to contrast with some of those he found in Virginia, providing a picture of points where the Scottish origin of the approach to reading that he had learned from Witherspoon's Fithian is at odds with his (white) Virginian contemporaries.

In addition, I have drawn on manuscript sources in the National Library of Scotland. The Fletcher of Saltoun papers document a family of minor Scottish nobility who played an important role in the nation's civic life, serving in government and on the judiciary. Most of the documents are letters and include material on the young women of the family and their entertainments, including reading, as well as some reading lists drawn up by the family tutor for the youngest son. A second manuscript source is the diary of a Highland school teacher. This man was funded by a Christian charity to educate poor children in English, rather than the Gaelic spoken by some pupils, and consolidate their Protestant faith. Unlike Fithian's diary, it does not give a rich account of the relationship between his pupils and their books but does give some hints of how the power relationship between English-speaking master and Gaelic-speaking pupils informed the relationship of those pupils to their books. Finally, I consider the diary of Amelia Steuart of Dalguise, a gentlewoman of distinguished family, who educated her own children at home.

In each of the three sections that follow, I return to all of these sources, examining and comparing them in each section from different perspectives, creating a tentative account of how freedom to read varied with socioeconomic class, nature of occupation, access to books, and family attitudes. I organize this in three sections, looking first at freedom to read alone; second, at freedom to choose what to read; and finally at freedom to interpret what was read. As the analysis will show, this survey of sources suggests, perhaps surprisingly, that those children who were least free, mainly because of poverty, to choose their own preferences from a wide range of potential reading, may in fact have been most free to read those texts they could access without interference or supervision, and therefore more free than their wealthier contemporaries to interpret what they read without reference to the expectations or desires of anyone else.

FREEDOM TO READ ALONE

Grenby's evidence covers children's reading practices from multiple angles, drawing on extensive and varied sources, including examination of many thousands of copies of children's books. He finds that "the impression we get from many descriptions of children's book use, outside school at least, is . . . that children read where and when they wanted" and that although "whether or not children should have unrestricted access to their books was a subject of intense dispute," "many children seem to have read in regulated sessions throughout the day, with little obvious distinction between lessons and leisure."[30] The evidence is, then, that children were required to read, but that the reading itself was of a kind they could enjoy and that they could at least partially fulfill that requirement as and when they wished, allowing for free, solitary reading. In addition, Grenby's findings suggest that ownership of children's books was associated mostly with the middle class.[31]

How consistent is this picture with the evidence from eighteenth-century Scotland that I survey here? Grenby's account of child reading in comparatively prosperous homes is consistent with evidence from Elizabeth Hamilton's autobiography. Hamilton (1756–1816) was from a merchant's family who fell on hard times when her father died, and as an adult she wrote novels and essays on education. Her autobiography was written late in life, when her health was poor, and without a clear purpose of publication (though it was published after her death):

I sit down to recall and to record every event which I can imagine to have been in any way conducive to the formation of my character and sentiments. Should what I now write never be seen by human eye, the retrospect may at least to myself be useful; as where it gives rise to reflections that mortify, the mortification may be salutary; where it produces a more lively view of the divine goodness, that view must be attended with corresponding sentiments of pious gratitude.[32]

The "biographical fragment" was in fact published after her death, and the quotation suggests a status for the text somewhere between an instrument of self-scrutiny and an interesting read for her existing reading public. Elizabeth's mother compared her son, at boarding school, with his industrious sister, who, "When she is not employed about something necessary and useful . . . entertains herself with a book for the improvement of her mind."[33] This suggests a happy coincidence of the freedom to read silently and for her own entertainment, with a parent's desire to see the mind improved.[34] The young Elizabeth had a somewhat solitary childhood, but "In books, she soon discovered a substitute even for a playmate," again suggesting that she had considerable freedom to read in solitude during leisure hours.[35] There were limits to this freedom, however. Elizabeth, "perused many books by stealth," evading the supervision of a guardian who worried that a "display of superior knowledge" might give the impression of "pedantry."[36] So her freedom to read in solitude was not time limited.

The diary of the gentlewoman Amelia Steuart of Dalguise, part written in her own early adulthood, and part later, as a mother, reflects to some extent her piety, and a Rousseau-like interest in recording minutely her children's moral development. It appears to have been written for private use but with an awareness that family members might read it; it contains nothing scandalous. Steuart's children, like the young Elizabeth Hamilton, had leisure and permission to read alone, which her daughter chose to exercise more often than her sons, for whom she wished "to contrive amusements & employments . . . when they are not at lessons, meals or walks," "for their sister can amuse herself many ways & is fond of work reading, drawing &c."[37]

Alexander Monro (1697–1767), an eminent Edinburgh surgeon and anatomist, composed his "Essay on Female Conduct" in the form of a series of letters for the benefit of his own daughter, unpublished until the twentieth century. His advice reflects a similar view of solitary reading as a happy coincidence of a parent's desire for improvement and a child's choice of entertainment: "Reading assists us to pass our time in an agreeable manner when it might otherwise be very dully perhaps wrong employed."[38] Monro clearly has silent reading in mind here, as he goes on to say that "a girl" ought in addition to this "to learn to read well" aloud, to "entertain her Companions," and later "amuse and instruct her Husband."[39] Like Elizabeth Hamilton's guardians, he too fears that "a Taste for Books" or reading to pass the time (i.e., most likely, silent reading, not amusing or instructing friends or husband through oral reading) might make a daughter unpleasant company, warning that if she was to start displaying unusual knowledge and "uncommon words," he will "let you remain as ignorant as I can of everything beyond what relates to the plainest domestick life."[40] Again, freedom to read alone and at leisure is a good thing for girls, so long as it does not go too far.

The possible results of such a childhood freedom for girls to read can be seen in the adult reading of the gentlewomen of the Fletcher of Saltoun family, whose role in the public world of letters has been studied by Katharine Glover.[41] These women were a group of sisters and cousins who had grown up together in a family of minor, but politically and intellectually distinguished, Scottish nobility. The family papers discussed here consist of letters to and from family members, especially the young women, as well as a reading list drawn up for a young male Fletcher by his tutor. As adults, the young Fletcher women were in one of several occasional verses written for them teased affectionately by their father (or, for one cousin, uncle) about their love of reading and its potential to distract them from female domestic tasks.[42] They all read extensively for pleasure, to a degree that made them fit correspondents and companions for learned men such as Edward Young and William King, the principal of St. Mary Hall in Oxford. Like Elizabeth Hamilton and Monro's daughter, these women had been discouraged or prevented from learning classical languages as children; Monro allowed his daughter to learn the rudiments of Latin along with her brothers but did not "propose to make you so learned that you can have any Pretensions to be a Critick in Languages" or to show off the "uncommon words," as mentioned above. So their freedom to read was encouraged insofar as it might make them fit companions, and discouraged if it went further than that, as this might make them less fit to be feminine companions.[43] The adult Amelia Steuart of Dalguise also read in ways suggesting she had enjoyed a similar level of freedom in her own childhood: as an innocent form of amusement but not without limits. In the diary she kept, in her early twenties, before her marriage, she often reads socially in the evenings, and apparently alone before breakfast:

> I read a little History before breakfast & ended the 2 vol. of Smollet. Nothing remarkable but that the Barons have got the better of the King & obliged him to do what they please.

> after tea we had a little dance in the dining room. My father *open'd the ball* with a short minuet with Aunt Harriet. At 8 o'clock we had a little lotter of 3 prizes & 5 blanks—& concluded with a few pages of our French book in which were the following anecdotes.[44]

In Steuart's case, history and English-language novels provide reading for the mornings, in solitude. French language reading is shared, perhaps because the well-bred females were needed for their French skills, skills which made them fit companions. Her later 1806 diary concentrates on her work educating and bringing up her three children, which included supervised oral reading. At one point, as she details her daughter Harriet's faults, she mentions "tricks such as biting her nails lolling when reading or repeating &."[45] The "reading" here looks as though it is oral and under supervision, accompanied as it is by Harriet "repeating" to her mother, but the reproof for "lolling" or spreading oneself across an armchair while reading may have applied to silent reading.

What of poor children? The evidence here suggests that parents could vary extensively in their views on children's reading and that freedom to read in solitude could depend not only on these views but also on the kinds of labor the children were needed for. Those tasked with herding cattle or sheep and who could get their hands on a book may have had more time entirely free from adult reading supervision than rich children, as they spent hours at a time alone in the fields. Elizabeth Cairns, for example, was the daughter of Scottish Covenanters, a religious group experiencing political persecution at the time of her birth in 1685, and her family lived in extreme poverty.[46] She and her sister looked after sheep unsupervised from the age of five.[47] Her mother taught her to read not long before she was eight, an experience Elizabeth (1685–1741) associated with religious epiphany. Cairns's *Memoirs*, published after her death by admirers of her piety, were written "some years before her death" in the tradition of Calvinist spiritual diaries and autobiographies, genres often shared in manuscript with family members, especially after death, when they could serve as a spiritual inspiration and example.[48] Her epiphanic experience of learning to read was followed, not long afterwards, with sole responsibility for looking after her father's cattle:

> From the eighth year, to the tenth year of my age, I was much delighted with my book, so that I was not only content with the reading of it, but so retained it on my mind, that when I had not time to read, I might have it to meditate on. All the day-time, I was still in the fields alone, with my flock; but in the winter seasons, especially in the long nights, I was busy getting lessons, from any that would teach me, and when ever I could read distinctly by myself, I carried my book always with me, and as I read, there shined a light on my mind, so that I was filled with wonder, at everything I read.[49]

The only books mentioned in the memoir itself are the Bible, the *Shorter Catechism* (of the 1647 Westminster Assembly of reformed ministers), and, at an unspecified later point, Thomas Vincent's 1675 commentary on this catechism. Even this limited selection of books may have constituted a great luxury; life was so hard that even when the Cairns themselves had acquired a little more land, Elizabeth shared her allowance of oatmeal with the daughter of a hungry neighbor who "kept the sheep along with me" and "when I was extremely hungry, I did eat the grass."[50] The book that Elizabeth loved to read, and was free to read silently and unsupervised, then, was the Bible alone, but there was no fear that having "too great a taste for it" would make her unfit for polite society in this impoverished, Calvinist family, and in any case, no one need know of her extensive reading in the fields unless she wished it.

Marion Shaw (1700–1764) also came of very pious and "creditable parents."[51] Shaw, by her own account, could not write until she was fifty-eight years old, when she took up the pen to write a record of "the wonderful love of God and the care of his providence towards me," as well as to offer advice to those she would leave behind on death.[52] Her parents had a kiln, perhaps for lime, as well as livestock. They "carefully instructed me to read," and Shaw kept her father's sheep in the summer, though in the winter she went to school.[53] For Shaw, too, keeping sheep provided solitude for reading: "being oft in the fields out of the view of all others, save the Omniscient eye, I took my catechism along with me, and learned better alone than at school, and also my Bible."[54]

A third reader who enjoyed the freedom that herding livestock brought was the poet and novelist James Hogg (1770–1835), now considered one of Scotland's greatest writers. Hogg's "Memoir of the author's life" was published with his *Familiar Anecdotes of Walter Scott*, at a time when Hogg's fame was well established.[55] Like Cairns, Hogg came from a family of herders often close to, or enduring, financial ruin. Hogg learned the Shorter Catechism and Proverbs of Solomon at a school house "almost at our door," before taking up work when he was seven as a local farmer's cow herd.[56] Again, the memoir highlights the freedom this work could afford children: "I was wont to strip off my clothes and run races against time, or rather against myself."[57] The following year he had a second and final period of time at school before returning to several years of cow herding. During this time, until the age of eighteen, he had no "access to any book save the Bible" and the Scottish metrical psalms, which he learned by heart, though he managed to buy, and teach himself to play, a violin.[58] Like Cairns, he had a great deal of freedom to read the only two books he had access to.

Janet Hamilton (1795–1873), the daughter of a shoemaker and embroiderer/lacemaker on the tambour frame, could not recollect when she learned the alphabet and claimed to have been reading "Bible stories and children's half-penny books" before five (though it is not clear if "read" means oral reading, aural reading, or silent reading).[59] Like Marion Shaw, she learned to read late in life, but went on to publish a range of works including essays and poetry, and her "autobiographical sketch" was first prefixed to the second edition of *Poems, Essays and Sketches* in 1863, in response to being asked,

"How I came to acquire the power of language and ability for composition, which is necessary in writing a book that would pass muster with the press, and the public."[60] At "about eight," she "found to my great joy, on the loom of an intellectual weaver, a copy of *Paradise Lost* and a volume of *Allan Ramsay's Poems*. I carried them off in triumph to the kitchen, returning day after day to devour the contents."[61] This account is consistent with what we know of Scottish weavers, who were often able to read and work at the same time.[62] She lived in a community, then, with comparatively extensive access to books: "About this time my father became a subscriber to the village library."[63] She also had sufficient freedom in childhood from her own labor, in the form of spinning and working at the tambour, to indulge her "unquenchable thirst" for reading in places of her choice (such as the kitchen).[64] On the other hand, her mother disapproved of Janet's "ballad singing, poetry, and novel reading, and would often threaten to burn my precious store."[65] Silent reading in the kitchen or elsewhere may have been the best way for her to evade her mother's watch, but she lacked the freedom from supervision enjoyed by Elizabeth Cairns, Marion Shaw, and James Hogg when reading in the fields.

One further glimpse into the freedom or otherwise of poor children to read alone emerges from the diary of Andrew Rule, a school teacher in the first half of the eighteenth century, tasked with bringing the English language and a sound Protestant faith to poor Gaelic-speaking Catholic children in the Highland parish of Glenmuick who may have been viewed as less zealous than their Lowland, Scots, or English-speaking contemporaries.[66] The diary is mostly an account of books bought and received, and of annual visitations, or inspections, of the school, almost certainly intended for his own recordkeeping. The examples of Janet Hamilton and Andrew Rule confirm the evidence from Cairns, Shaw, and Hogg that the catechism was considered a foundational text for poor children. Where copies of English grammars, dictionaries, and Virgil occur in booklists, the *Shorter Catechism*, "Guthries Trials" (likely the speeches before execution of James Guthrie, a Presbyterian minister hanged at the restoration of the monarchy in 1661), and titles such as *The Danger of Popery* and *The Protestant Resolution* appear in the half-dozens and dozens.[67] These numbers suggest that some of Rule's very poor pupils, in situations similar to those of Elizabeth Cairns and James Hogg, both of whom had access to a catechism, could at least have temporary ownership of some of these books, and therefore both the means and, while herding, the opportunity for silent, solitary reading.

To sum up, both well-off and poor children in Scotland enjoyed some freedoms to read in silence and solitude as they pleased. But the very poorest children, those who herded livestock, while having only the barest of means to read at all, sometimes enjoyed that freedom to the greatest degree of all, measured both by time and by parental approval or disapproval.

FREEDOM TO CHOOSE WHAT TO READ

The evidence here is consistent with Grenby's: children in prosperous homes both owned and had access to a much wider range of potential reading material than those in poor homes. We have seen that Elizabeth Cairns was limited to the Bible and catechism alone and that as a child James Hogg was restricted to the Bible and the Scottish metrical psalms. Marion Shaw mentions only the Bible and the catechism, though she does not specify that no other books were available to her. Andrew Rule's Highland schoolroom for the poor had a much wider range, including Ovid, Virgil, and "Tully's offices in English" (Cicero's "De Officiis"), but in too few copies for any but a handful of the pupils to take elsewhere.[68] Janet Hamilton, however, who lacked the herding freedoms of Cairns, Shaw, or Hogg, and whose mother disapproved of too much reading, was able to access, through neighbors and the village library, a much wider range of reading, including Milton and Ramsay at the age of eight, and, when her father joined the village library, "history, geography, biography, travels and voyages," although the library had "no poetry, novels or light reading."[69]

Better-off children likely enjoyed freedoms greater still than Janet Hamilton's. Elizabeth Hamilton was able to read, between the ages of eleven and thirteen, at the very least "Blind Harry's Lays" (of the Scottish medieval hero William Wallace), "two or three of Shakespeare's historical plays," "the history of England," and "Ogilvie's translation of Homer's Iliad."[70] Alexander Monro expected young girls to learn basic skills and accomplishments such as writing, dancing, and music by instruction, and then "generally without being desired," they "study Poems Plays Novels and Romances."[71] This implies that they have ready access to these poems, plays, novels, and romances.

However, Monro's guidance on what to read is ambiguous. On the one hand, he felt that reading poems was "rather hurtfull" until readers were of an age to exercise good judgment; that "the promiscuous Reading of plays" was dangerous; and that young people who read novels indiscriminately were likely to confuse romance with history.[72] On the other hand, he allowed that each of these genres included virtuous examples which would benefit girls. In each case, his advice was similar: to "let some judicious friend choose" sound examples of poetry; to read no plays "except such as are recommended to her by one whose judgement and sincere friendship she can rely on"; to read the novels or romances he himself recommended, such as Fenelon's

Telemachus and Richardson's *Pamela*; and to rely once more on "some judicious friend" to recommend appropriate "Books of Wit and humour."[73] In each case, Monro silently assumes that an outright ban of faulty texts is impracticable, perhaps because a well-off girl in a town like Edinburgh, with its high levels of sociability, would always be able to access a wide range of books, or because Monro himself considered it too time-consuming to vet and censor books coming into the home. The Fletcher of Saltoun library catalogue has "Travels of Cyrus for children, Edin 1732, octavo" alongside the octavo "Rosenhaugh Modern eloquence of the bar Edin 1711," suggesting children's books and adults could be equally accessible.[74] Grenby describes illustrations of children accessing their own books from cabinets, illustrating both freedom and a sense of transgression (e.g., because the cabinet was too high for easy access by a child).[75]

Certainly some wealthy homes had locked libraries, and even adults had to ask for a key. This was the case in the house of the Robert Carter III, a wealthy Virginia plantation owner, who employed Philip Fithian as tutor to his eight children. Fithian was a graduate of Princeton, then under the leadership of the Scottish Presbyterian John Witherspoon. The Princeton Library when Fithian was a student had fewer than 2,000 books, 300 of them volumes of pamphlets donated by Witherspoon himself.[76] Despite his experience of the Princeton Library, however, Fithian's letters suggest that Carter's library struck him as unusually large, reporting that Carter had an "overgrown library of books which included law, Latin and Greek Classicks," a "vast number of Books on Divinity," and "almost all the late famous writers, as Locke, Addison, Young, Pope, Swift, Dryden &c."[77] In a later entry, we find out that the family library also included lower status items: Fithian spent a day time on *The New Amusements of the German Spa*, a work "Designed entirely for Amusement" which he "took out of the library to read for entertainment."[78] Fithian also thought it worth recording that Carter senior guarded the key to the book cases, and even Fithian had to ask for it if he wished to read any books that he did not own.[79] Additional books in the house might be kept in the schoolroom or near sofas and chairs, but by no means all books were there for the taking.[80] Fithian, then, seems to have been more accustomed to an attitude of greater freedom in access to books, even from much smaller collections, than his wealthy employer displayed, suggesting that Witherspoon, at least, was a Scot used to lesser wealth of books but freer access to them.

Fithian also seems to have been struck that the Carter parents did not play a very active role in their children's education: Carter "informed" Fithian "concerning his desire as to the Instruction of his children," but was frequently away, and neither he nor Mrs. Carter seems to have played the kind of active role in their children's learning that, for example, Amelia Steuart did, or that Fithian himself seems to have expected.

But neither do the Carters seem to have been keen on having the children educate themselves. Fithian was given the keys of the bookcases on specific occasions, but there is no evidence that this freedom was granted to the children. Instead, there was a strictly utilitarian approach to the children's reading. The family wished the elder son to have a university education at Cambridge (it's not clear from the letters if this is Cambridge, Mass, or the English Cambridge).[81] But there was less interest in the achievements of the younger children, the aims of improving the mind being to do better in "each useful and ornamental undertaking to which you may be directed."[82] The children shared this utilitarian approach to learning; a younger son asked for instruction in Latin, at that point reserved for his elder brother, because "Mrs *Taylor* told him he must not have either of her Daughters unless he learn'd Latin."[83] The tutor often had to battle his pupils' indifference to the texts chosen for them, even the promising elder son Ben: "Ben seem'd scared with his Greek Lesson, he swore, & wished for Homer that he might kick Him, as he had been told Homer invented Greek."[84] Again, Fithian's faithful recording of these attitudes suggests that they contrasted to those he was accustomed to at Princeton and in his Presbyterian home. This was a wealthy home then, and one well stocked with books, but not a house where children were free to choose their own books, or encouraged to read for pleasure, nor one in which parents got involved with their children's reading or encouraged them to discuss it. Fithian's response to this home suggests that it was very different from the way he had been educated himself by Witherspoon.

However, Fithian's education in an all-male institution, with comparatively free access to books without supervision, may have differed from that of Scottish girls. Readers like Elizabeth Hamilton "constantly perused many books by stealth," and "once hid a volume of Lord Kaims's Elements of Criticism under the cushion of a chair, lest she should be detected in a study which prejudice and ignorance might pronounce unfeminine."[85] Francis Fletcher of Saltoun was a student in 1749, when he drew up an extensive list of books he owned in his own right, but which had been bought under his masters' instructions, with a heavy emphasis on ancient languages, mathematics, and geography, but also included *Hudibras*.[86] These were not books he chose to buy without direction, but he did own them personally and could therefore read as he chose in ways that his sisters, who did not learn ancient languages, could not, and who, like Alexander Monro's daughter and Elizabeth Hamilton, would likely be discouraged from attempting through self-instruction.

Wealth, then, was a very powerful index of a child's freedom to choose what she or he wished to read. But poorer children who lived in communities of artisans, like some wealthy young men and boys, could access a surprisingly wide range of texts. Wealthier children's parents were concerned with controlling their access to some kinds of texts, though they clearly did not always succeed or even, as in the case of Munro, hope to succeed, trusting instead to their children's discretion.

FREEDOM TO INTERPRET WHAT IS READ

As Michelle Cohen has shown, eighteenth-century approaches to education, particularly in the family, emphasized the importance of relaxing normal spoken decorum in favor of conversation, with parents both questioning children and inviting their questions. This included questions about what the children had been reading.[87] Isaac Watts suggested that during social calls, one person could take a book while the others could "ask any question."[88] Regarding her own reading, Amelia Steuart not only records what she has read but comments on it: "I began to read the Pilgrims progress today," she writes on March 3, 1806, and adds, "I think I shall be one of his admirers if I like all his allegory as well as I do the beginning."[89] Elsewhere she laments that "I read so little today, I have few remarks to make."[90] Again, this suggests that reading should be talked about, and an understanding of texts as requiring more than simply reading the words and understanding their meaning. Her own practice as maternal tutor certainly reflects what might now be called "active learning:" "I was proposing to Marg^t that we should compose a dictionary of every thing that ought to be thought of on every occasion—such as a Journey—a Wedding—a Funeral."[91] This active approach to learning and reading can be found in other eighteenth-century mothers who worked as their children's tutors, most notably Jane Johnson.[92] This is a clear distinction from working-class homes like those of Janet Hamilton and Elizabeth Cairns, whose mothers worked and would not have been able to devote themselves in this time-consuming way to their children's education. So while Steuart's children were much more closely supervised in their reading, it is possible that their mothers' pedagogy encouraged the idea that they, the children, were responsible to some extent for their own learning, and potentially for their own interpretation of texts.

In the same entry, Steuart also mentions what she has been reading communally with her children and then comments on the texts:

> Yesterday & today I was sometimes reading or hearing part of two new Works called the miseries of human life & the art of tormenting [the first is by James Beresford, 1806, and the second by Jane Collier, 1753, reprinted in 1806]. They seem to be by the same Author. The first is divided into *groans* some of them deserve the name, others I think shd be called only annoyances even to Testy & Sensitive the two utterers of groans.[93]

We do not hear from the diary what the children made of the texts they read with their mother, but we can infer that at least some of their reading was reading to her, or hearing her read and that it was her practice to comment on what she read. What the diary does not tell us is to what extent, if at all, her children offered interpretations of their own, or were encouraged to do dispute those of their mother.

Elizabeth Hamilton, as well as an enthusiastic silent reader, was an oral reader of "distinctness and propriety," schooled in this "rare accomplishment" by the aunt who brought her up, an accomplishment which, as she reveals in her *Letters on Education*, she exercised during her sewing lessons at the request of the sewing mistress.[94] At the age of thirteen, she felt secure in interpreting the scriptures alone, or "by stealth," successfully finding arguments to refute the skepticism of a family friend.[95] In the *Letters on Education* she encourages parents to excite children's interest in Biblical passages and let them read them themselves as a treat, with parents intervening to avoid harmful errors. "A very little pains bestowed by the parent," for example, will prevent "the pupil's imbibing improper notions of the Deity from the Jewish representation of his attributes."[96] Here, Hamilton treats an area with the potential for profound theological dispute (the attributes of God as revealed in the Old Testament) as a supposedly simple affair of warning against Jewish views in what are, after all, Jewish scriptures. Her declared tolerance for "variety of opinion" elsewhere in the Letters, then, should perhaps be seen as a lack of insight into the range of opinions potentially available,[97] rather than a genuine acceptance of difference in textual interpretation. It is perhaps to be expected that free interpretation of religious texts might be particularly discouraged, and may serve as a reminder that the eighteenth-century encouragement of independent thought in children may assume that the children will independently come to agree with their parents and superiors. This is an approach to textual interpretation with a long pedigree; see, for example, James Simpson on the reformed insistence that believers must read the Bible for themselves but only so that they may reach the same conclusions as the reformers did.[98]

As adults, the very well-read Fletcher women showed a similar mixture of deference and independence in their evaluation of different kinds of texts. In two letters, they ask the advice of learned men (Edward Young and Dr. King) on what to read. But they also form, to give one example, a robust view of Warburton's essay on Pope.[99] Fletcher family letters also reveal Andrew Fletcher's plans for a parish school in 1714, with the intention that "all those quo [Scots orthography for 'who'] live in ye parish should be obliged both by ye government and ye founders of such Schools to breid yr children at ym."[100] It was accepted that although "it takes a long while for a master to teach such a number of Children to any purpose," there was "time destined"

either for exercise or for "a conversation with ye Master."[101] This suggests
that some children even in parish schools would interpret texts through conversation with a superior. These children might vary in rank from the poorest
of laborers' children to children of the petit bourgeoisie but were unlikely
to include gentry children who were usually educated either by tutors, as
the Fletcher children were, or at single-sex schools, often for boarders, in
Edinburgh or other cities. In Andrew Rule's Highland school, where pupil
numbers could be as high as 117, with no record of a paid assistant, two of
his scholars qualified to teach schools themselves.[102] This implies that they
had attained competence in Latin. Rule's diary records regular purchases of
a range of Latin texts in small numbers, from Rudiman's *Latin Rudiments* to
Buchanan's Psalms, and Salust, Virgil, and Ovid. This level of education was
not, it appears, a priority with the visitors and funders: none of the visitations
featured a display of expertise in classical literature.[103] But it does suggest
that at least some of these very poor students had the opportunity for close
instruction in texts, including classical texts, looking at interpretation as well
as mere translation and that such conversation with their master may have
been their only opportunity to discuss the texts with others.

Janet Hamilton's recollections of reading Milton as a child suggest that
either then or later she was aware of the standard critical reception of Milton.
She refers to "the sublimity of Milton's imagery, and the grandeur of his ideal
conceptions."[104] Hamilton had access to the *Spectator*, and her interpretation
of Milton in terms of sublime images and grand ideas, first formulated by
Addison, was influential in the eighteenth century across all ranks of society.[105] She associates Ramsay's work, on the other hand, with "beginning
to get rich in the Ballad pleasures of my country about that time," suggesting that the printed text was contextualized by a continued oral practice.
Hamilton associates reading and singing as a continuous practice of textual
pleasure, condemned by her mother.[106] Her reading of the Bible, on the other
hand, was highly socialized as a daily practice with her mother and may have
been interpreted through her mother's prayers: "Every night when I laid my
head on the pillow, my mother's mouth was close at my ear, praying for me,
and teaching me to pray for myself."[107]

Marion Shaw, who went to school in winter and herded animals in summer, taking her catechism with her, found that she "learned better alone than
at school." When she "first began to notice the promises and threatenings"
while reading the Bible in the fields, "the one to the righteous, and the other
to the wicked, which was a mean to restrain me from many evils I saw prac-
tised and was inclined unto," and was at times troubled with envy, "so that
since I can scarce either read or hear the lxxiii. Psalm."[108] Her solitary reading
then seems to have had a much greater influence on her interpretation of the
Bible than her reading in school. Even the usual pious background of social

interpretation through sermons, home prayer, and Bible reading may have been weaker than usual, since Shaw "had seldom opportunity of attending public ordinances."[109] And a socioreligious framework of this kind could lead to innovation in the way scripture was interpreted in ways that might be less likely through the parent-child dyad of wealthier homes. During the 1741 religious revival in Cumbernauld, for example, the twenty-six-year-old servant Anne Wylie was moved by communal psalm singing to a rapturous and highly personalized recall of lines from a pietist poet she had read two months earlier.[110]

Elizabeth Cairns also recalls ecstatic experiences of the Bible while out in the fields with her herd: "I carried my book always with me, and as I read, there shined a light on my mind, so that I was filled with wonder, at every thing I read."[111] She also noted changes in her solitary experiences of Bible reading between the ages of ten and sixteen: "in the former two years, wherein I was filled with wonder, the word was all alike to me; but now there were passages sent into my mind with power suitable to my case."[112] Cairns's experience here—of Biblical texts of surprising aptness appearing in her mind—was a common one in Calvinist communities.[113] Cairns, like Shaw, interprets the Bible both in sometimes ecstatic and apparently undirected solitude, and in a social context shaped by a devout Calvinist community.

James Hogg's experiences of impoverished, solitary reading while herding livestock also involved a very personal response to the only books he had access to, the Bible and the Scottish metrical psalms: "I was greatly taken with our version of the Psalms of David, learned most of them by heart, and have a great partiality for them unto this day."[114] Hogg left home young, working for a sequence of masters in his childhood and teens, and his memoir does not suggest a social framework of devotion comparable to Shaw's or Cairns's. He did not, it seems, find in the psalms ecstatic religious experience or a particular application to his own sins, and his enjoyment seems to have been personal and pleasurable. When he gained access to a wider range of works at the age of eighteen, his responses again suggest a freedom from the influence of received interpretations. He was "immoderately fond" of Blind Harry's *Wallace* and Ramsay's *The Gentle Shepherd*. The first is a fifteenth-century heroic poem in over 11,000 lines, the second a popular Scottish pastoral drama from the eighteenth century, both in decasyllabic couplets. Despite his deep affection for these works, Hogg "could not help regretting deeply that they were not in prose . . . or, I thought if they had been in the same kind of metre with the Psalms, I could have borne with them," as his rusty skills in reading made the verse hard to understand (the Scottish metrical psalms are in stanzas of four lines, alternating between eight and six syllables).[115] This is not a response to the verse I have encountered else-where among eighteenth-century laboring class readers, though many shared

Hogg's love of the Scottish metrical psalter.[116] Similarly, the religious texts
lent by one of his master's wives were enjoyed in unconventional ways. In
Burnet's *Theory of the Conflagration of the Earth*, for example, he

> did not understand . . . for the little of it that I did understand had nearly over-
> turned my brain altogether. All the day I was pondering on the grand millen-
> nium, and the reign of the saints; and all the night dreaming of new heavens and
> a new earth—the stars in horror, and the world in flames![117]

Hogg was a reader of exceptional determination and would become a writer
of exceptional and idiosyncratic talent, author of what in the twentieth century is one of the most esteemed novels in English. It is not surprising that
he shows remarkable independence in his interpretation of literary texts.
But it is worth noting that his freedom as a teen reader from the pressure of
received interpretations arose in an exceptional degree of isolation from family, school, or religious communities of reading, again suggesting that those
child readers so poor that they herded animals may sometimes have been
more free to respond to and interpret what they read than any other group of
children in society.

On the question of freedom of interpretation, then, we again see distinctions between the very poorest children, those obliged to herd animals
in isolated, laboring class communities, readers situated in stable artisan
communities of fellow readers, and the better off, who could possess their
own books and whose reading was integrated into a supervised program of
parental (more specifically, maternal) education. The evidence of the Steuart
and Fletcher families, and of Elizabeth Hamilton as child reader and adult
pedagogue, suggests that child readers were brought up to interpret as well as
to read, and to interpret independently. However, the independence consisted
of learning to converge on a received interpretation, whether of the Bible or
of secular texts. As Alexander Monro put it:

> Most Mothers teach their Children some Prayers and make them repeat some
> Catechism & Chapters of the Bible, which are most to their own taste; but then
> they don't explain to the young Creatures the meaning of the Words which they
> repeat, so that little other Benefit than the Exercise of the Memory is got by this
> trouble.[118]

"Explaining the meaning," the example of Hamilton suggests, could move
invisibly from explaining literal meanings to identifying correct interpretations, an ambiguity reinforced by the emphasis on correctness in oral reading
in these parental settings.[119] These privileged child readers were encouraged
to interpret for themselves, but in doing so reach the correct, shared view.

Readers from laboring class communities of readers such as Janet Hamilton's, typically artisans in towns or villages with some access to books, may not have had the leisure, expertise, or desire to instill this kind of reading in their children. But those children who wanted to learn correct interpretation could potentially do so through access to printed criticism such as Addison's.[120] At the same time, they might maintain, as Janet Hamilton did, access to an oral community of, for example, ballad singing, something she associated with reading poetry and novels for pleasure, and which was not necessarily framed in the same way by polite critical consensus. Children at charity schools were often too numerous to memorize both verbatim texts and their interpretation, but there seems to have been room for a few advanced students to share the kind of conversational teaching with their masters that the Fletcher and Steuart families enjoyed at home.

The very poorest, the children who herded animals in isolated settings, had more idiosyncratic responses to texts, even when their chief reading was the Bible and Catechism, both deeply entrenched in the shared interpretation of a religious community. Marion Shaw, Elizabeth Cairns, and James Hogg all experienced the Bible intensively, both in the "intensive reading" sense of frequency and emotionally, spiritually, and aesthetically, making their own choice of key passages which sometimes generated ecstatic experiences and individualized interpretations. In the case of Hogg, this laid the foundation for highly original responses to the much wider range of texts he encountered from the age of eighteen.

CONCLUSIONS

This is a small selection of texts, and these findings highlight only possible ways in which social rank or class could mediate children's reading, rather than providing definite answers. Hagglund concludes from her study of literacy, schooling, and education in Scottish women's autobiographical writing that "while availability of books was significant in determining a girl's involvement in reading and study, the existence of a familial and/or community literary culture seems to have been equally significant."[121] We could add, however, that those children with less access to books enjoyed some freedoms from mediation by their social superiors not available to those with both more access and more adult support for, and supervision of, reading. The very poorest children, who neither helped in social, artisanal work nor spent their days in home or school education, often herded animals in solitude. As a result, they were free to read for long periods alone and without scrutiny or oversight, and to respond to what they read with few constraints.

NOTES

1. Richard Baxter, *A Treatise of Self-Denial,* 2nd ed. (London, 1675), 157; Francis Kirkman, quoted in Louis B. Wright, *Middle-Class Culture in Elizabethan England* (Chapel Hill, NC: University of Carolina Press, 1935), 86–87.

2. Matthew Grenby, *The Child Reader, 1700–1840* (Cambridge: Cambridge University Press, 2011).

3. Elspeth Jajdelska, *Silent Reading and the Birth of the Narrator* (Toronto, ON: University of Toronto Press, 2007).

4. Paula McDowell, *The Invention of the Oral: Print Commerce and Fugitive Voices in Eighteenth-Century Britain* (Chicago, IL and London: University of Chicago Press, 2017); Carey McIntosh, *The Evolution of English Prose 1700–1800: Style, Politeness, and Print Culture* (Cambridge: Cambridge University Press, 1998); Susan Whyman, *The Pen and the People: English Letter Writers 1660–1800* (Oxford: Oxford University Press, 2009).

5. Adam Potkay, *The Fate of Eloquence in the Age of Hume* (Ithaca, NY: Cornell University Press, 1994).

6. McDowell, *Invention of the Oral.*

7. Adam Smith, *Lectures on Rhetoric and Belles Lettres,* ed. J.C. Bryce (Oxford: Clarendon Press, 1983), 26.

8. William Gouge, *Of Domesticall Duties: Eight Treatises* (London: John Haviland for William Bladen, 1622), 282.

9. James Nelson, *An Essay on the Government of Children* (London: for R. and J. Dodlsey, 1753), 176.

10. Elspeth Jajdelska, *Speech, Print and Decorum in Britain, 1600–1750: Studies in Social Rank and Communication* (Abingdon: Routledge, 2016), 32–56.

11. Michele Cohen, "'Familiar Conversation:' The Role of the 'Familiar Format' in Education in Eighteenth- and Nineteenth-Century England," in *Educating the Child in Enlightenment Britain: Beliefs, Cultures, Practices,* eds. Mary Hilton and Jill Shefrin (Farnham: Ashgate, 2009), 99–116; Grenby, *The Child Reader,* 229.

12. Jajdelska, *Speech, Print and Decorum,* 74.

13. William St Clair, *The Reading Nation in the Romantic Period* (Cambridge: Cambridge University Press, 2004).

14. George Coade, *Letter to the Right Honourable W.P. Esq; by George Coade, merchant, of Exeter* (London: for and by J. Scott, 1758), 5.

15. Abigail Williams, *The Social Life of Books: Reading Together in the Eighteenth-Century Home* (New Haven, CT: Yale University Press, 2017), 34 and elsewhere; Jajdelska, *Speech, Print and Decorum,* chapter 7.

16. Elspeth Jajdelska, "'The Very Defective and Erroneous Method': Reading Instruction and Social Identity in Elite Eighteenth-Century Learners," *Oxford Review of Education* 36, no. 2 (2010): 141–56; Soe Marlar Lwin, "Capturing the Dynamics of Narrative Development in an Oral Storytelling Performance: A Multimodal Perspective," *Language and Literature* 19, no. 4 (2010): 357–77.

17. Alexander (Primus) Monro, *The Professor's Daughter: An Essay on Female Conduct Contained in Letters from a Father to a Daughter* (Cambridge: Library edition, 1995), 2, 3.

18. Grenby, *The Child Reader*, 180–85; 209; 211; 224–42.

19. Grenby, *The Child Reader*, 284.

20. Grenby, *The Child Reader*, 244, 245.

21. Grenby, *The Child Reader*, 252.

22. Grenby, *The Child Reader*, 203; David Vincent, *Bread, Knowledge and Freedom: A Study of Nineteenth-Century Working Class Autobiography* (London: Europa, 1981).

23. Betty Hagglund, "The Depiction of Literacy, Schooling and Education in the Autobiographical Writings of Eighteenth-Century Scottish Women," in *Women in Eighteenth-Century Scotland: Intimate, Intellectual and Public Lives*, eds. Katie Barclay and Deborah Simonton (Farnham: Ashgate, 2013), 115–32.

24. Jonathan Rose, *The Intellectual Life of the British Working Classes* (New Haven, CT: Yale University Press, 2001), 16; Elspeth Jajdelska, "'Singing of Psalms of Which I Could Never Get Enough': Labouring Class Religion and Poetry in the Cambuslang Revival of 1741," *Studies in Scottish Literature* 41, no. 1 (2016): 88–107.

25. T.C. Smout, "Born Again at Cambuslang: New Evidence on Popular Religion and Literacy in Eighteenth-Century Scotland," *Past and Present* 97 (1982): 114–27. Alexander Murdoch, "Literacy," in *The Edinburgh History of the Book in Scotland*. Vol. 2, *Enlightenment and Expansion 1707–1800*, eds. Stephen W. Brown and Warren McDougall (Edinburgh: Edinburgh University Press, 2012), 287–96.

26. Jajdelska, "'Very Defective and Erroneous Method.'"

27. Jajdelska, *Silent Reading*.

28. Philip Fithian, *Journal & Letters of Philip Vickers Fithian, 1773–1774: A Plantation Tutor of the Old Dominion*, ed. Hunter Dickinson Farish (Williamsburg, VA: Colonial Williamsburg, Incorporated, 1945), 46.

29. John Witherspoon, *The Selected Writings of John Witherspoon*, ed. Thomas P. Miller (Southern Illinois University Press, 1990), 110.

30. Grenby, *The Child Reader*, 209.

31. Grenby, *The Child Reader*, 284.

32. Elizabeth Hamilton, *Memoirs of the Late Mrs Elizabeth Hamilton* (London: Longman, Hurst, Rees, Orme and Brown, 1819). Vol. 1, 6.

33. Hamilton, *Memoirs of the Late Mrs Elizabeth Hamilton*, vol. 1, 31.

34. Hamilton, *Memoirs of the Late Mrs Elizabeth Hamilton*, vol. 1, 31.

35. Hamilton, *Memoirs of the Late Mrs Elizabeth Hamilton*, vol. 1, 35.

36. Hamilton, *Memoirs of the Late Mrs Elizabeth Hamilton*, vol. 1, 50.

37. Amelia Steuart, *Diary of Amelia Steuart of Dalguise, Journals of Mrs Steuart of Dalguise*, National Library of Scotland MS 983, f.101.

38. Monro, *The Professor's Daughter*, 2.

39. Monro, *The Professor's Daughter*, 2.

40. Monro, *The Professor's Daughter*, 11.

41. Katharine Glover, "The Female Mind: Scottish Enlightenment Femininity and the World of Letters. A Case Study of the Fletcher of Saltoun Family in the Mid-Eighteenth Century," *Journal of Scottish Historical Studies* 25, no. 1 (2005): 1–20.

42. Fletcher of Saltoun, *Papers of the Family of Fletcher of Saltoun*, National Library of Scotland, MS 17890.

43. Hamilton, *Memoirs of the Late Mrs Hamilton*, vol. 1, 37; National Library of Scotland MS 16688, f.78; Glover, "The Female Mind."

44. Steuart, *Diary of Amelia Steuart*, National Library of Scotland MS 983, f.1: March 12, 1789, March 15, 1789.

45. Steuart, *Diary of Amelia Steuart*, National Library of Scotland MS 983, f.94: October 9, 1806.

46. Elizabeth Cairns, *Memoirs of the Life of Elizabeth Cairns* (Glasgow: John Greig, 1762), 11.

47. Cairns, *Memoirs of the Life*, 13.

48. Jajdelska, *Silent Reading*, chapter 5.

49. Cairns, *Memoirs of the Life*, 15.

50. Cairns, *Memoirs of the Life*, 21.

51. Marion Shaw, *Elijah's Mantle, or, the Memoirs and Spiritual Exercises of Marion Shaw* (Glasgow: printed by John Bryce, 1765), 13.

52. Shaw, *Elijah's Mantle*, vii.

53. Shaw, *Elijah's Mantle*.

54. Shaw, *Elijah's Mantle*, 14.

55. James Hogg, *Familiar Anecdotes of Sir Walter Scott* (New York: Bloodgood, S. Dewitt, 1834). Modern edition consulted here in James Hogg, *Altrive Tales: Featuring a Memoir of the Author*, ed. Gillian Hughes (Edinburgh: Edinburgh University Press, 2003).

56. Hogg, *Altrive Tales*, 12.

57. Hogg, *Altrive Tales*, lii.

58. Hogg, *Altrive Tales*, 14.

59. Janet Hamilton, *Poems, Essays and Sketches* (Glasgow: James Maclehose, 1870), viii.

60. Hamilton, *Poems, Essays and Sketches*, vii.

61. Hamilton, *Poems, Essays and Sketches*, viii.

62. Jajdelska, "Singing of Psalms," 100.

63. Hamilton, *Poems, Essays and Sketches*, ix.

64. Hamilton, *Poems, Essays and Sketches*, ix.

65. Hamilton, *Poems, Essays and Sketches*, ix.

66. Andrew Rule, *Diary of Andrew Rule*, National Library of Scotland MS 34.7.12.

67. See for example, Rule, *Diary*, ff. 10 and 15.

68. Rule, *Diary*.

69. Hamilton, *Poems, Essays and Sketches*, vol. 1, viii–ix.

70. Hamilton, *Poems, Essays and Sketches*, vol. 1, 35–36.

71. Monro, *The Professor's Daughter*, 2.

72. Monro, *The Professor's Daughter*, 9.

73. Monro, *The Professor's Daughter*, 8–11.

74. Fletcher, Library Catalogue for the family of Fletcher of Saltoun, *Papers of the Family of Fletcher of Saltoun*, National Library of Scotland MS 17866, ff.1, 4.

75. Grenby, *The Child Reader*, 211.

76. David Zubatsky, "The History of American Colleges and Their Libraries in the Seventeenth and Eighteenth Centuries: A Bibliographical Essay," *Occasional*

Papers 140 (Champaign, IL: University of Illinois Graduate School of Library Science: October 1979), 39.

77. Fithian, *Journal & Letters*, 35.

78. Fithian, *Journal & Letters*, 159–160.

79. Fithian, *Journal & Letters*, 61.

80. Fithian, *Journal & Letters*, 61, 185.

81. Fithian, *Journal & Letters*, 35.

82. Fithian, *Journal & Letters*, 281.

83. Fithian, *Journal & Letters*, 103.

84. Fithian, *Journal & Letters*, 72.

85. Hamilton, *Memoirs of the Late Mrs. Elizabeth Hamilton*, vol. 1, 50.

86. Fletcher, Account of books bought by Francis Fletcher, younger son of Andrew Fletcher, Lord Milton. *Papers of the Family of Fletcher of Saltoun*, National Library of Scotland MS 17065.

87. Cohen, "'Familiar Conversation;'" Jajdelska, *Speech, Print and Decorum*, 38–39.

88. Isaac Watts, *The Improvement of the Mind: Or a Supplement to the Art of Logick* (London: for J. Brackstone and T. Longman, 1749), 130.

89. Steuart, *Diary of Amelia Steuart*, National Library of Scotland MS 983, f.92.

90. Steuart, *Diary of Amelia Steuart*, MS 983, f.97.

91. Steuart, *Diary of Amelia Steuart*, MS 983, f.93v.

92. See also the educational practice of Jane Johnson in, for example, Evelyn Arizpe, Morag Styles and Shirley Brice Heath, *Reading Lessons from the Eighteenth Century: Mothers, Children and Texts* (Lichfield: Pied Piper, 2006).

93. Steuart, *Diary of Amelia Steuart*, October 9, 1806, National Library of Scotland MS 983, f. 93.

94. Elizabeth Hamilton, *Letters on Education* (Dublin: for H. Colbert, 1801), 153–54.

95. Hamilton, *Memoirs of the Late Mrs Elizabeth Hamilton*, vol. 1, 34–35.

96. Hamilton, *Letters on Education*, 145.

97. Hamilton, *Letters on Education*, 94.

98. James Simpson, *Burning to Read: English Fundamentalism and Its Reformation Opponents* (Cambridge, MA: Harvard University Press, 2007).

99. Fletcher of Saltoun, *Saltoun Family Letters*, National Library of Scotland, MS 16688, f.78; MS 16746 f.233; MS 16693, f.222; for a fuller discussion, see Glover, "The Female Mind."

100. Fletcher of Saltoun, *Saltoun Family Letters*, National Library of Scotland MS 16503, f.69.

101. Fletcher of Saltoun, *Saltoun Family Letters*, National Library of Scotland MS 16503, ff.69–70.

102. Rule, *Diary*, f.92.

103. See D.J. Withrington, "The S.P.C.K. and Highland Schools in Mid-Eighteenth Century," *Scottish Historical Review* XLI 132 (1962): 89–99, 97, footnote 4.

104. Hamilton, *Poems, Essays and Sketches*, viii.

105. Hamilton, *Poems, Essays and Sketches*, ix; Jajdelska, *Speech, Print and Decorum*, 147, 167.

106. Hamilton, *Poems, Essays and Sketches*, ix.

107. Hamilton, *Poems, Essays and Sketches*, x.

108. Shaw, *Elijah's Mantle*, 14.

109. Shaw, *Elijah's Mantle*, 15.

110. Elspeth Jajdelska, "'Singing of Psalms.'"

111. Cairns, *Memoirs of the Life*, 15.

112. Cairns, *Memoirs of the Life*, 16.

113. Jajdelska, *Silent Reading*, 31–32.

114. James Hogg, *Memoir of the Author's Life* in *The Poetical Works of the Ettrick Shepherd*, Vol. 5 (Glasgow: Blackie and Son, 1840), 8.

115. Hogg, *Memoir of the Author's Life*, xvii; Francis Rous modified by the General Assembly of the Church of Scotland, translators, *The Psalms of David in Meeter* (Edinburgh: printed by Evan Tyler, 1650).

116. See Jajdelska, "'Singing of Psalms.'"

117. Hogg, *Memoir of the Author's Life*, xviii.

118. Monro, *The Professor's Daughter*, 8.

119. Jajdelska, *Speech, Print and Decorum*, 22–24, 186–89.

120. Jajdelska, *Speech, Print and Decorum*, 166–68.

121. Hagglund, "The Depiction of Literacy," 132.

Chapter 2

Enlightenment Reading Lists

Domestic Curricula and the Organization of Knowledge in Novels by Women

Rebecca Davies

The location of women as educators within domestic systems of childhood education, during the long eighteenth century, imbued women with some limited social power. This in turn allowed women to participate in key Enlightenment debates connected to educational discourse, such as covert female participation in Enlightenment discourse regarding human under-standing and systemization of knowledge.[1] Literary treatments of domestic educative projects from the period often include implicit and explicit guid-ance on the "use" of books—a broader systematization of book-based learn-ing including suggested reading lists and, in older learners, the creation of their own reading lists. In what Matthew Daniel Eddy has recently described as the "spaces of print" in education, child and young-adult book-users learned the patterns and structures to process and mediate knowledge; read-ing was not a linear process of working through a "list," but rather a complex system of knowledge organization and processes of learning. As Eddy notes, however, it is difficult to assess "how students internalized the information."[2] One way to explore conceptualization of internalized knowledge is through an examination of literary fictional treatments of reading and knowing, which combine psychological interiority of characters with Enlightenment systems.

This chapter examines the fictional treatment of systems for organization of knowledge and individualized understanding in works by Jane Austen, Mary Wollstonecraft, and Amelia Opie. In the light of histories of human understanding, I explore how these contemporaneous writers balanced notions of reading-based knowledge acquisition with concepts of indepen-dent thought, internalized understanding, and creative imagination in narra-tives of female education. Drawing on Clifford Siskin and William Warner's paradigm-shifting redefinition of Enlightenment as located in the systems of mediation rather than in the ideas themselves, I argue that both Austen in *Emma* (1815) and Opie in *Adeline Mowbray* (1801) represented a conflict between mediated systems of knowledge and individual cognition in young female characters.[3] Both authors, I posit, rank *bildung* over full integration of those inherently misogynistic systems, to present implicit challenges to the accepted notion of what it means to be an educated woman. While *Emma* represents the ostensible re-education of the misguided young Emma Woodhouse into the traditional marriage plot, the lesser-known *Adeline Mowbray* shows the dangers of an overly liberal education. Adeline—whose education has been guided by an intellectual mother with a focus on radical essays—has a child with a philosopher, Frederic Glenmurray. Steadfastly following Glenmurray's own philosophical tenets, Adeline refuses to marry him, a decision that leads to social alienation and condemnation. The eponymous characters of both novels accurately identify what books they "should" read and understand, demonstrated through reading lists and library choices, but suffer from faulty and misguided interpretive practices. However, the authors imply the systems, rather than female understanding, are flawed.

In order to demonstrate women's negotiation between individualized understanding and systemized knowledge, this chapter also examines how these women writing in the early nineteenth century mediate and critique the late-Enlightenment systematization of knowledge through print. Specifically, how did novels of education, or female *Bildungsromane*, negotiate the complexity of the learning process—the importance of structured written knowledge, balanced with individual cognition, association, and understanding? In order to contextualize the fictional accounts, I examine Mary Wollstonecraft's representation of structured female education through reading in *The Female Reader* (1789), her own understanding in *Letters from Sweden, Norway and Denmark* (1796), and also touch upon Austen's treatment of knowledge in *Mansfield Park* (1814). My contention is that they are laying claim to a form of female "property" in knowledge, akin to what Matthew D. Eddy refers to as a "stock of knowledge," in their representation of systems of understanding and processing.[4] As Eric Rothstein has noted:

> The interplay of different kinds of "system," with different kinds of validity for readers and characters, . . . dominates discussions of method in England and on the continent in the eighteenth century. As Ernst Cassirer says, "The whole theory of knowledge of the eighteenth century strives to confirm this distinction" between the inductive and rational "esprit systématique" and the deductive, rationalistic "esprit de système." . . . Although in practice this ideal often got causal treatment, the conceptual framework was ubiquitous . . . [and therefore it was natural that authors of novels would engage with systems in

representing the intellectual development of their characters. The authors of novels engaging, through their characters, with] the relationship of empiricism and personal systems.[5]

These female characters are not just passively being inscribed with appropriate knowledge, to serve as exemplars, they also demonstrate the use of subjective systems to enable individualized understanding.

In addition, even if the writers of these novels do not lay down the store of knowledge themselves through discovery and insight, they have ownership in that knowledge by identifying what is important enough to claim a space in what John Guillory has termed a canon of "national vernacular." Reading lists and anthologies create a proto-canon of literature that teaches certain themes and rhetoric.[6] However, the novelistic interpretations of the process through which systematized reading informs practice and decisions demonstrates that what the women have gained through reading is still a store of personalized knowledge as property, not just an exercise in rhetoric, or "appropriate" knowledge.[7] Because knowledge could be acquired, it offers a form of social power in terms of knowledge as a "property." Part of what I am interested in here, in addition to the female authority displayed in the interrogation of knowledge systems, is the way that women writers at the end of the eighteenth century conceptualized the relationship between reading and thinking; the role reading, and planning of reading, played in human understanding and subjective cognition.

As Mark Towsey has demonstrated, women's experience of Enlightenment in the long eighteenth century was largely based on their reading practices, more so than for men, who were more likely to have access to formalized education. Towsey observes that "female readers became 'thinkers,' capable of engaging in the public realm of information and politics to a far greater extent than before."[8] Similarly, Richard de Ritter offers Maria Edgeworth's representation of the reading practices of her eponymous heroine, Belinda, as the kind of "symbolic . . . labour that is required to make the developmental self cohere."[9] The quote used by de Ritter to illustrate Belinda's *bildung*-focused reading-labor—"I read that I may think for myself"—also demonstrates the coterminous nature of structured reading and independent thought, which I am presenting as central to women's role in Enlightenment concepts of progress through systems of knowledge and learning.

Both Austen and Opie depict women, often on the cusp of adulthood, or at least adult understanding, who have grasped the concept of improving their knowledge through focused and selective reading, or systematized reading lists, but struggle to move beyond the abstracted concept to useful inculcation of knowledge.[10] This provides a self-conscious commentary on the social restrictions placed on women's understanding—implying that childhood education can only be completed through complete integration of externally ordered knowledge and individual cognitive understanding. Thus, they are partially challenging, and partially reinforcing, the restricted nature of what Eddy terms "panoptic knowledge."[11] The systems of power-knowledge required by Enlightenment conceptions of intelligence and understanding inscribe women as inferior in status and judgment. Therefore, to be considered intelligent, a woman must acknowledge her sex's inferiority. The novelists discussed here demonstrate that subverting such social "knowledge" is ill-advised, or even dangerous, but in part because the system is flawed, rather than purely because of their female characters' personal errors in judgment. In following Immanuel Kant's directive to "have courage to use your *own* understanding," the female characters in these novelists' works often find themselves in conflict with social mores and systems.[12] In this way, these women writing about domestic education explore broader Enlightenment discourse concerning human understanding and individualism through rational interrogation of systematic, and systematized, learning. Thus, in these novels, Mary Wollstonecraft's contemporaneous feminist call for women's "conscious virtue" through rational individualism can be extrapolated to active interrogation of the nature of intellectual understanding.[13] The way novelists wrote about reading and learning in this period can help us better comprehend how they viewed the process of thinking and understanding, the relationship between structured external knowledge and internal "thinking." It also helps us appreciate the relationship between "knowledge" in a generalized sense and individuals' learning: in other words, the difference between knowledge and knowing.

The notion of active internalized knowledge, or understanding, in the long eighteenth century almost invariably refers directly to John Locke's conceptualization of "reasoning:" "As far as we can comprehend Thinking, thus *Ideas* seem to be produced in our Minds."[14] Simplistically, the externally constructed "knowledge" women learned from books would need to be organized and connected internally, through their rational faculties. By externalizing the process of association—depicting female protagonists drawing up lists or constructing clear written systems of understanding—women writers demonstrated women's reasoning power. Alexander Gerard's *An Essay on Genius* (1774) provides a useful conceptualization of the process of systematizing knowledge:

> Regularity arises in a great measure from such a turn of imagination as enables the associating principles, not only to introduce proper ideas, but also to connect the design of the whole with every idea that is introduced. When the design is steddily [*sic*] kept in view, and the mind so formed as to be strongly affected by that associating quality by which the design is related to the means of executing

it, the imagination can scarce fail of being regular and correct. Any conception that is present, will introduce most readily those ideas which are related to the main design, as well as to itself, though there should be a thousand others bearing the same relation to itself, but unconnected with the general subject.[15]

The selection of "appropriate" knowledge, dismissing anything irrelevant to the "whole design" of associated ideas, is thus a demonstration of good reasoning powers. By structuring knowledge in (to employ Eddy's apposite term) "spaces of print," through lists, plans of reading, headings, and explicit references to reading, women writers such as Opie and Austen demonstrated women's active reasoning, or powers of association. To put it another way, they presented a written framework for rational thought and, through their *Bildung* plots, showed how this could be incorporated into an intelligent life of active reason. For women, the limitations placed on this "active" knowledge are twofold. First, unfettered creative thinking is socially restricted; female characters cannot be depicted as fully independent because they would then pose a threat to patriarchal authority. Kant acknowledged this particular restriction on women in the aside that "the entire fair sex" had been persuaded to remain in a constant state of dependence on external guidance, because internalized self-guidance is considered too dangerous.[16] Second, women's limited authoritative social position as educators—or "self-appointed guardians" of knowledge systems in Kant's terms—relied on knowledge being conceived as stable and continuous, rather than individualized and dynamic. Creative imagination—and associated notions of original "genius"—challenged this conception and thus also challenged the limited power that women had gained as guides through, and guardians of, systematized knowledge. It was consequently in the interest of authoritative female educators to reinscribe knowledge as a stable schema which could be passed down to future generations without any shocking innovation or challenging of the status quo. In an apparent novel of internalized character development and education— such as Austen's *Emma* and Amelia Opie's *Adeline Mowbray*—to completely halt the process of learning at the point of schematizing knowledge seems to run counter to the purpose of the genre. But by representing female characters who never get around to reading proposed books, or who select the wrong knowledge to incorporate into their understanding and the wrong way of schematizing this knowledge, these authors do not represent the process of formal learning as closing with schemata. As this chapter argues, rather than circumscribing women's knowledge and understanding by an overt focus on the systems that reinforce and reproduce epistemologies, these authors are applying Kant's notion of separation between rational public scholarship and private social behavior.[17] In this manner they open up space for women to maintain authority in educating future generations, while allowing them to question their position as eternal minors under guardianship of men through a demonstration of women's enlightened individual rationality.

Unfortunately, despite his distinction between private scholarly freedom and public duty, Kant's notion of an enlightened individual is closely connected to the concept of original genius, which itself is associated with the complete rejection of educational systems and tools.[18] This is problematic for women, whose limited authority in this period rests in their governance over consistent systems of education and recognized structures of learning through reading. If the public consensus was that women could pass information on to future generations, and were not individualized "thinkers," it was important that education and syllabi remain fairly stable. Siskin and Warner offer an alternative to Kant's "formulation of a self that dares to know—that has the courage to use—as he emphasized—its own understanding," by looking back at Bacon's earlier acceptance of "the necessity of tools—tools that work. We can't create—at least create very well—on our own."[19] The tools, or media, employed by Austen and Opie are shared systematizations of reading, understanding, and knowledge: book lists, library catalogs, appropriate reading materials, selective and selected knowledge. In this way, women writers were able to enact progress within existing protocols; the systems are not overturned by radical suggestions, but their limitations *are* revealed through the damage caused to women who dare to over-trust their own understanding within these systems of power. The subversive nature of the commentaries in these novels comes from the covert implication that the systems, and not women's understanding, are at fault.

The knowledge imparted by books is not limited to the content. Reading any approved books will provide the reader with an understanding of the systems used to construct understanding in the context of her society, through the use of written machinery such as chapters, headings, or even personalized choices regarding where to start and stop reading within an assigned period of time. These written codes order knowledge in consumable ways and provide women novelists with models through which they can demonstrate the developing individualized understanding of their protagonists.

The written ordering of knowledge in approved books is schematic, and female writers such as Opie and Austen were demonstrating familiarity with shared schemata in the way they portrayed development of understanding in their characters. Matthew D. Eddy suggests that the learned graphic ordering inscribed by Enlightenment education "explains why specific kinds of visual order were repeatedly employed by the adult authors and readers who were taught such practices."[20] While Eddy emphasizes the physical print layout over conceptualization of cognitive order in the association of ideas explored by adult authors, both of these elements are present in the works of Austen and Opie. They present an examination of women writers' relationship to organized knowledge—external and physical, and internal and cognitive—through their treatment of female educators and readers. These writers are, I posit, demonstrating an understanding of a social version of what Siskin and Warner have described as "protocols . . . the rules, codes, and habitual practices that help to secure the channels, spaces, and means of production and communication. They control for the sake of growth."[21] In order to present women as active and important contributors to the field of knowledge exchange and development, these writers had to inscribe them within recognized systems and practices that were understood in the associations of the readers; the representation of female readers and writers following structured concepts of knowledge reinscribed the association of women with idealized education, employing codified systems of knowledge, and associating it specifically with women as educators and readers.

Here, I am drawing on, but not contributing to, reader and pedagogical history. My concern is not what was actually happening in terms of reader experience in the period, but how writers of fiction were interpreting and conceptualizing the role of reading in developing female minds, and the representation of cognition through female characters. How were these writers using books as markers of knowledge fields, both socially dictated and taboo, relative to young female minds? Furthermore, how did they represent the independent interaction of female learners' minds with these systems of knowledge? Reading, as represented in the novels discussed in this chapter, demonstrates first a cultural understanding of shared knowledge as a systematized model which privileges some texts as "important," and second that understanding the *system* is culturally required, regardless of whether the content of the books is read and assimilated into the reader's thoughts and understanding. This categorization and subdivision of knowledge into understandable and attainable portions creates a definition of "required knowledge" and thus demonstrates what these writers perceived as essential for young women's construction of self, if we view the understanding and knowledgeable "mind" as coterminous with selfhood. Texts included in reading lists are thus interpolated into (or excluded from) the understanding of appropriate knowledge for women and recognized as such by their inclusion in the system of education. The process of "learning" makes a space for these texts to be listed, read, discussed, and understood. What I am interested in drawing out is the way that the novelists balance individualized interiority with the disinterested nature of systems of knowledge relative to individual subjects.

LEARNING THROUGH READING

Reading, in many ways, systematizes knowledge and ideas in a way that smooths the path to individual reasoning. Externally structured "book knowledge" is associated through signifiers contained in book titles, "heads"—or headings—within books, repeated phrases and socially understood concepts, and intertextual references to other books. In his *Dissertation on Genius* (1755), heavily influenced by Locke's *Essay Concerning Human Understanding*, William Sharpe represented auto-didacticism through reading as worthy of the title "education" explicitly *because* it is systematic and structured, rather than random and chaotic: "It is one principal drift and business of education to methodize instruction, and if this aim is accomplish'd without it, then it is an education to all the purposes of improvement as much as if it were conducted with the strictest regularity under the most accomplish'd masters."[22] Books, in a sense, pre-order knowledge, making association and reasoning more straightforward than knowledge gained through other means. This concept of order influencing intelligence and associative thought is also a notion exemplified by Mary Wollstonecraft in the introduction to her "Female Reader," a selection of appropriate texts for teaching girls, "whatever tends to impress habits of order on the expanding mind may be reckoned the most beneficial part of education."[23] Jane Austen also explicitly acknowledges the relationship between structure and a reading-based education for women. In *Mansfield Park*, Edmund Bertram's encouragement of Fanny Price's learning is based on his trust in an effectively planned reading-based curriculum: "He knew her to be clever, to have a quick apprehension as well as good sense, and a fondness for reading, which, properly directed, must be an education in itself." Edmund's direction is an important component in Fanny's education through reading because he forms "her judgment," a central component in the structured aspect of the reading process since it forms the structured foundation of the cognitive process.[24] As John Locke defines it:

> If in having our Ideas in the Memory ready at hand, consists quickness of parts; in this of having them unconfused, and being able nicely to distinguish one thing from another, where there is but the least difference, consists, in a great measure, the exactness of Judgment and clearness of Reason, which is to be observed in one Man above another. . . . *Judgment*, . . . lies . . . in separating carefully, one from another, *Ideas*, wherein can be found the least difference, thereby to avoid being misled by Similitude, and by affinity to take one thing for another.[25]

Thus, Fanny Price's education is formed by a combination of externally defined "appropriate knowledge," as defined by Edmund, and her own "quickness of parts," which can associate the ideas she has inscribed in her memory without being led to inaccurate conclusions by a lack of cognitive ability, or poor "judgment."

Austen, through Fanny, comments explicitly on the mechanical functioning of the human understanding, while demonstrating the association of ideas through "trains of thought," earlier in the novel:

"How wonderful, how very wonderful the operations of time, and the changes of the human mind!" And following the latter train of thought, she soon afterwards added: "If any one faculty of our nature may be called more wonderful than the rest, I do think it is memory. There seems something more speakingly incomprehensible in the powers, the failures, the inequalities of memory, than in any other of our intelligences. The memory is sometimes so retentive, so serviceable, so obedient; at others, so bewildered and so weak; and at others again, so tyrannic, so beyond control! We are, to be sure, a miracle every way; but our powers of recollecting and of forgetting do seem peculiarly past finding out."[26]

While Fanny is not specifically discussing memory in service of book-learned knowledge here, it is impossible to overlook the relationship of her statement to Locke's theories of *ideas*. Her observations on remembering and forgetting demonstrate a clear understanding of the individualization of mind, or intelligence: or "quickness of parts."

We can trust in Fanny's own good sense because Edmund's approbation of her intelligence is conveyed through Austen's narrative, but she is also able to display her understanding of the interiorized system of knowledge through an appropriate selection of books for her sister, Susan. This transference of learned knowledge structures through reading lists designed for others is also seen in Emma Woodhouse's guidance of Harriet Smith, although "Her views of improving her little friend's mind, by a great deal of useful reading and conversation, had never yet led to more than a few first chapters."[27] Instead of reading, Harriet collects a book of riddles, assisted by Emma. Austen's tone in relation to Harriet's literary endeavors is ironic, but it does again acknowledge Emma's exquisite understanding of the intersection of systems of print and memory—significantly placing importance on both form and content—through which knowledge could be organized and digested:

In this age of literature, such collections on a very grand scale are not uncommon. Miss Nash, head-teacher at Mrs. Goddard's, had written out at least three hundred; and Harriet, who had taken the first hint of it from her, hoped, with Miss Woodhouse's help, to get a great many more. Emma assisted with her invention, memory and taste; and as Harriet wrote a very pretty hand, it was likely to be an arrangement of the first order, in form as well as quantity.[28]

The fact that Harriet's understanding of processing "literature" in this format came from her teacher demonstrates that the processes of excerpting and inscribing, in order to assist memory and invention, are effective educational programs. Although the subject is a little trivial, Austen's treatment of the process, in the context of Enlightenment systems of learning and knowing, demonstrates its effectiveness.

The systematizing of knowledge through lists and collections is another way in which order, understanding, and association can be given a written form. Matthew D. Eddy directly connects list making and commonplace books with systemized learning as

> a manually reinforced act of graphic order instantiated by the vertical alignment of words in neat sentences, lists, and tables. Within the associationist milieu of Scotland, transcribing information in this manner was believed to be an effective pedagogical tool because it shaped the mind through an act of embodiment. Put another way, it was seen as a cognitively important practice, one that could be expanded later by adults in commonplace books, diaries, letters, and university notebooks.[29]

In the same way, "readers" or anthologies, lists and libraries of planned reading, and Opie's wrongly educated protagonist all demonstrate a consciousness of the links between written systems of knowledge and personal, internalized cognitive development.

The act of reading, or preparing to read, demonstrates a self-aware engagement with the publicly agreed schemata of knowledge and provides the individual with "ideas," or knowledge, that can then be associated by the independent, individualized, mind. Knowledge of the schemata demonstrates one is "educated" within the confines of the system. Jane Austen demonstrates this process in *Emma* through the completion of the protagonist's education in spite of—instead of through—a plot that never requires the completion of a program of reading. Emma is criticized by Mr. Knightley for continually embarking on a "course of steady reading" which never develops beyond the creation of "excellent" reading lists.[30] Ultimately, however, Emma Woodhouse's education is not completed through guided reading, neither is Harriet Smith's successful marriage achieved through following the reading lists that Emma draws up for her. This representation of the limits of "reading lists" in Austen's *Emma* demonstrates that the second stage of "understanding," one requiring individualized cognitive ability, was more necessary for full integration into society: the young female protagonists are not just passive vessels for "book-learning" but part of a more complex systematized understanding. If material books in private and circulating libraries and shops represented the inscription of a material "knowledge," then reading lists, or recommended reading, offered an implied potential for completion of this knowledge; if one were to read the "right" books, comprehensive wisdom would be achieved. Matter thus became ideas, and reading the contents of the physical book would turn them into something less tangible—wisdom, ideas, and knowledge. Austen and Opie demonstrate the flaws in this belief in the "wholeness" of knowledge, by presenting the importance of more nuanced individual cognition through their female novel characters. The combination of systematized knowledge and individual thought is required for true female wisdom.

The woman on whom Opie allegedly based the character of Adeline, Mary Wollstonecraft (a contemporary of Opie and a writer who had explored female cognition and education in much of her feminist writing) had reflected on this notion of the material prerequisites of learning, or being "learned," when on a visit to Risør in Norway.[31] In her Scandinavian *Letters* from 1796, describing the fate of the bookless inhabitants as intellectually "bastilled . . . shut out from all that opens the understanding, or enlarges the heart," Wollstonecraft finds the solitude helpful to her own thought processes because her "mind was stored with ideas" in advance. We can infer these ideas were gained through her previous reading. Through her solitary walks she finds these ideas are associated "with astonishing rapidity," demonstrating her familiarity with the systems required to construct understanding from consumption of knowledge in books or to extract relevant information from one's own store of knowledge to create original thought.[32] This recognition of association of ideas through systematized reading is more explicitly demonstrated in her *Female Reader* (1789), where subjects are "carefully disposed in a series that tends to make them illustrate each other; linking the detached pieces seemed to give an interest to the whole."[33] Wollstonecraft's representation of the relationship between ideas as laid out in written forms, and in her description of cognitive associationism of her own "mature" mind through the employment of imagination, demonstrates a broader epistemic model: the systematized connection of ideas and subjects leads to coherence and wholeness of understanding. There is a "truth" that can be attained by carefully structured knowledge acquisition and then contemplation of the ideas accumulated in this manner. In warning against purely memorizing text, Wollstonecraft urges "the fond mother" to teach her daughter to "read *well*," suggesting a systematic inculcation of understanding that lasts into adulthood.[34] Although many of Austen's characters fail to read at all, they do demonstrate the nuanced understanding that is implied in the phrase "read well"; they understand the systems even if they do not do the work.

CONTROLLING KNOWLEDGE: SYSTEMS AND READING LISTS

Mary Wollstonecraft thus shares with Jane Austen and Amelia Opie a notion of knowledge as controlled, rather than circumscribed, by structures of knowing and reading. Emma Woodhouse's "excellent" reading lists are not an eternally broken promise to read, but a demonstration of a woman's ability to, in Alexander Gerard's terms, "introduce proper ideas" to the "design of the whole."[35] In Umberto Eco's 2009 interview with *Der Spiegel* he usefully conceptualizes the control invoked by listing, describing lists as "a cutout of infinity"—a way to try and find order in the incompletable infinite of knowledge. However, he also explains his refusal to codify and list his own personal library catalog, which constantly changes as his interests change, thus demonstrating a conceptualization of the individualized mind as less fixed than a catalog of written documents. A book catalog, it is implied, would put a limit on his personal knowledge—an ever-expanding, boundless knowledge—which is given material form through his book collection.[36] This notion of knowledge as infinite, however, elides the fact that knowledge is circumscribed by social codes, which must also be learned through a "correct" education. This is especially true for eighteenth-century women's education through reading. Knowledge of how to order what "should" be learned is thus a key part of the educational process, and learning the wrong systems for knowing can be more damaging than having read the wrong books, or no books. It is through comprehending what one "should" know that Emma Woodhouse achieves acceptable knowledge, and lack of such knowledge dooms Adeline Mowbray. Similarly, Eco suggests he is better able to gain reliable knowledge from Google lists than children are, because he, as an older man, has developed his understanding in a non-digital, implicitly more reliable, realm of print. The implication being that to conceptualize the knowledge contained within lists, one must already have the knowledge to judge the worth of the list. This notion of pre-gained knowledge providing a roadmap to individualized understanding is present in a pre-Google eighteenth-century form in Wollstonecraft's claim in Risør, mentioned earlier, that her mind was ready-stocked with ideas, and therefore not adversely affected by the intellectual sterility of her environment. This biographical account mirrors Austen's depiction of Fanny Price's return to a bookless home in *Mansfield Park*, where she is able to bring knowledge to her sister, Susan, through her preceding reading and access to a circulating library.[37] However, because eighteenth-century women's knowledge must be within acceptable confines, the individual's understanding must simultaneously fit the socially defined systems. Not all knowledge from the "infinite" is equally valued. Writing personal reading lists of planned or suggested reading demonstrates an intersection of personalized knowledge with an awareness of socially constructed "appropriate" knowledge systems.

Eco's concerns about the unfiltered excesses of internet-based knowledge, given structure through Google lists, echoes the eighteenth-century attempts to find order in the Enlightenment era of information, in an age when old systems were being questioned and replaced. Christina Lupton cites Chad

Wellmon's *Organizing Enlightenment* (2015) in defining the Enlightenment machinery at work in intellectual institutions in the period:

> Wellmon, looking at the late-eighteenth-century German case of "information overload," describes indexes, charts and encyclopedias as explicitly designed to contain and synthesize this excess. His focus is on a broad form of cultural endeavour, an institutional response to print production that leads finally to new technologies of disciplinary inquiry and subject formation channeling that surplus of book-bound knowledge . . .[38]

Women, who were not allowed to be part of the universities and scientific societies that form the center of Wellmon's study, also employed systematized controlling mechanisms such as reading lists, directed reading, and commonplace books, in order to limit the intake of ideas to a manageable level. However, as Austen and Opie's treatments demonstrate, the process of learning is not passive, and the cognitive processes—or "associations of ideas"—that take place internally give women a sense of autonomy and subjective understanding within the structures of learning. Just because women learned by reading, it did not mean their curriculum was not externally structured and controlled.

Mary Wollstonecraft's preface to *The Female Reader* epitomizes the notion that immature minds require structured knowledge in the form of selected reading:

> It is universally allowed that many poems, tales, and allegories, are scattered through our best authors, particularly calculated to affect a young heart and improve an opening understanding, which the gay and thoughtless seldom have patience to look for, or *discernment to select*; and many collections have been made, in order to present in one point of view the most useful passages of many volumes, where various other subjects are mixed that were once *written for minds matured by experience*.[39]

Here, Wollstonecraft is not just offering reading that is necessary to develop knowledge—"essential reading" if you will—she is suggesting that texts contain both appropriate knowledge and knowledge that is beyond the comprehension of a still-developing understanding. She is also presenting a mediated version of appropriate knowledge that mirrors magazines in being what Siskin and Warner have described as "store-houses" of previously printed materials, which worked as "part of a cumulative, collaborative, and ongoing enterprise."[40] Wollstonecraft was not providing a collection of her favorite pieces of writing; she was participating in a recognized systematized educational system of knowledge based on printed material. This systematized printed knowledge is what Austen demonstrates her characters' familiarity with, and Opie shows the risks of lacking.

In emphasizing the significance of reading as a bedrock of female education, Mark Towsey notes the caveat that "women had to maintain a careful balance—reading could enhance virtue, domesticity, and reason, but reading the wrong kinds of books or the right books in the wrong way was thought to breed idleness, vanity, and sexual indiscretion."[41] Of course, Opie overtly critiques Editha Mowbray for the latter sort of reading—reading to support self-love rather than social duty and to show off her intellect rather than improve her useful knowledge. However, the treatment of her daughter, Adeline's, reading is more complex. Adeline undoubtedly suffers from being allowed to read some of the wrong books but more from lack of social contact, unsystematic reading, and, most damagingly, the inability to integrate systemized knowledge into lived experience.

Adeline Mowbray is, on the surface, a critique of the organization of knowledge and inquiry through a priori rational systems. Adeline is educated in philosophy without context, which would have been provided through the "real life" experiences represented in novels, and therefore lives her life in a way that is socially condemned. In this way, the novel can be read as a direct challenge to the Enlightenment conceptualization of intelligence as an ordered and systematized mind. However, this is an overly simplistic reduction of Opie's warning: implicitly Adeline and Glenmurray's system (which views marriage as unnecessary) is owned to *be* rational and morally defensible, and Adeline's letter of repentance to the suitor she could not marry because of her poor reputation, Colonel Mordaunt, employs exactly the same *methods* of reasoning and rhetoric, albeit to draw the opposite conclusion to her apparently erroneous views at the beginning of the novel. The beginning of each paragraph in Adeline's letter builds up her thesis in a persuasive and rhetorically recognizable empirical structure; "It is evident . . . Hence it follows . . . On this ground, therefore, this strong ground, I venture to build my present opinion, [based on] the reverend experience of ages."[42] Thus, Adeline's letter demonstrates the schemata of organizing knowledge and understanding can be employed to represent two completely opposing views. In demonstrating the limitations of strict logic, Opie appeals to another existing schema: that of *moral* right, while simultaneously seemingly undermining the notion of judging moral right through socially defined frameworks. Throughout the novel, Adeline maintains more than a pathetic hold on the reader's sympathies; Opie employs ethos and logos too. Opie supports Adeline's negative views of the social institutions of marriage through the numerous exploitative, mercenary, and cruel marriages experienced by women in the novel, not least Editha and Adeline's marriages to profligate libertines. The reader never once doubts Adeline's true virtue and worth, and her insistence on honesty and her stance against hypocrisy are also persuasive. It is only, therefore, the implied reader's understanding of morality as socially defined that should undermine the persuasiveness of Adeline's original stance. Opie seems to self-consciously acknowledge this genre-flaw in the novel as educational exemplar through Adeline's insistence at the end of the novel that she *must* die lest her daughter not understand her example as a warning against immorality.[43] If novels are supposed to bridge the reading gap between real experience and abstract theoretical systems, here Opie makes the constructed written nature of that reality more explicit. In doing so, she also refers to Adeline's story as a "biography," a genre missing from Adeline's youthful reading scheme causing her lack of understanding of social expectations. This is because her mother in turn had never followed this program of reading in her education:

> For her, history, biography, poetry, and discoveries in natural philosophy, had few attractions, while she pored with still unsatisfied delight over abstruse systems of morals and metaphysics, or new theories in politics; and scarcely a week elapsed in which she did not receive, from her aunt's bookseller in London, various tracts on these her favourite subjects.[44]

Biographies and novels are, therefore, self-referentially inscribed into the novel as essential reading for a rounded education. This is reemphasized in the itemizing of the immoral Sir Patrick's lascivious library in comparison with Mrs. Mowbray's, which highlights important gaps in Adeline's novel-reading, while demonstrating that not all novels are equally appropriate:

> Scarcely had the works of our best poets found their way to her library; and novels, plays, and works of a lighter kind she was never in the habit of reading herself, and consequently had not put in the hands of her daughter. Adeline had, therefore, read Rousseau's *Contrat Social*, but not his *Julie*; Montesquieu's *Esprit des Loix*, but not his *Lettres Persannes*; and had glowed with republican ardour over the scenes of Voltaire's Brutus, but had never had her mind polluted by the pages of his Candide.[45]

As a result of this lack, Mrs. Mowbray mistakenly tells her daughter that Rousseau's *Nouvelle Heloise* is inappropriate reading and curtails the potentially useful broadening of her book-based education.

Biography, as an important genre in women's reading-based education, is more explicitly connected to the print-based "systems of learning" outlined in the introduction to this chapter. When describing how Mrs. Beauclerc tells people Adeline's biography, Opie writes that she "took care to tell those who mentioned the subject to her, the *heads* of Adeline's story."[46] In his writing on the graphic nature of written education, Matthew Eddy particularly emphasizes the significance of "heads, lists, and tables [which] created a collective image that helped students remember and organize information."[47] He goes on to suggest that the "spatial knowledge" of educational texts in schools "laid the foundation for the forms of systematic classification that undergirded the Enlightenment vision of an ordered mind and, by extension, panoptic knowledge."[48] In employing this meta-graphical description within her story of systems and informational processing gone wrong, Opie both demonstrates a cognizance of collective systems of understanding and useful knowledge and suggests to the reader a process through which they could recollect the "important" aspects of the moral tale following completion of the reading process.

That Mrs. Beauclerc wishes to exonerate Adeline because of the morally sound reasoning behind her refusal to marry, but is unable to because Adeline's position as a teacher of young women makes her an unsuitable example, illustrates Kant's caution against conflating the public scholar and the private citizen. In Kant's example, he suggests a pastor can criticize doctrine in his public scholarly writing, but that these views should not affect the performance of his role as a pastor because he "is bound to instruct his pupils and his congregation in accordance with the doctrines of the church he serves, for he was employed by it on that condition."[49] While Adeline is self-employed, in the respect of running her own private school, she is employed in a social system of education, and thus holds the position of guardian of socially approved knowledge. As such, she and Mrs. Beauclerc are both aware that she must present social doctrine in an externally defined system and that the "heads" of Adeline's story within that system represent, in a recognizable format, the social doctrine of a fallen woman led astray by inappropriate education.

Adeline's own life-as-example, or more specifically as warning, is inscribed as a written biography, a maternal legacy for her daughter:[50] "Now, when she shall see in my mournful and eventful history, written as it has been by me in moments of melancholy leisure, that all my sorrows were consequent on one presumptuous error of judgment in early youth, and shall see a long and minute detail of the secret agonies which I have endured."[51] The construction of the necessity of "minute detail" and extraordinary length of text in order to convey the moral message provides an alternative method to Mrs. Beauclerc's "heads" for conveying knowledge and information. Adeline's autobiography provides an intimate, psychological study of the effects of rejecting social systems of morality in favor of pure rationality. The people to whom Mrs. Beauclerc was providing the information regarding Adeline's moral errors were members of respectable society; therefore they could access their prelearned moral schemata in order to comprehend the moral knowledge conveyed by summary "heads." However, Adeline's infant daughter, prevented by Adeline's untimely death from receiving a personal education from her reformed mother, needs to follow the detailed and lengthy explanation of morality contained in Adeline's text. By reading her mother's story, which will empirically demonstrate the ill-effects of her mother's mistaken schemata, Adeline's daughter will not be led into the same heuristic errors.

Opie's partial, or ambiguous, reinforcement of systematized morality—which seems to invite contradiction from a rational reader's casuism, as Adeline is not immoral as assessed through purely theory-based deductive judgment—can be read as an acknowledgment of Kant's rationale that "a public can only achieve enlightenment slowly."[52] In representing the dangers of systems through the narrow reading practices, and understanding, of Mrs. Mowbray and, consequently, her daughter, Opie also implicitly criticizes the inflexible system of public morality, or "modes of thought," that views Adeline as a fallen woman, in spite of her firm belief in monogamy that cannot even transcend the death of her partner. The overall message of Opie's novel, therefore, does not seem to be a warning against scholarly women, but rather guidance in balancing individual reasoning and scholarship with obedience to social conventions. While Opie does seem to criticize the hypocrisy of not aligning one's scholarship with one's private actions, particularly through the figure of Glenmurray who refuses to lose face by correcting his mistaken theories against marriage, Adeline's inability to distinguish between scholarly theoretical reasoning and appropriate private behavior is more overtly criticized. The ultimate fault, however, lies with her mother's misguidance and neglect of Adeline's book-based curriculum.

TIME TO LEARN

In addition to the limitations imposed on systems of knowing by socially unacceptable knowledge, women's reading was temporally constrained, and in need of defining and limiting through lists in order to feel achievable. Knowledge, as contained within material books, if not infinite, as claimed by Eco, is impossible to attain in a lifetime.[53] As Christina Lupton argues in *Reading and the Making of Time in the Eighteenth Century*,

> book reading develops its own character as an activity valued because it can offset newer and faster kinds of reading. Books pile up, get given, preserved, recycled, purchased, deferred, and absorbed at special rates because they are not punctual or as urgently demanding of attention as news or occasional writing.[54]

The marking out of sections and chapters of writing is, as both Lupton and Matthew Grenby have pointed out, also a marking of time.[55] Austen demonstrates a mis-functioning of the systematization of knowledge within the system of time in her novels depicting the education of young women; Mrs. Morland of *Northanger Abbey* does not have the time to find the appropriate passages for Catherine to read, saying, "I will look it out for you some day or other, because I am sure it will do you good"; Emma Woodhouse never finds the time to read the works on her list; and Fanny Price in *Mansfield Park* is an avid "collector" and "rentor" of books as material objects of comfort and in relation to their *potential* to impart knowledge.[56]

These temporal limits do not indicate a lack of knowledge on the part of the characters, however, they merely show that appropriate "ways of knowing" are not purely contained within externally defined systems and that individual cognition plays a part in navigating and understanding the way the world works. In her recent book on unreformed protagonists, Stephanie Insley Hershinow persuasively argues, in opposition to most modern critics, that Emma's refusal to finish reading projects demonstrates that formal endings were not part of the realist novel, rather than indicating a failure in the character. *Emma*, Hershinow suggests, is Austen's wry commentary on novels of inexperience and *bildung*. This is, in part, because Emma is in her early twenties, and therefore not an inexperienced naïve at all, but also because Emma "does not read endings . . . Emma is drawn to new beginnings."[57] Thus Austen implicitly acknowledges that the learning process is never "complete," and the potential of knowledge is perceived, for the human mind, as infinite. Hershinow suggests this refusal to finish is indicative of Emma's "desire to be more than one person, to live out more than one possible path," but I suggest it also demonstrates an engagement with the ordering processes of Enlightenment intellectual society; the extent of the unknowable, through acknowledging the ordering rather than the actual learning, forms the process of improvement.[58] As Richard De Ritter has noted in his examination of Maria Edgeworth's relationship to female knowledge in a manner that dismantles the public/private gendered social divisions of the eighteenth century, women had "leisure to be wise." Austen's heroines, however—or in the case of Catherine Morland, her mother—demonstrate the marginalization of the time allocated to reading. If knowledge is to be gained through reading, then reading for women needs to be prioritized and organized, albeit while not impeding more important feminine duties like mothering, as illustrated by Opie's Mrs. Mowbray. There is a necessary self-reflexivity in the treatment of reading in the works explored here; the implicit shared agreement being that the reader is *not* wasting her time in the present moment of reading. A compromise is reached in the identification and organization of future reading projects.[59] De Ritter suggests that Edgeworth demonstrates a balance is needed between the breadth of knowledge and organized and structured focus, because the former is associated with lack of substance and application.[60] Simply by drawing up the lists, or knowing what one "should" read, Austen's heroines demonstrate necessary focus, and an ability to navigate the information overload of the Enlightenment, whether they find the time to read the books or not.

Whereas Austen's protagonists understand the systematization of knowledge, albeit while not always completing the integration of that knowledge into their understanding through reading, Opie represents the dangers of reading outside of socially agreed systems, and the creation of new systems. Nevertheless, this is also an issue of time mismanagement. In Opie's *Adeline Mowbray*, the system, rather than the process of reading, is incomplete. Adeline is an avid reader but has been given a limited collection of books to learn from, and therefore she has dedicated a vast amount of time to learning the wrong things. Adeline's mother's lack of time management is, in addition, a contributing factor to her poor judgment. The only time in which she lives in the moment, as a mother should according to Opie, is when Adeline is feared mortally ill. The rest of her time is spent reading and planning a system, allusive to Sterne's "Tristopædia," for her daughter's education. Mrs. Mowbray comes to the realization that she has misspent her time in this manner through her conversation with the wise Quaker, Mrs. Pemberton. Mrs. Pemberton, in reply, emphasizes the importance of not putting off to the future, the task that needs immediate attention:

> A child's education begins almost from the hour of its birth; and the mother who understands her task, knows that the circumstances which every moment calls forth, are the tools with which she is to work in order to fashion her child's mind and character.[61]

The mention of "hours" and "moments" in the context of a child's life and education makes explicit, through specific measurements, the temporal limitations which life places on reading for knowledge. Once motherhood becomes the pressing obligation in a woman's life, the period for leisurely reading is limited, and following existing systems of education is essential. Individual understanding, or in Lockean terms "quickness of parts," must be integrated into socially defined systems of appropriate, temporally and visually organized knowledge.

CONCLUSION

In part, what I have argued here is that the process of writing reading lists is an act of learning in itself; it shows an awareness of the organization and categorization of what constitutes "knowledge" in building a curriculum for a process of knowledge acquisition through reading. Even if Emma never read the content of the books she added to her list, her list was "excellent," while Adeline Mowbray was an avid reader of inadvisable books when not countered by a balanced reading list. As Matthew D. Eddy has observed, form and content of educational texts both have value, and it is my contention that "required reading," or thinking about what should be read, takes on a textual form. It is an acknowledgment that reading for knowledge acquisition is a structured process that needs order, and preexisting knowledge, to be effectively implemented. In other words, learning through reading was an active and reflective process, but it was also pre-organized, not individualized. However, the writers studied in this chapter actively demonstrate their understanding of the contribution their novels make to the systematization of knowledge and association of ideas, while covertly suggesting that these systems should not be accepted unquestioningly. They achieve this through meta-graphic descriptions of "heads," descriptions of anthologies inscribed through memory, and the completion of plans for reading and learning. In this way, Austen and Opie covertly demonstrate women's reasoning powers through their, and their female characters', ability to connect parts—or individual ideas—to the whole. In other words, they demonstrate the intersection of individual reasoning with systematized "approved" systems of knowledge. Emma is not an exemplar, demonstrating "correct" knowledge, but she demonstrates how to combine individuality with systems of knowing without being dangerously independent. Similarly, Adeline Mowbray's self-conscious realization that in order to provide the perfect textual warning to her daughter, she must perish for her faults is Opie's self-conscious commentary on the preordained systems of novels, implicitly encouraging her readers to question the fixity of moral systems in literature. The foregrounding of the systems for mediating knowledge, over the ideas of the texts themselves, confirms Siskin and Warner's redefinition of Enlightenment as "an event in the history of mediation."[62] These are novels of Enlightenment, in that they require their readers to have the courage to think for themselves, while apparently working as systems of social guardianship.

NOTES

1. See, for example, Mary Hilton, *Women and the Shaping of the Nation's Young: Education and Public Doctrine in Britain 1750–1850* (London and New York: Routledge, 2007); Rebecca Davies, *Written Maternal Authority and Eighteenth-Century Education in Britain: Educating by the Book* (London and New York: Routledge, 2014); Sarah Knott and Barbara Taylor, eds., *Women, Gender and Enlightenment* (Hampshire: Palgrave MacMillan, 2005); Mary Hilton and Jill

Shefrin, eds., *Educating the Child in Enlightenment Britain: Beliefs, Cultures, Practices* (Farnham: Ashgate, 2009).

2. Matthew Daniel Eddy, "The Shape of Knowledge: Children and the Visual Culture of Literacy and Numeracy," *Science in Context* 26, no. 2 (2013): 215–45, 220.

3. Clifford Siskin and William Warner, eds., *This Is Enlightenment* (Chicago, IL and London: University of Chicago Press, 2010).

4. Eddy, "The Shape of Knowledge," 228.

5. Eric Rothstein, *Systems of Order and Inquiry in Later Eighteenth-Century Fiction* (Berkley, Los Angeles, CA, and London: University of California Press, 1975), 9, 10.

6. See John Guillory, "Literary Capital: Gray's 'Elegy,' Anna Laetitia Barbauld, and the Vernacular Canon," in *Early Modern Conceptions of Property*, eds. John Brewer and Susan Staves (London and New York: Routledge, 1996), 389–412.

7. In *This Is Enlightenment* John Guillory suggests that Condorcet identified the mediation of knowledge through print as the turning point in Western education, from rhetoric and persuasion to transmission of knowledge in writing. This is especially true for women readers reliant on a book-based education, as I will demonstrate in this chapter. Guillory, "Enlightening Mediation," in Siskin and Warner (2010), 37–63, 38.

8. Mark Towsey, "Women as Readers and Writers," in *The Cambridge Companion to Women's Writing in Britain, 1660–1789*, ed. Catherine Ingrassia (Cambridge: Cambridge University Press, 2015), 21–36, 22.

9. Richard de Ritter, "Leisure to Be Wise: Edgeworthian Education and the Possibilities of Domesticity," *Journal for Eighteenth-Century Studies* 33, no. 3 (2010): 313–33, 327.

10. The main focus of this chapter is Austen's *Emma* (1815) and Opie's *Adeline Mowbray* (1805), but I also consider the reading practices of other Austen protagonists, Fanny Price in *Mansfield Park* (1814) and Catherine Morland in *Northanger Abbey* (written 1798/9, published 1817). Much has been written about misguided reading in *Northanger Abbey*, so I will not cover that here.

11. Eddy, "The Shape of Knowledge," 221.

12. Immanuel Kant, *An Answer to the Question: What is Enlightenment?*, trans. H. B. Nisbet (London and New York: Penguin, 2009), 1.

13. Mary Wollstonecraft, *A Vindication of the Rights of Woman with Strictures on Political and Moral Subjects* (London: J. Johnson, 1796), 48.

14. John Locke, *An Essay Concerning Human Understanding* (Oxford and New York: Oxford University Press, 2008), 249–50.

15. Alexander Gerard, *An Essay on Genius* (London: W. Strahan, T. Cadell and W. Creech, 1774), 46.

16. Kant, *What Is Enlightenment?*, 1.

17. Kant's distinctions between public and private are a little confusing in this context, because "public" means written scholarship, and "private" means public performance of duties within dogmatic systems (such as religious ministry, teaching, government etc.) Neither are, therefore, domestic or "secret histories" traditionally associated with women.

18. See Paul Bruno, *Kant's Concept of Genius: Its Origin and Function in the Third Critique* (London and New York: Continuum, 2010).

19. Clifford Siskin and William Warner, "If This Is Enlightenment Then What Is Romanticism?" *European Romantic Review* 22, no. 3 (2011): 281–91, 282.

20. Eddy, "Systems of Knowledge," 242.

21. Siskin and Warner, "If This Is Enlightenment," 284–85.

22. William Sharpe, *A Dissertation upon Genius, Or, an Attempt to Shew that the Several Instances of Distinction, and Degrees of Superiority in the Human Genius Are Not, Fundamentally, the Result of Nature, but the Effect of Acquisition* (London: Bathurst, 1755), 119.

23. Mary Wollstonecraft in Moira Ferguson, "The Discovery of Mary Wollstonecraft's 'The Female Reader'," *Signs* 3, no. 4 (1978): 945–57, 949.

24. Jane Austen, *Mansfield Park* (Oxford and New York: Oxford University Press, 1989), 22.

25. Locke, *An Essay Concerning Human Understanding*, 92.

26. Austen, *Mansfield Park*, 208–9. I am grateful to Kjetil Myskja for drawing my attention to this quote.

27. Jane Austen, *Emma* (Oxford and New York: Oxford University Press, 1989), 69.

28. Austen, *Emma*, 69–70.

29. Eddy, "The Shape of Knowledge," 223.

30. Austen, *Emma*, 37.

31. For discussions of the novel as a commentary on Wollstonecraft and Godwin see Patricia A. Matthew, "Biography and Mary Wollstonecraft in *Adeline Mowbray* and *Valperga*," *Women's Writing* 14, no. 3 (2007): 382–98.

32. Mary Wollstonecraft, *A Short Residence in Sweden* (London and New York: Penguin Classics, 1987): 131.

33. Wollstonecraft in Ferguson, "The Discovery of Mary Wollstonecraft's 'The Female Reader'," 949.

34. Ferguson, "The Discovery of Mary Wollstonecraft's 'The Female Reader'," 952. Emphasis mine.

35. Gerard, *An Essay on Genius,* 46.

36. Susanne Beyer and Lothar Gorris, "We Like Lists because We Don't Want to Die," interview with Umberto Eco, *SPIEGEL International*, November 22, 2009, https://www.spiegel.de/international/zeitgeist/spiegel-interview-with-umberto-eco-we-like-lists-because-we-don-t-want-to-die-a-659577-2.html, accessed 27.12.19.

37. Austen, *Mansfield Park*, 398.

38. Christina Lupton, *Reading and the Making of Time in the Eighteenth Century* (Baltimore, MD: Johns Hopkins University Press, 2018), 7.

39. Wollstonecraft in Ferguson, "The Discovery of Mary Wollstonecraft's 'The Female Reader'," 949. Emphasis in the original.

40. Siskin and Warner, "If This Is Enlightenment," 285.

41. Towsey, "Women as Readers and Writers," 22.

42. Amelia Opie, *Adeline Mowbray* (Oxford and New York: Oxford University Press, 1999), 237–38.

43. Opie, *Adeline Mowbray*, 239.

44. Opie, *Adeline Mowbray*, 4.

45. Opie, *Adeline Mowbray*, 55.

46. Opie, *Adeline Mowbray*, 171. (Emphasis mine.)

47. Eddy, "Structures of Knowledge," 219.

48. Eddy, "Structures of Knowledge," 221.

49. Kant, "What is Enlightenment?" 5.

50. For more information on the tradition of maternal legacy writing see Jennifer Heller, *The Mother's Legacy in Early Modern England* (Farnham: Ashgate, 2011).

51. Opie, *Adeline Mowbray*, 239.

52. Kant, "What Is Enlightenment?," 3.

53. Christina Lupton has noted the fear of being overwhelmed by material books expressed in response to the huge proliferation of print media during the eighteenth century. See Christina Lupton, *Knowing Books: The Consciousness of Mediation in Eighteenth Century Britain* (Philadelphia, PA: University of Pennsylvania Press, 2012), 4.

54. Lupton, *Reading and the Making of Time in the Eighteenth Century*, 6.

55. Matthew Grenby, *The Child Reader, 1700–1840* (Cambridge: Cambridge University Press, 2011), 194–235; Lupton, *Reading and the Making of Time in the Eighteenth Century*.

56. Jane Austen, *Northanger Abbey* (London and New York: Penguin, 1994), 225; *Mansfield Park*, 151, 398.

57. Stephanie Insley Hershinow, *Born Yesterday: Inexperience and the Early Realist Novel* (Baltimore, MD and London: John Hopkins University Press, 2019), 131.

58. Hershinow, *Born Yesterday*, 132.

59. In this way Opie and Austen also participate in what Lupton has described as "a moment where such reflexivity was so deeply embedded in popular culture that it can be described as a fashionable and technological impulse . . ." Lupton, *Knowing Books*, 1.

60. De Ritter, "Leisure to be Wise," 325.

61. Opie, *Adeline Mowbray*, 250–51.

62. Siskin and Warner, *This Is Enlightenment*, 1.

Part II

PROGRAMS AND COLLECTIONS

Chapter 3

Mediating the Archives

Child Readers and Their Books in Special Collections

Suzan Alteri

For practical, altruistic, or nostalgic reasons, and sheer zeal, book collectors of children's literature, mostly women, amassed books that gave the fledgling field of children's literature legitimacy in academia. But their practical, often no-nonsense approach to book collecting was at odds with the real and romanticized idea of the book collector—one that was wealthy, male, and philanthropic. The gendered aspect of their book collecting, in addition to that of their collecting area, children's literature, has important implications for the fields of children's literature and childhood studies. The mediation of not only what they collected but also of their decisions on cataloging and access prompts, determines, or prejudices scholars and their views on the reading habits of child readers.

Beginning in the 1950s, through the 1980s, the collection building activities of Dr. Ruth M. Baldwin (University of Florida's Baldwin Library of Historical Children's Literature), Dr. Lena Y. de Grummond (University of Southern Mississippi's de Grummond Collection), Dr. Eloise Ramsey (Wayne State University's Eloise Ramsey Collection of Books for Young People), and Betsy Beineke Shirley (Yale University) illustrate how collecting and curating books have influenced the fields of children's literature and childhood studies. Since each collector differed slightly in philosophy and judgment about what children should read and what books should be preserved, the "how" of collection building coupled with the "why" is still crucial to understanding how scholars interact with the primary sources of child readers. Each of the collections discussed in this essay, while not all great or major, represents many different adult intercessions into the world of children and their books. That each collection was built by a woman born during eras of severe gendering in higher education, particularly in obtaining a doctorate, and achieving equal pay, adds further layers of complexity. Nonetheless, through their collection building efforts, these women collectors—Dr. Ruth Baldwin, Dr. Lena de Grummond, Dr. Eloise Ramsey, and Betsy Beinecke Shirley—gave authenticity not only to their work but to larger fields of study as well. By unpacking their motivations for collecting, I will demonstrate how children's literature archives and special collections shape our views about child readers and their reading habits.

BOOK COLLECTING AND CHILDREN'S LITERATURE

The collecting of books began not long after movable type came to Europe from the East in the mid-fifteenth century. At this time, the making of a book was done entirely by hand. Paper was made from rags, type was set letter by letter and then run through a wooden press, men proofed the pages, and finally men had to create binding boards and sew the pages together. The cost of such business was expensive, and when coupled with the low literacy rates in Western Europe, it's understandable that the buying of books was not always for reading or education, but for status as well. Just like their printing, the buying and reading of books remained the domain of wealthy white men. Women in Western Europe, most of whom lived without access to formal education well into the nineteenth century, were rarely collectors of books. Even as income levels and literacy rose throughout the nineteenth and early twentieth centuries, the collecting of rare books remained a predominantly rich, white male activity until the 1950s and 1960s.

What these men collected—largely the works of other great, white men or books considered to be classics of science, medicine, art, and literature—is important to understand when considering how, in the late 1950s and early 1960s, the world of book collecting became more welcoming of women and of cheap, mass-produced works. Much of the Western world's history of rare book and research collections rested largely on three values—the reputation of the author, the age and condition of the book. Very few book collectors preserved popular books and writings of their time, such as broadsides, chapbooks, and penny dreadfuls. Children's literature was in an even more precarious position. Trivial, transient, and predominately written by women, children's books were often relegated to the dustbin once the child reader reached an age for real literature. Children's literature did not exist as a field of study and special collections libraries largely eschewed these examples of popular culture in favor of fine printing and the works of great civilizations.

In the more romantic writings about book collecting, collectors are usually seen as people who "perform an inestimable service to literature."[1] They are often likened to detectives excited by the thrill of chasing down rare books and rescuing them from oblivion. "The true book-hunter considers himself a discoverer rather than a purchaser, and it is the essence of his skill to find value in those things which in the eye of the ordinary possessor are really worthless," John Herbert Slater wrote in 1891.[2] Later, reflecting on his own book collecting, cultural theorist Walter Benjamin echoed similar sentiments, recognizing that collectors have "a relationship to objects which does not emphasize their functional, utilitarian value—that is, their usefulness—but studies and loves them as the scene, the stage of their fate."[3] Book collecting is focused on acquisition of the physical item rather than comprehension of contents, which is what separates a collector from what is traditionally called a book lover. Reading is not necessarily their entertainment; it's the attainment that fuels their desire. "The period, the region, the craftsmanship, the former ownership—for a true collector the whole background of an item adds up to a magic encyclopedia whose quintessence is the fate of his object," Benjamin mused.[4]

Other essays and guides about book collecting emphasize more combative aspects. In *A Gentle Madness*, Nicholas Basbanes refers to the words of Clifford Waller Barnett:

> He must be distinguished by his rapacity. If he does not covet and is not prepared to seize and fight for every binding, every issue and every state of every book that falls even remotely within the range of his particular bibliomania . . . throw him back.[5]

The Victorian scholar and university administrator Gordon N. Ray routinely mentioned the joy of possession when speaking of himself and other book collectors. Even Benjamin alludes to the battle-like atmosphere of collecting when he writes about "the fervor with which he guards his borrowed treasures"[6] and that "the smallest antique shop can be a fortress, the most remote stationery store a key position."[7] While many mid-twentieth century and earlier book collectors discussed the invade-and-conquer aspects of book collecting, more contemporary collectors are either hesitant to acknowledge the more competitive atmosphere or completely overlook the idea that possession is, perhaps, the ultimate goal. Baldwin was rather shameless in her need for ownership—she wanted every Anglophone printed book prior to 1900. And her approach to collecting illustrated her business-like, practical manner. As a single woman, making a lower salary than a man as a college professor, Baldwin would buy books in bulk and then resell the duplicates to other academic universities, usually in lots. After hearing of Baldwin's death, many collectors spoke fondly of her when earlier they demeaned her purchasing methods of buying entire shelves of juvenile books in calling her "buy the book" Baldwin. The earlier dismissal of her work was based on equal parts gender—a strong and rather stubborn woman—and her callous approach to collecting.

Book collecting is a solitary experience with collectors often hoarding their book treasures throughout their lives. It is only after they have donated their collections, and, in some cases, their life's work to libraries, archives, and museums that we can discover what indicators mark important collections. According to Carolyn Clugston Michaels, who wrote one of the more important guides to children's book collecting, important collections must "demonstrate depth and internal balance and contain highlights of text, authors, decoration, and illustration. . . . It must not leave a great many questions to be answered."[8] For most collectors, significant aspects of building a collection involve depth and balance. The idea of depth—which combines insight, deep learning, and measurement into one concept—is not a new one. For book collectors, depth usually signifies the extent (size or amount) of books as objects but can also characterize one subject or person. Someone who collects illustrators, for example, could be seen to have depth if they have all the illustrated works by one artist, or depth could be seen as having all illustrated works from one time period. Libraries also use the concept of depth when describing their collections. In the 1980s, the Research Library Group (RLG), a U.S. library consortium of over 150 prominent research libraries, archives, and museums, created the *RLG Conspectus*, which measured collecting levels and intensity for research libraries. Level 5 of the *Conspectus* is the comprehensive level and is defined as "a collection which, so far as is reasonably possible, includes all significant works of recorded knowledge . . . in all applicable languages, for a necessarily defined and limited field. This level of collecting intensity is one that maintains a 'special collection.' The aim, if not achievement, is exhaustiveness."[9] When the RLG merged with the Online Computer Library Center, the creators of WorldCat, the Library of Congress updated the conspectus and still uses its collecting levels today. All three groups remain the driving forces behind American research libraries and the information profession in the United States.

Other hallmarks of great book collections include variety, condition, uniqueness, and focus. Of course, what makes a truly important or good collection is usually a matter of value judgment often applied by others. In the words of Gordon N. Ray, who published a series of essays about the rare book world from the 1950s through the 1980s, "the rare book world is perhaps best symbolized by the great shrines of the book—the Folger, the Houghton, the Huntington, the Morgan, and latterly the Beineke and the Lilly. In these sumptuous buildings are preserved the greatest triumphs of the mind of man in literature."[10] In 1965, he remarked that there was still an "inescapable amount of exclusiveness in the very idea of a rare books collection."[11] But already, there had been signs that this was about to change. One of the largest changes was the explosion of American research libraries, most of which were housed at universities with policies that allowed for a larger degree of exposure to rare books than the previous four centuries combined. By his third essay, written in 1974, Ray noted that "as more and more becomes known about every conceivable subject, new collecting horizons are constantly opening."[12] His observations about the rare book world mirror the world of children's book collecting that Baldwin, de Grummond, Ramsey, and Shirley were familiar with. With the exception of Shirley, all benefited from the greater inclusiveness of the rare book collecting world that slowly included women and more acceptance of nontraditional subjects, such as children's literature.

Children's books represented one area the rare book world grew to love during the mid-to-late twentieth century. Few guides to book collecting even mentioned children's books prior to F. J. Harvey Darton's multivolume work *English Books 1475-1900: A Signpost for Collectors*, written with Charles J. Sawyer and published in 1927. Darton was the great-great-grandson of William Darton, one of the early pioneers of children's book publishing in the late eighteenth century, and his book has one chapter devoted to "Nursery Treasures." In it, Darton and Sawyer walk the reader through some of the treasures from two centuries of children's literature. While mentioning children's books published prior to the mid-nineteenth century, the focus is on the lasting books of childhood—*Alice's Adventures in Wonderland*, the fairy tales of Hans Christian Andersen and the Grimm Brothers, the illustrated editions by Kate Greenaway, Randolph Caldecott, and George Cruikshank as well as children's works by Charles Lamb. For Darton, a lasting book is one that was either "so scarce as to be almost unique" or "shared by three children year-after-year, turn-after-turn."[13]

While much has been written about the scarcity of works by Isaac Newton or incunabula, the rarity of children's books is almost never touched upon, perhaps because they are thought of as ephemeral—something that lasts only as long as its owner has use of it. Not many think of their children's books as prized possessions. Still, there are other reasons for the infrequent appearance of children's books on the rare book market up until the mid-1970s. If their owners didn't manage to destroy the book through ripping, coloring, or other abuse, it was adults who found another use, as noted by Baldwin in her unpublished notes on book collecting: "In the early days I began to think of my collecting as a rescue mission as I was frequently told that I should have come sooner. They'd been using my kind of book to stoke the furnace in winter."[14]

Those who did think that children's literature might be worth preserving, people who could see beyond the "patina that has been deposited by unwashed children's hands,"[15] as Benjamin quipped, fell roughly into three main types: those who collected for children, those who collected as a more general hobby, and those who built collections for their work. While there were some important men who collected large quantities of children's books—A. S. W. Rosenbach, d'Alte Welch, F. J. Harvey Darton are among the better known—most prominent research collections were built solely by women.[16]

This gendered aspect to collection building plays no small role in how children's literature archives function in academia. When Francelia Butler, one of the founders of children's literature studies, first thought about establishing the field, she was met with derision from many of her colleagues, most of whom were men. In her article "Scorned but not Defeated," Butler discussed some of the major criticisms (that she faced):

> "It's not even recognized as a legitimate field by the Modern Language Association," one said. "It has no scholarly journal comparable to those in other fields of literature," said another. "It has no professional organization which is humanities-oriented," explained a third.[17]

Butler, along with Anne Devereaux Jordon, set about addressing these "concerns," with the first session on children's literature occurring at the Modern Languages Association conference in 1969, and the Children's Literature Association and its journal *Children's Literature* following in 1972. While professors of literature today find the archive to be an indispensable resource for research and scholarship, the children's literature archives' ability to transcend disciplinary boundaries is more limited despite allowing for research into childhood, heritage, and history. As early as 1927, Darton remarked on the social and cultural history inherent in children's literature: "Consider in what ways the heirs of all the ages have come into their legacy. *Cinderella*—a *citoyenne* of the world, if the anthropologists are right, for her life is told in all civil and most savage tongues."[18] But children's literature remains firmly entrenched in Education and English, the two fields where it began. While book historians have paid some attention to children's books, the study of children's literature still has not infiltrated auxiliary academic fields like history, and an adjacent and equally important field, childhood studies, still languishes in relative obscurity even with the Society of the History of Childhood and Youth's establishment of its journal in 2008.[19]

Emphasis on childhood isn't just in its materials. The return to childhood is commonly evoked by scholars who research children's literature and collectors of children's books alike. William Targ, an American book editor and book collector, likened his activities to a second childhood: "It is a kind of return to the first, euphoric childhood of memory, the recalled world of fantasy and adventure, mirrored in the magic of printer's ink and paper."[20] Memory, sentiment, and innocence appear to cohabit in the children's literature archive, which represents "the hope that adults can recover the texts of childhood experience thereby preserving and understanding childhood itself."[21] Thus books collected, on the surface, seem like tangible reminders of childlike innocence and delight. But the prominence afforded the idea of the inner "child" of the founders of children's literature is inconsistent with their methods of many collecting children's literature.

The two dominant themes running through the female founders of the children's literature archive are hobbyist and educator. Betsy Beinecke Shirley, daughter of Walter Beinecke, one of the brothers who helped create the famed special collections library at Yale University, began her passion for book collecting as a grandmother who wanted her grandchildren to understand American literature and history through its children's books. Her collection at Yale "presents a selection covering three hundred years of American children's literature—defined by examples from the colonial days to the best-loved favorites of our space age."[22] Shirley is the only major female founder of a children's literature archive who speaks of the more romantic side of collecting, writing in *Read Me a Story, Show Me a Book* that "Collecting children's books is an education, an adventure, it's playing Sherlock Holmes (or Nancy Drew), it's a treasure hunt—it's a disease."[23]

The impetus behind two other major collections of children's literature founded by women was far more practical in scope. The smallest of these, the Eloise Ramsey Collection of Literature for Young People, arose from Dr. Ramsey's method of using children's literature to "cultivate a child's slumbering literary sense and image making power,"[24] a concept she learned from studying the work of former principal of the Detroit Normal School, Harriet M. Scott. Ramsey taught English Education, first at the Normal School then in its later incarnations as the Detroit Teacher's College and Wayne State University's College of Education. Her personal collection was used in teacher training courses to provide student teachers with examples of what she thought were good children's books. In this way, students could look at, handle, and work with books for children. After the Detroit Teachers College merged with other city institutions to become Wayne State University, Drs. Ramsey and Gertha Williams along with Lois Place from Library Science formed an education laboratory where teachers could have real training with books.

The Ramsey Collection reflects the practical and educational motivations behind its origins and is selective of the trends in children's literature it covers. The works chosen by Ramsey are "representative of the development of concepts and forms in imaginative writing and illustration in publications intended for English-speaking children."[25] The collection includes single works that were landmarks in children's literature and is organized along with Ramsey's specific categorization scheme of religion, subject-matter books, and literature adopted by young people. In her work *Handbook of Children's Literature: Methods and Materials,* which she cowrote with Emelyn Gardner in 1927, Ramsey discusses the "intelligent" selection and interpretation of literature for children. "The thought or content of the books selected for children should be worth while [*sic*]. . . . Literature that excites disgust, contempt, and despair with reference to people, conditions, and life itself should have no place in children's lives."[26] Of series books, long the bane of children's librarians and teachers in the early and mid-twentieth century, Ramsey noted that children will "read the entire series, filling his mind with useless chaff instead of golden grain."[27] While our modern-day conceptions of what is good children's literature has changed, Ramsey's collection is important not only for the books it holds but also for the manner in which it was collected. Her belief that "students [needed to] read as exhaustively as possible from the truly great literature of children" is reflected in the books that remain three-quarters of a century after her death.[28] Ramsey defined great literature by the standards established by Caroline M. Hewins in the early twentieth century, to "Broaden the horizon of children . . . and add to their stock of general knowledge."[29] But, Ramsey's mediating factor between children and their books was one of suggestion. She wanted future teachers to learn about children's literature so that they would instill the idea of literary value and appreciation for knowledge, and this still has great influence of what remains in her children's literature collection.

Dr. Lena Y. De Grummond's collection reflects what she believed was important for future librarians to know about how books were produced for children. She did not begin her collecting in earnest until she retired as the state supervisor of School Libraries in Louisiana. Offered a teaching position in the School of Library Science at the University of Southern Mississippi, de Grummond asked and was allowed to create a collection that was to be used for teaching library science students about children's literature. She highlighted how children's books were created by their authors and illustrators. As former assistant curator Anne Lundin stated, "Lena de Grummond began her collection with the mission of education and outreach."[30]

De Grummond's collection did not focus on books per se but rather on materials that enrich a collection. Emily Murphy's article on de Grummond's letter writing campaign illustrates how this collector would order copies of an author's book and then write them asking for "materials which enrich a collection—manuscripts of published books, illustrations, 'dummies,' scripts, proofs, sketches, rough notes, etc."[31] In particular, de Grummond focused on materials that many authors at that time would throw away after publication. She taught classes in the School of Library Science at night so as to give herself time to write letters during the day. And the materials did come, first slowly, and then more regularly, until the collection grew to be the second-largest children's literature archive of manuscripts in the United States. Like Ramsey, de Grummond's collection began as a resource for students—in this case future librarians—who would shape how children reacted to books. De Grummond also wanted to share her experiences as a former school librarian by giving students the opportunity to study the creative process behind how a book is made. The intent behind her collection was to complement the University of Southern Mississippi's history as a teaching college.

Dr. Ruth M. Baldwin's collecting efforts were a bit more enigmatic. Aspects of her collecting habits fit certain stereotypes of the romanticized book collector, particularly in seeing book collecting as a game of war. But in other ways, Baldwin is the antithesis of the idealized collector, with a no-nonsense approach to building her collection as reflected in her ability to bargain and resell duplicate texts to fund her book expeditions. Ironically, the Baldwin Library of Historical Children's Literature's origin is not with Baldwin herself but with her parents, who purchased a few children's chapbooks from McLeish's bookshop in London as a birthday present to her in 1953. At that time, Baldwin was thirty-five years old and working on her PhD in Library Science at the University of Illinois. During the rest of 1953 and most of 1954, her mother purchased in London and sent to Illinois between 300 and 400 children's books. While many of Baldwin's letters are lost, a few remain. On October 10, 1953, she wrote her mother that she was "perishing to see the books."[32] A month after receiving her first package, she wrote, "here I am well started in a collection and loving it."[33]

Although Baldwin was born into a family of collectors, she herself did not collect books until after the arrival of those children's books. Her father, Dr. Thomas W. Baldwin, was a Shakespearean scholar and book collector. Both of these pursuits had caused Ruth to swear off book collecting, but she couldn't resist the bundles of books her mother sent, less because she felt sentimental about her childhood and more because they represented an area of publishing that was full of small bibliographic problems. As her mother wrote to her toward the end of 1953, "I have another bunch in a corner on the floor—one a German of the same period and style of as the Kate Greenaway. How you'll delight in the problem of which came first—and who copied who."[34] Baldwin wasn't a collector in the narrowly defined bibliographic sense nor did she buy from more well-known, first-tier book dealers in postwar Britain or the United States. Instead, she would scour piles of books in rural antique stores, Goodwill, and other out-of-the-way bookshops. In her own words, she "never learned how to book shop in the large cities."[35] This was a trick she had learned from her mother, who bought from markets around London or in the barrows outside the *Daily Worker*.

Baldwin's collecting philosophy focused less on aesthetics, scholarship, or teaching, and more on the practicalities of purchasing large quantities of books on a female professor's small salary. In the initial stages of her collecting, Baldwin didn't have an overarching philosophy outside of wanting to create the largest collection of children's literature. It was only as her library grew that she looked back and realized she was building the largest private collection of children's literature in the United States. Part of Baldwin's refusal to think of her collection as a source for research was that she didn't want to be linked with her book-collecting father. She was always emphasizing that her collection had no connection to her father's academic collection building. The practicalities of her collecting also surfaced through other approaches to book buying and collecting, most notably her ability to buy in bulk and then resell duplicate books to academic libraries throughout North America. While other collectors mediated—or intervened—in determining which children's books were preserved for scholarship, Baldwin's mediation came less from the idea of wanting to save only the best of children's literature or materials to use in teaching and more from a desire to own everything published for children during the long nineteenth century. New York bookseller Daniel Hirsch remembered that Baldwin felt

> that for a research collection to be truly such, it had to represent the printing history of each title, from the expensive deluxe editions to the inexpensive trade editions, to the later cheap reprints or editions gobbled up by children of all means.[36]

In fact, Baldwin valued most of the books that children had actually loved and used. Books dated with inscriptions, written or colored in, and assorted other abuses were important to her since they formed the cultural history of children's literature and child reading.

MEDIATION IN THE ARCHIVES

Archives and libraries were often seen as independent constructs for most of their histories. It has only been in the last thirty years that scholars in the humanities have begun interrogating the archive as an object worthy of study. This turn, often noted as the "archival turn," has meant that institutions with large historical holdings have to justify what they contain. In "History and Memory: The Problem of the Archive," Francis X. Blouin Jr. noted that "what constitutes the archive has become a question fundamental to how our knowledge of the past is acquired and shaped."[37] Those who collect books and archival manuscripts, whether institutionally or personally, make significant selection decisions that inevitably affect how we interpret human culture and history. Not only what is preserved in the archive but also what is absent is "reflective of our politics, our biases, and our preoccupations."[38] An archivist's, collector's, or curator's mediation in selection, description, reference, and research support influences how the past, or in the case of this chapter childhood, is viewed by scholars. William Rosenberg noted that archivists "serve essentially as mediators between the documents and their readers, between the types of knowledge creation by the formation of artifacts themselves and the ways and form in which that knowledge is accessible and capable of scholarly use."[39]

Terry Cook writes extensively on the concept of mediation and worthiness in the archive, encouraging archivists to look inward at their biases in how the past and memory are shaped through their actions (or inaction) with records. The same could also be said for librarians who make several intercessions after selecting a title and prior to its appearance on a shelf for public view. For Cook, the "why" behind collecting may be more important than what is collected because "certain voices will be heard loudly and some not all; that certain views and ideas about society will in turn be privileged and others marginalized."[40] Since archivists and librarians work as organizers of documents and books as well as gatekeepers to rare materials, they serve as mediators between the objects of study on the one hand and researchers on the other. Because preservation, access, and description are crucial to the process of conceptualizing the past, "archivists . . . will need to examine very consciously their choices in the archive-creating and memory-formation process."[41]

Returning to the collectors of children's literature, we see how the decisions behind what these three women did and didn't collect have meaningful implications for how the field of children's literature was shaped as it developed in the academy. By selecting, collectors will "inject their own values, experiences, and education, and reflect those of various external pressures, into all such research and decision-making."[42] The idea of lasting books—books that have survived, if you will—sounds like social Darwinism. To conserve or preserve something—a text, document, photograph—is, according to scholar David Greetham, "culturally self-referential, even self-laudatory: we want to preserve the *best* of ourselves."[43] To put it more bluntly, most collectors of children's literature, particularly those whose emphasis was pedagogical, selected what was ideologically desirable. Of the collectors studied here, Baldwin was less interested in saving the finest children's literature, but by only selecting titles in English (Baldwin spoke only English and French), it's clear she felt that children's literature was largely an Anglo-American phenomenon. Even after selection, other mediating factors such as how to allocate resources (personnel, financial), what material is cataloged or described, and what is promoted and researched are central in determining accessibility. Cook, in fact, delineates a whole list of choices that are made in archives and libraries, particularly in our era of limited resources—"which systems, which functions, which programmes, which activities, which ideas and discourses, and indeed which related records, will get full, partial, or no archival attention."[44]

The next form of mediation is determining what documents are processed, or, in the case of books, which titles are cataloged. Without proper cataloging and organization, visitors to an archive or library have no way of locating material or discovering what is available for research. Cook notes that we are now in the second era of very limited resources in terms of money and personnel for libraries and archives. As the creation, dissemination, donation, and purchase of materials for researchers continues to grow, librarians, curators, and archivists are forced to prioritize what is processed or cataloged.

To do so, they assess institutional research and teaching programs and demands on resources. In this case study of the Baldwin Library, when Baldwin donated her collection to the University of Florida (UF), it was not cataloged along any system. Baldwin, who had a phenomenal memory, simply knew how her collection was organized and where certain books were located. For anyone else, the collection appeared haphazardly organized and difficult to use. In 1981, Baldwin completed the three-volume *Index to the Baldwin Library of Books in English Before 1900*, which included all eighteenth- and nineteenth-century titles in her collection when it was donated to UF in 1977. At the time, libraries operated from card catalogs rather than online databases, and Baldwin spent years prior to coming and after her arrival at UF creating an intricate card catalog system that was only partially useful. It wasn't until 1983 that online catalog software (Dynix) along with the rise of MARC standards existed so that catalogs could be accessible to users not only at a physical location. But even with sophisticated tools, the Baldwin Library was slow to respond to technological and classification developments. As late as 1987, one library administrator at UF lamented that "the [Baldwin] library does not meet modern standards of either physical control or accessibility. By physical control I mean that each item in the Baldwin Library can be found easily and quickly and by accessibility. I mean that the bibliographic records can be searched and retrieved in the national utilities [OCLC] and the Library's online catalog by author, title, and subject."[45] In a report drafted by Richard Fyffe (former library director at the Essex Institute) who was asked to consult on the feasibility of machine-readable cataloging for the Baldwin Library, something which Baldwin strenuously objected to, he stated that automation would increase visibility of the "sadly underused" collection.[46]

The gradual inclusion of the Baldwin Library's holdings into the Online Public Access Catalog (OPAC) was due in no small part to Baldwin's refusal to open her collection to all, especially students and faculty. In her *Index to the Baldwin Library*, she stated in the preface that the collection is "open for room use . . . by persons with a serious purpose who have exhausted all other resources."[47] Baldwin also noted that because of limited staff, she could not "undertake reference work for inquirers."[48] The *Index* was a photocopy of all the catalog cards of the collection; albeit without the index, they had to contact her or visit the library. But visiting was often difficult. It was a well-known legend that Baldwin did not consider many people to be "serious" enough to work with her materials. Her narrow definition of who could use the collection was a constant source of disagreement between Baldwin and library administration, particularly since UF is an institution with a public mission. "Her reputation was legendary on campus," Rita Smith told Nicholas Basbanes in an interview for his book *A Gentle Madness*. "Ruth Baldwin controlled her collection with an iron hand, and if she didn't think your reason for wanting to see something was good enough, you were gone."[49] It wasn't until after her retirement and death that the Baldwin Library was cataloged almost in full and added to WorldCat, the largest online union catalog in the world.

Cataloging and processing of books and other materials in special collections and archives are crucial to scholarly endeavors because the stacks are closed off to users. Researchers and other patrons are not able to browse closed stacks as they can in many other libraries. The only way for someone to see, specifically, what is held in special collections and archives is through the OPAC or other finding aid. Cataloging has often been viewed as a neutral activity—describe the material (book, document, or photograph) so that users can find and select it for their research. But, in truth, there can be many exclusionary aspects of this process as well. Any search through an OPAC will reveal an array of different levels of cataloging. Some books will receive more detailed descriptive information than others, which is particularly apparent when looking at subject headings.[50] In order to provide efficient cataloging services, most libraries have established tiers or priorities that serve as guidelines for the work of catalogers. Certain books will receive the highest priority—complete original cataloging with a detailed description of the physical appearance of the book along with at least four or five different subject headings. Books that are lower on the priority list receive less cataloging. Since researchers rely on descriptive information, like subject headings, to find archival and other primary sources, the omission of certain subject headings can almost make a resource invisible.

While the catalog (and subsequent digital collections) is the main resource for discovering materials to research, often scholars who travel to a specific special collection also rely on librarians, curators, and archivists to guide them toward materials in the collection, either related to a specific research question or to begin research in an entirely new area. When Gillian Avery, a children's writer and historian of childhood visited to dedicate the Baldwin Library in 1982, she was inspired to write about American children's books. In personal correspondence, Avery replied to Baldwin that "it will be wonderful to be among your books again; it was the sight of them that originally made me want to write something about American children's books" and that her "AMKID book (as the word processor calls it) owes its whole being to the Baldwin Library."[51] The book Avery mentions is *Behold the Child: American Children and Their Books, 1621-1922,* and Baldwin's assistance pointed Avery to previously undiscovered children's books. Baldwin also assisted bibliographer Marjorie Moon with her work, *Benjamin Tabart's Juvenile Library: A Bibliography of Books for Children Published, Written, Edited and Sold by Mr. Tabart, 1801-1820,* another influential work for children's literature scholars.

Jennifer Douglas also speaks to the cyclical relationship between curators, archivists, and librarians when discussing the idea of creation and creators in the archive, noting that "an archive is recreated each time it is activated by a user. Creation by activators relates to the effect of previous interpretations of an archive's content and meaning on subsequent interpretations of the same archive."[52] In the act of doing research, scholars are constantly reevaluating and reinterpreting content held within archives and special collections. But in the act of mediation, curators, archivists, and librarians are also consistently reinterpreting the archive. Use of materials in archives plays a crucial role in the enterprise of the scholarly endeavor. A researcher's continued use of materials on a certain topic or theme combined with a curator's sense of curiosity will ensure that more materials are discovered and more purchased. In this cyclical subtle way, mediation plays a pivotal part in the creation and re-creation of a specific archive.

Over the past fifteen years archivists, curators, and librarians have struggled over how to define their role as mediators. Pushed by scholars outside the fields of archives management and library science, we are entering an era where preservation of the records of any given culture is a joint effort between the public, professionals, and scholars. Since the archive serves as the back-drop to scholarly research, it's crucial not only to understand how libraries and archives function but also how libraries and, in particular, archives are viewed by those outside. In the field of children's literature, literary scholars have been hesitant to work with librarians and archivists. As late as 2013, Sara Schwebel remarked that "Anxiety about status within English departments and the humanities has led children's literature scholars to distance themselves from child readers, from peers in schools of education and library science, and from research or publications that might be deemed 'applied.'"[53]

CHILDREN'S LITERATURE AND THE ARCHIVE

As a site of knowledge production and interpretation, the archive (or library) is strongly influenced by the ideas scholars produce and, vice versa, the materials in an archive impact what scholars choose to research. Since the archive and the researcher are intimately connected, scholars are naturally concerned with how the archive functions and provides legitimacy to academic fields. Thomas Osborne, in analyzing the work of Michel Foucault, wrote about how the archive functions as "a sort of bottom-line resource in the carving-out of claims to disciplinarity."[54] In the humanities, the archive provides a certain amount of credibility to a discipline, particularly early on in a field's creation. Since childhood is seen as a transient time period, the materials of childhood—such as literature or toys—were not deemed significant to preserve up until the mid-twentieth century. Prior to that book collecting was primarily concerned with the works of the great men of science, medicine, art, and the humanities. It was only after the growth of fields such as educational psychology and child development that the "things" of children took on growing importance both in society and in the academy. Still, the motivations for preserving childhood were, as Karen Sanchez-Eppler pointed out, "less as the result of intentional acts of preservation than because someone, at some point, did not bother to throw them away."[55] In the latter half of the twentieth century, the rare book world and academic fields began a process of inclusion— of women, people of color, popular culture—as part of changes brought on by social movements and the material turn. The shift from studying greatness to studying all aspects of culture coupled with the small, perhaps accidental, intercessions into preserving things made by children was an important first step in children's literature and childhood studies.

But it wasn't until the collecting work of women who realized that literature for children and younger people was an important aspect of cultural history that the children's literature archive was created. Their collecting efforts and later institutional commitment contributed much of the academic legitimacy for the fledgling field of children's literature. As noted by Kenneth Kidd, "By preserving children's materials, and conferring upon them special (primarily historical but also affective) value, the archive asserts the research value of children's literature within the broader culture of academic and university research."[56]

One of the key aspects of research in the archive is that the materials function almost as raw data. The data, or manuscripts and books, inside the archive require interpretation and analysis. Rather than providing users with the story of cultural history, the archive represents what has been made available and what has been presented. Therefore, the archive is a site where the mediation of book collectors and curators becomes crucial to scholarship. By "bringing together objects that are worthless on their own yet priceless when put together,"[57] as in the case of children's books, the archives of children's literature helped build, and now continue to influence, the fields of childhood studies and children's literature. The founding of these collections also is a valuable part of children's literature history, in particular the how and the why of building children's literature archives and special collections developed in the first place. Anne Lundin, former curator of the de Grummond Collection, and others have noted that

> Special collections of children's literature demonstrate in their holdings that collections are not islands either, that texts are connected in a whole indeed greater than the sum of its parts. . . . These collections speak of how traditions deconstruct, canons re-form, and the old makes new.[58]

Seeing a large children's literature archive for the first time is a daunting experience for scholars. The archive in all its "greatness" reminds scholars that only a small fraction of books are destined to become classics and that newer methodologies like distant reading may be more important than close reading of a few texts. While children's literature scholars often want to distance themselves from the connection to practical, applied fields, the relation of teaching and librarianship to the children's literature archive is necessary to understand how child readers develop not only reading habits, but also their understanding of the world. It is equally important for the archive to "locate in the historical record the child's voice and aspirations, to find traces of what children 'are.'"[59]

Baldwin's collecting of much-loved books is one way to locate the child in children's literature, and it has been an influence on the ability for researchers to study what children actually read rather than what has been mediated for them by adults. Regardless of her motive, the inscriptions, marginalia, scribbles, and notes located in many of the books from her collection allow those in children's literature and childhood studies to examine how children used their books outside of reading while also serving to illustrate "how these objects open a window into the intellectual and emotional lives of young people in the past."[60] Ramsey and de Grummond focused their collecting efforts on the teaching of children's literature to children. At first glance, it seems more difficult to find the child in their collections, but both provide an opportunity to interrogate the school and library reading of children—vitally important since many children had access to books only through these two institutions.

But regardless of the origins of these collections—pedagogy, materiality, detection—they all directly influence how and what scholars research. Baldwin's collection, for example, provided inspiration for scholars writing broad historiographies on what children actually read as opposed to what adults wanted them to read. The de Grummond Collection has provided scholars with unparalleled access to how illustrators create books, while the Ramsey Collection is an excellent resource for studies on what children's literature was taught by teachers and librarians. Or perhaps the true value in these collections is, as Ruth Baldwin proclaimed in an interview, "its contributions to the social and cultural history of our nation."

NOTES

1. Nicholas Basbanes, "Collectors and Libraries: Some Studies in Symbiosis," *Rare Books and Manuscripts Librarianship* 8, no. 1 (1993): 37–48, 17.

2. J. Herbert Slater, *Round and about the Book-Stalls: A Guide for the Book-Hunter* (London: L. U. Gill, 1891), 35–36.

3. Walter Benjamin, "Unpacking My Library," in *Illuminations*, ed. Hannah Arendt, trans. Harry Zohn (New York: Schocken Books, 1969), 59–68, 60.

4. Benjamin, "Unpacking," 60.

5. Nicholas Basbanes, *A Gentle Madness: Bibliophiles, Bibliomanes, and the Eternal Passion for Books* (New York: H. Holt & Co., 1995), 39.

6. Benjamin, "Unpacking," 62.

7. Benjamin, "Unpacking," 63.

8. Carolyn Clugston Michaels, *Children's Book Collecting* (Hamden, CT: Library Professional Publications, 1993), 70.

9. "Collecting Levels," Library of Congress, accessed May 2019, https://www.loc.gov/acq/devpol/cpc.html.

10. Gordon N. Ray, *Books as a Way of Life: Essays*, ed. G. Thomas Tanselle (New York: Grolier Club, Pierpont Morgan Library, 1988), 47.

11. Ray, *Books as a Way of Life,* 48.

12. Ray, *Books as a Way of Life*, 97.

13. Charles J. Sawyer and F. J. Harvey Darton, *English Books 1475–1900: A Signpost for Collectors* (London: Chas. J. Sawyer, Ltd, 1927), 115.

14. Ruth Baldwin, Notes on book collecting, n.d., Ruth M. Baldwin Papers, George A. Smathers Libraries, University of Florida.

15. Walter Benjamin, "Old Forgotten Children's Books," in *Selected Writings: Volume 1 1913–1926*, eds. Marcus Bullock and Michael W. Jennings (Cambridge, MA: Belknap Press of Harvard University Press, 2002), 406–13, 406.

16. One significant exception was also Irving Kerlan, who developed a large collection of children's literature that is housed at the University of Minnesota.

17. Gillian Adams, "The Francelia Butler Watershed: Then and Now," *Children's Literature Association Quarterly* 25, no. 4 (2000): 181–90, 183.

18. Darton, *English Books 1475–1900*, 131.

19. Joseph M. Hawes and N. Ray Hiner, "Hidden in Plain View: The History of Children (and Childhood) in the Twenty-First Century," *Journal of the History of Childhood and Youth* 1, no. 1 (2008): 43–49, 43.

20. William Targ, *Bibliophile in the Nursery: A Bookman's Treasure of Collectors' Lore on Old and Rare Children's Books* (Cleveland, OH: World Pub. Co., 1957), 12.

21. Kenneth B. Kidd, "The Child, the Scholar, and the Children's Literature Archive," *The Lion and the Unicorn* 35, no. 1 (2001): 1–23, 2.

22. Betsy Beinecke Shirely, *Read Me a Story, Show Me a Book: American Children's Literature, 1690–1988 from the Collection of Betsy Beinecke Shirley* (New Haven, CT: Eastern Press, 1991), 7.

23. Shirley, *Read Me a Story*, 7.

24. L. L. Hanawalt, *A Place of Light: The History of Wayne State University* (Detroit, MI: Wayne State University Press, 1968), 134.

25. Joan Cusenza, *The Eloise Ramsey Collection of Literature for Young People: A Catalogue* (Detroit, MI: Wayne State University Libraries, 1967), 1.

26. Emelyn E. Gardner and Eloise Ramsey, *A Handbook of Children's Literature: Methods and Materials* (Chicago, IL: Scott, Foresman and Company, 1927), 13–14.

27. Gardner and Ramsey, *A Handbook*, 16.

28. Eloise Ramsey, "Michigan State Fair," n.d., in *Eloise Ramsey Papers*, Walter P. Reuther Library, Wayne State University.

29. Caroline M. Hewins, *Books for Boys and Girls: A Selected List* (Chicago, IL: American Library Association Publishing Board, 1915), 5.

30. Anne Lundin, "A 'Dukedom Large Enough': The de Grummond Archive," *The Lion and the Unicorn* 35, no. 1 (2001): 303–10, 305.

31. Emily Murphy, "Unpacking the Archive: Value, Pricing, and the Letter-Writing Campaign of Dr. Lena Y. de Grummond," *Children's Literature Association Quarterly* 39, no. 4 (2014): 551–68, 553.

32. Ruth M. Baldwin to her mother, October 10, 1953, Ruth M. Baldwin Papers, George A. Smathers Libraries, University of Florida, Box 4.

33. Ruth M. Baldwin to her mother, November 10, 1953, Ruth M. Baldwin Papers. Box 4.

34. Elizabeth Baldwin to Ruth Baldwin, n.d., Ruth M. Baldwin Papers. Box 4.

35. Notes on book collecting, n.d., Ruth M. Baldwin Papers. Box 2.

36. Daniel Hirsch to Rita Smith, June 1992, Ruth M. Baldwin Papers. Box 5.

37. Francis X. Blouin, Jr., "History and Memory: The Problem of the Archive," *PMLA* 119, no. 2 (2004): 296–98, 296.

38. Francis X. Blouin, Jr., "Archivists, Mediation, and Constructs of Social Memory," *Archival Issues* 24, no. 2 (1999): 101–12, 102.

39. Blouin, Jr., "Archivists," 108.

40. Joan M. Schwartz and Terry Cook, "Archives, Records, and Power: The Making of Modern Memory," *Archival Science* 2 (2002): 1–19, 14.

41. Terry Cook, "Archival Science and Postmodernism: New Formulations for Old Concepts," *Archival Science* 1 (2001): 3–24, 24.

42. Terry Cook, "Evidence, Memory, Identity, and Community: Four Shifting Archival Paradigms," *Archival Science* 13 (2013): 95–120, 102.

43. David Greetham, "Who's In, Who's Out: The Cultural Poetics of Archival Exclusion," *Studies in the Literary Imagination* 32, no. 1 (1999): 1–28, 9.

44. Terry Cook, "Evidence, Memory, Identity, and Community," 102.

45. Sam Gowan to Ruth M. Baldwin, May 27, 1987, Ruth M. Baldwin Papers.

46. Richard Fyffe, Consultant's Report: Machine-Readable Cataloging for the Baldwin Library, University of Florida, January 14, 1988, Ruth M. Baldwin Papers. Box 1.

47. Ruth M. Baldwin, *Index to the Baldwin Library of Books in English before 1900, Primarily for Children* (Boston, MA: G. K. Hall, 1981), v.

48. Ruth M. Baldwin, *Index*, vi.

49. Nicholas Basbanes, *A Gentle Madness*, 368.

50. Compare the two catalog records for two of Jane Marcet's books: http://uf .catalog.fcla.edu/permalink.jsp?20UF029418294 and http://uf.catalog.fcla.edu/permalink.jsp?20UF027208231.

51. Oral History with Gillian Avery, n.d., Ruth M. Baldwin Papers.

52. Jennifer Douglas, "A Call to Rethink Archival Creation: Exploring Types of Creation in Personal Archives," *Archival Science* 18 (2018): 29–49, 40.

53. Sara Schwebel, "Taking Children's Literature Scholarship to the Public," *Children's Literature Association Quarterly* 38, no. 4 (2013): 470–75, 470.

54. Thomas Osborne, "The Ordinariness of the Archive," *History of the Human Sciences* 12, no. 2 (1999): 51–64, 53.

55. Karen Sanchez-Eppler, "In the Archives of Childhood," in *Children's Table: Childhood Studies and the Humanities*, ed. Anna Mae Duane (Atlanta, GA: University of Georgia Press, 2013), 213–237, 218.

56. Kenneth B. Kidd, "The Child," 9.

57. Emily Murphy, "Unpacking," 563.

58. Anne Lundin, "A 'Dukedom Large Enough,'" 310.

59. Sanchez-Eppler, "In the Archives," 215.

60. Katharine Capshaw, "Archives and Magic Lanterns," *Children's Literature Association Quarterly* 39, no. 3 (2014): 313–15, 313.

Chapter 4

Bookbug

The Mediating Effect of Book Gifting in Scotland

Emma Davidson and Tracy Cooper

This chapter explores the mediating effects that parental support can have on families' relationship to children's reading. We do this by examining "Bookbug," one of the Scottish government's flagship early years programs run by Scottish Book Trust.[1]

In collaboration with local authorities and health boards, Bookbug gifts bags of books and resources to every child in Scotland, from birth to Primary 1 (the first year of primary school) and supports a network of practitioners to deliver free song and rhyme sessions (Bookbug Sessions) across the country. Scottish Book Trust has a dedicated team that coordinates the distribution of the bags. The team also develop and deliver training for professionals who work with children and families, often referred to as practitioners due to their active role in supporting families. The training audience includes representatives from healthcare, library, education, and social work, and volunteers from charities, or third sector. The courses on offer aim to facilitate effective gifting of the Bookbug Bags and support for those running Bookbug Sessions in community settings (such as support workers or specialist services). All Bookbug training is evidence-based and features key messages about how family engagement with stories, songs, and rhymes can contribute to better outcomes for children. There is also a strong emphasis on practical activities which aim to boost the key skills of professionals and offer a space for discussion and reflection.

Based on the principles of universal entitlement and non-stigmatization, the overall aim of the Bookbug program is to provide parents, carers, and children with the opportunity to share books from birth. Drawing on a growing body of scholarly evidence on the benefits of sharing stories, songs, and rhymes, the program seeks to positively impact on bonding and attachment within families; develop children's language and writing skills; boost children's confidence; and encourage families' enjoyment and love of reading.

Using evidence from a two-year evaluation of the Bookbug program conducted by Davidson et al. from the Centre for Research on Families and Relationships, and the direct experiences of a practitioner delivering the program, this chapter examines the ways Bookbug can be conceived as "mediating" the reading practices of families in Scotland, and the extent to which such mediation is justified by its social benefits.[2] We begin with a brief overview of the literature on literacy and the home learning environment, giving specific attention to inequalities. We move on to discuss the Bookbug model in detail, and how it is delivered to families in Scotland. We discuss the program's role as mediator by proposing that Bookbug is making a contribution to what, how, and when children read in Scotland. These examples illustrate not only the forms of mediation implicit within the program but also the possibilities that exist for children and their families to interpret, engage, and direct these. We conclude by arguing that three key factors underpin the success of Bookbug's approach: its promotion of booksharing to *all* parents; an emphasis on encouraging families to develop their own family reading practices; and a recognition of children's agency within this.

APPROACH AND METHODS

In addition to the literature review which follows, this chapter draws on data from two sources, a two-year evaluation of Bookbug and the direct experiences of a practitioner delivering the program. This approach to writing extends the collaborative ethos that was at the heart of the evaluation study. Through the research, it sought to engage practitioners delivering Bookbug in the research process by sharing new knowledge, undertaking collaborative analysis, and discussing emergent findings. Beyond this, the process of writing together can help fill the gap that often exists between practitioners and academics by recognizing the value of different forms of knowledge and the respective strengths of reflecting on an issue from an inside and outside position.

The evaluation was commissioned by Scottish Book Trust and conducted by a team of researchers based at the Centre for Research on Families and Relationships between 2015 and 2017,[3] with the aim of understanding the impact of the Bookbug program on parents and carers, children and early years professionals. In relation to parents and carers, the research sought to explore how the Bookbug Bags and the sessions were experienced and their range of impact on attitudes to reading, signing, and library use. We also sought to examine parents and carers' perceptions of the benefits of the Bookbug program. Areas explored included confidence, language development, and relationships. In terms of those working with children and families, the focus of the research was on the contribution that Bookbug made to professional practice. How, for example, Bookbug fit within the different professional roles, and what impact (if any) does the program have on their wider practice? Finally, we were interested in building an understanding of who was accessing the program and in what way. In particular, we wanted to determine whether there were barriers to accessing the program for certain groups, and if so, what support could be offered. Finally, it is notable that the research examined Bookbug as a program, rather than looking at bags, session, and training in isolation. In this way, we wanted to look at the linkages between the program from both the perspective of professionals and the end users (the child, parent, or carers). In this way, we aimed to look at the cumulative impact of the program as a whole.

Rather than seeking to understand Bookbug in a vacuum, the evaluation used "Contribution Analysis," a theory-based approach to evaluation.[4] The approach has emerged in response to growing recognition of the challenges presented in identifying causal pathways that link an intervention to a particular change or impact. Identifying and evidencing such cause and effect pathways are especially difficult for evaluation research within social policy, where impact is influenced by a wide array of contextual factors and players.[5] Contribution analysis thus provides researchers a means through which to draw reasonable conclusions about the part a program plays—its contribution—to observed results. To do this, the approach sets out to create, then verify, the theory of change behind a program, while taking account of other influencing factors.

The value of contribution analysis to this research was clear. Our initial investigation quickly demonstrated that the Bookbug program was embedded in a complex policy context, straddling both national and local decision-making relating to strategic prioritization and resourcing. Being delivered in diverse local contexts introduced further complexity in terms of socioeconomic circumstances, and cultural norms and expectations.

By focusing on contribution, rather than impact per se, this approach allows us to accept the impossibility of attributing social impact to specific interventions and instead seeks to identify the unique contribution that the Bookbug program brings to families and professionals. Contribution analysis also helps to highlight all stages of project work, rather than focusing purely on the end result.

Several different ways of exploring parents', carers', and professionals' experiences to assess the impact of the Bookbug program were used. These include looking at existing research about book gifting programs; conducting

Figure 4.1   **The Context of Bookbug Program Delivery.** *Source:* Scottish Book Trust.

surveys of parents, carers, and professionals; and analyzing six locality-based case studies. In total, the evaluation surveyed 627 professionals and 4,387 parents and carers. Forty-six parents and carers were interviewed in-depth by telephone. The six case studies each involved extended time on-site in the local area (in libraries, nurseries, and in third sector settings) with the aim of understanding how local circumstances shape and affect Bookbug's impact on families and professionals. In total, the case studies comprised interviews with 55 professionals and 141 parents and carers, as well as observations of 12 Bookbug sessions and eight parent and toddler/family groups.

LITERACY AND THE HOME
LEARNING ENVIRONMENT

A strong and well-established body of research has shown that the social, emotional, and physical circumstances of a child's early years can have a significant impact on literacy and language development,[6] cognitive development,[7] and later academic abilities.[8] This work has given particular attention to the significance of the home learning environment on emergent literacy.[9] Not only is the home where language and literacy are first encountered, it can, for example, provide young children with opportunities to engage with literacy materials, observe literacy activities, and take part in shared reading and writing activities with their family.[10]

Booksharing, in particular, is considered beneficial given the dedicated interaction it prompts between parents and children; the use of more complex language in books compared to everyday conversations; and the ability to reinforce new knowledge through repetition.[11] Suzanne Mol and Adriana Bus, for example, found that children who are read to more frequently enter school with larger vocabularies and more advanced comprehension skills,[12] while Kathy Sylva and colleagues concluded that parental reading with children, along with songs, rhymes, and games with letters and numbers, was associated with higher intellectual and behavioral scores.[13] Scott Gest et al. similarly concluded that parental involvement in reading activities can influence language comprehension and expressive language skills.[14] Evidence can also be found in the longitudinal study "Growing Up in Scotland," which has been tracking the development of thousands of Scottish children and their families since 2005.[15] It has found that children regularly exposed to reading and visiting libraries have higher cognitive ability than those with less experience with reading and reading environments. Moreover, it concluded that frequent home learning activities, such as reading and singing from an early age, were associated with better cognitive ability (vocabulary and problem-solving) at age three. This held up even after correcting for sociodemographic factors. This evidence shows consistency across different research paradigms and focuses,[16] and is now recognized to apply across different cultural, social, and economic contexts (illustrated by initiatives such as EU READ, a consortium of European reading promotion organizations).

Others have sought to highlight the affective aspects of booksharing, referring to the physical and emotional closeness that comes from reading together. Laurie Makin describes early literacy as concerned with "relationships and the development of dispositions," while for Guy Claxton and Margaret Carr, it is where attitudes, habits, and values are learned and developed.[17] This has led to the analysis of interactions taking place during booksharing, including helping the child understand and interpret the text, and making explicit the child's connections between the text and other texts, or their own personal experiences.[18] Nicholas Dowdall and colleagues highlight the evidence on the role booksharing has in allowing parents a space to talk about mental states and promote children's social understandings.[19] This casts booksharing as an active and relational practice, which integrates children's own wider knowledge, experiences, and relationships.[20] This personal context is arguably what makes booksharing at home distinctive from reading in other settings:

> What appears to be particularly significant about booksharing in the home, as distinct from booksharing in the classroom or pre-school, is that it takes place between an adult and a child who know each other well, share the same cultural context and therefore share understandings, interests and experiences.[21]

Evidence on the importance of the home environment, and the parent-child relationship, is compelling. However, many variables influence the beneficial qualities of booksharing, given that families have different social and cultural characteristics and differing abilities to participate in both programs and booksharing practices. Van Kleeck points to aspects of the parent-child interaction, such as pre-literacy skills, context, materials, and interactional styles, as examples of such factors. One further example may be the extent of a child's level of participation in booksharing and the ability they have (or opportunity they are given) to interact and direct "talk" around the book.[22] For Makin, supporting a child's active participation should be a core focus of shared book reading, sitting alongside the goals of scaffolding of knowledge and fostering of engagement.[23] In their excellent book on children reading picture books, Arizpe and Styles highlight booksharing as an interactive and, fundamentally, social act. They emphasize the vital role that a mediator can have in supporting and enabling children toward achieving "deeper and, eventually, more critical meaning-making," while at the same time recognizing that such meaning is "culturally saturated."[24] Notably, Van Kleeck places the book itself as a neglected aspect of the "adult-child-book triad." The characteristics of the book—its complexity, genre, or familiarity—Kleeck argues, is a significant factor in the quality of the interaction and, consequently, patterns of emergent reading.[25] Indeed, these issues are interconnected, especially for older children, since participation will relate to a child's ability to interact with the book and their agency in selecting the book being read.

The key point is that sharing books—or songs and rhymes—is not in itself beneficial. Rather, the benefits are influenced by the quality of instructional and affective "talk" surrounding the book, the frequency of the activity, and the overall form of the interaction. These factors, in turn, are connected to the wider social and cultural context of the interaction—for example, the carers' own biographical relationship to books and literacy; the dynamics and interests of the household; other caring responsibilities; and the pressures associated with managing work and family life. Primary caregivers will, of course, be central to mediating these processes. However, the evidence also highlights the importance of appropriately empowering families with the knowledge, understanding, and means through which to make their child's reading experiences as beneficial and rewarding as possible. We return to these issues in our discussion of Bookbug.

INEQUALITIES IN THE HOME
LEARNING ENVIRONMENT

This evidence on the social and emotional context of booksharing can help make sense of why, despite the solid connections between early home learning activities and language development, these benefits are not shared by all children and, in turn, why some families may benefit from more support than others. As research for Book Start (the equivalent program in England) points out, the knowledge, behaviors, and attitudes of different families are far more complex and subtle in meaning than can be understood by simplistic socioeconomic explanations.[26] Nonetheless, it remains important to acknowledge inequalities in home learning activities relative to the family's socioeconomic background and the parents' level of education. There is a relationship between socioeconomic status (SES) and many measures of childhood cognitive and academic achievement.[27] However, this is a complex relationship largely mediated by the quality of the home learning environment.[28] This is not to say that lower socioeconomic status families are directly associated with a low-quality home learning environment or that they are literacy impoverished. Rather, they will not benefit from the economic advantages afforded to more affluent households. Lower socioeconomic status families may, for example, have fewer reading resources available in their home and wider community, while diminished resources and economic security may produce barriers to learning in the home. This is therefore not an issue of class-based parenting styles but an issue of (in)equality of opportunity, as Jacob Cheadle points out:

> The home lives of children are unequal and that this inequality is translated into educational inequality that is part of larger systemic patterns of inequality that persist across generations.[29]

It is notable that there is relatively little research on ethnicity and parenting in the UK context.[30] However, given the well-evidenced relationship between child poverty, education outcomes, and ethnicity, it is reasonable to assume that black and minority ethnic families will be among those most affected by these systemic patterns of inequality.[31]

While the home learning environment can be a space of inequality, it can also act as a protective factor for children from disadvantaged backgrounds. The Millennium Cohort Study, for example, found that differences in the home learning environment (which included reading, sharing learning, visits to the library, songs, and rhymes) had a significant role in narrowing the cognitive gap between rich and poor.[32] Other studies have concluded that early exposure to reading may be more significant than socioeconomic status and parental education in accounting for individual differences in literacy attainment.[33] As will be discussed, for programs like Bookbug, this does not simply translate into an understanding that some parents and families need support, encouragement, and resources to access these activities but they also need help to capitalize on their benefits.

This is not to suggest that supporting parental involvement in home learning activities is a panacea for the effects of poverty and disadvantage (this, as Dimitra Hartas emphasizes, would be a gross oversimplification).[34] Lyn Tett and Jim Crowther have argued that dominant forms of literacy can privilege middle-class, school-based literacies and marginalize those of working-class communities. Although now twenty years old, Tett and Crowther's work powerfully illustrates the importance of programs which *work with* families, as opposed to imposing or dictating particular literacy practices:

> A family literacy programme that helps parents to be true partners in their own and their children's learning will be one which sees the role of the home and the school in learning as reciprocal. Paying attention to literacies that are culturally productive, through supporting the real life context of the family, is therefore more likely to result in positive outcomes for all.[35]

THE BOOKBUG PROGRAM

Before moving on to discuss how the Bookbug program relates to this evidence based on booksharing, it is useful, especially for readers outside the UK, to outline how the Bookbug program operates. For simplicity, we discuss here two core Bookbug activities—Bookbug Bags and Bookbug Sessions—although the program includes other notable elements. One of these is the Outreach program, launched in 2012, and supports Bookbug's principle of "targeted" or "proportionate" universalism. This principle is described as the resourcing and delivery of universal services at a scale and intensity that is proportionate to the degree of need. As such, it is not simply that a service is universally available but that it responds to the level of presenting need.[36] In the case of Bookbug, the outreach program is an acknowledgment that certain groups may face barriers in accessing the universal service. What the outreach program seeks to do is offer enhanced support to families identified locally as those who might benefit from support to access the benefits of the universal elements of Bookbug. To do this, Scottish Book Trust works closely with the thirty-two local authorities in Scotland, training specialist practitioners to deliver Bookbug Sessions (or elements of Bookbug) in the home environment.[37]

The program is best known in Scotland for the "Bookbug Bag," a canvas bag containing books and resources, gifted to every baby, toddler, and three- to five-year-olds in Scotland, and funded by Scottish government (see figure 4.2). Crucially, gifting is universal, meaning that all children in Scotland, regardless of location or financial circumstances, should receive four Bookbug Bags by the time they reach the age of five. The contents of each bag change each year and vary to include books and resources that will support or appeal to children at the designated age. However, typically the bags will include a selection of books, a CD of music, materials to inspire writing experiences (such as crayons in the toddler bag and colored pencils in the three-year-old's bag) and information leaflets including ideas for activities families can do together. Bookbug aims to be accessible and inclusive and therefore there are dedicated titles for children with additional support needs and information about Bookbug translated into a range of languages.

While Scottish Book Trust coordinates the program, bag gifting takes place in localities, and therefore successful delivery depends on local partners. There is a Bookbug coordinator based in each local authority area, usually within the library service. Although there is some local variation, generally health visitors gift Baby and Toddler Bags;[38] nurseries gift Explorer Bags to three-year-olds; and primary schools gift bags to five-year-olds. Library services are vital partners, being involved in local partnerships (e.g., gifting in partnerships with nurseries) or gifting individually to families (e.g., to those who have missed a bag). The bag, in itself, is not necessarily sufficient for encouraging parents to share the contents with their child and relies on families having knowledge of, or placing value on, the benefits of reading to their children. The expectation is that local partners do more than simply gift

Figure 4.2 Bookbug Baby Bag. *Source:* Scottish Book Trust.

the bag but use it as a tool through which to deliver key messages around the importance of reading, talking, and singing, and how this contributes to health, well-being, and language and communication development.

The second core activity is the "Bookbug Session," song and rhyme sessions run by a trained Bookbug Session leader. The groups are available in every local authority in Scotland and, like the bags, are free and accessible to all. At present, Bookbug sessions in Gaelic are delivered in ten local authorities, and a number of localities are running Bookbug Sessions for children with additional support needs (e.g., sessions for deaf children or children with autism). The majority are delivered within public libraries or early years settings (such as nurseries and third sector projects), although an increasing number of sessions are taking place in other community spaces, such as shopping centers and parent and toddler groups. Libraries also run Bookbug Sessions in partnership, for example, with nurseries to celebrate bag gifting. Like gifting, Bookbug Sessions aim to influence how families engage with songs and rhymes.

Although the content of a Bookbug Session is determined by the Session leader, Scottish Book Trust provides good practice guidelines and encourages leaders to plan within these. This includes a "hello" song, rhymes and songs, a book, activity with movement, more rhymes and songs, and finally, a "goodbye" song. Materials are available to those delivering sessions, including a Bookbug doll, Bookbug Bags, finger puppets, Lycra (stretchy material used to facilitate movement in sessions, and encourage parents and children to work together), and stickers. Specific resources for additional support needs (ASN) are also provided, including tactile ASN books and gifting guidance. Bookbug Session leaders model the session with a Bookbug empathy doll so the approach in the session is not instructional but rather seeks to model and influence. Importantly, songs and rhymes are used to encourage interaction and engagement during the session, with the intention that families will continue to share the stories, songs, and rhymes at home, and with other family members.

As program coordinators, Scottish Book Trust is responsible for developing and coordinating the distribution of Bookbug Bags; delivering free training to support gifting, sessions, and outreach activities; coordinating Bookbug Steering or Advisory Groups; and delivering one-off events. However, this is not only an administrative role. Notably, the quality and consistency of this program depend on strong national-local communication networks, and the maintenance of trust and commitment from local partners. Thus far, Scottish Book Trust has achieved this. Not only has the program grown significantly in the last five years (in 2016–2017 Scottish Book Trust and its local and national partners gifted 178,045 Bookbug Bags and delivered 146,616

Bookbug Sessions) but, as will be discussed, practitioners overwhelmingly described it as helping them to facilitate, support, and enable quality family reading practices.

BOOKBUG AS MEDIATOR

What role, then, does Bookbug play in mediating families' relationship to children's reading? First, we should start with a definition of mediation, which here we have taken to *relate to an* "intervention" in a process or a relationship. Such an intervention can be enabling or damaging for those concerned, with the outcome greatly dependent on the assumptions and values underpinning the action. As demonstrated by other chapters in this book, children's reading is an aspect of life which historically has been mediated by adult "others."[39] In this context, parents, teachers, librarians, early years workers, health professionals, writers, publishers, and governments have consistently been involved in decisions which have not only shaped what children should read but how they should read, and why. These levels of scrutiny continue and are not surprising given the central place that reading has assumed in children's early development, be it as a medium through which to teach moral values and manners, to support cognitive and socioemotional development, or as a form of play or entertainment.

We can define Bookbug's role as a mediator in two ways, the first being to select and provide families with physical resources which become part of their home and child's social world and the second is to universally support families to use these resources in the manner deemed most beneficial and rewarding. The intention, in other words, is not only that families will have physical resources "in hand" but that they are aware of their benefits and confident to use them in a way that suits their family. There is also the underlying intention that families will be encouraged to continue and develop their home literacy practice by seeking out other books. Bookbug's role in mediating children's reading may be less explicit, softer perhaps, than the term "intervention" implies. Nonetheless, the Bookbug program has significant reach. Whether its mediating role is positive or negative depends largely on the strategic values or ethos of the program; the agency it gives to the families it is delivering services to; and the extent to which professionals deliver the service "buy-in" to the program and do it locally as intended.

Scottish Book Trust articulates the aim of the program in the following way: to encourage parents and carers to share books with their children from as early an age as possible, and to inspire a love of books and reading in every child. This, in turn, should contribute to a number of outcomes:

- Families are reading, talking, singing, and cuddling more with their babies and children.
- More practitioners are confident and able to communicate the key Bookbug messages.
- Decision makers integrate the Bookbug approach into Early Years practice, local policy, and strategy.
- More children and families use libraries.

For the Scottish Book Trust staff interviewed as part of the evaluation, the program benefits were articulated as going beyond emergent literacy and language development. Emphasis, instead, was placed on attachment, bonding, and instilling a love of books as important goals in their own right. Here we see a vision of the program as capable of delivering holistic benefits, encompassing cognitive development, as well as social and emotional well-being:

> *The 360 degree benefits that come out of [Bookbug] aren't anything to do with literacy in itself, they're actually to do with building bonds, attachments, happiness and shared experiences. (staff member, interview)*

From the perspective of Scottish Book Trust, it remains critical that benefits should be available to all, not just those judged "in need." Central to this is the aspiration that the program is a "leveler," with every child receiving the same experience of reading and singing, without stigma or punitive intervention. During interviews for the evaluation, Scottish Book Trust staff also referred to the Bookbug program as both a community in itself and part of existing communities. It had, they argued, the potential to enable or facilitate "connections," "relationships," and a "common language" between early years professionals and families. In this context, Bookbug can be conceived as having a position at the center of a triangle composed of family, nurseries/school, and public libraries, strategically mediating between public and private domains, conveying and reinforcing the message that sharing books, songs, and rhymes are beneficial to children's early years.

WHAT SHOULD CHILDREN READ?

An aspect of mediation that may be overlooked is the selection of books for inclusion in the Bookbug Bags. As noted earlier, Van Kleeck (2003) suggests that the book itself is a neglected part of booksharing, despite its significance in shaping the quality and form of interaction. For Scottish Book Trust, central to the book selection is identifying a collection that will appeal to as diverse a group of children and families as possible, without being generic or oversimplistic. A range of attributes are considered, with books selected as appealing based on a combination of content, theme, and characters or physical attributes, such as format (board or paperback), mirrors, flaps, and other "novelty" features. For all bag types, the focus is on encouraging reading for pleasure. However, book selection has wider implications. Several practitioners commented that they knew children for whom the Bookbug books are the only ones they have at home. Others highlighted the trust and value parents and carers placed in Scottish Book Trust, and the likelihood that many receiving the bags will interpret the books, and the book suggestions, as examples of the "best" or most suitable for their child. These examples highlight the organizational responsibility placed on Scottish Book Trust to invest resources in book selection to ensure ongoing quality and inclusion.

Scottish Book Trust aims to be an evidence-based organization and ensures it draws on up-to-date research on the types of books suitable and engaging for different ages and stages of child. This knowledge is incorporated into its book selection criteria. For babies, publishers are asked to consider books with simple language, rhyme, rhythm or repetition, mirrors, flaps, bright and colorful or high contrast illustrations and photos of other babies. For toddlers, publishers are asked to submit for consideration books with themes that would resonate with toddlers, such as play, routines, or friends. These books should be more advanced than baby books, and may include concepts such as counting, opposites, or colors. One specific request is that publishers consider titles that will inspire children, either in their play or their interactions and conversations during the booksharing experience. The Explorer Bag does not need to contain books specifically linked to the explorer theme, but rather books that are engaging and relatable for children and their families. Example themes would be adventure; being outdoors; new experiences; counting; rhyme and rhythm; familiar stories retold; and emotions. For all the bags, there is an awareness that books need to appeal not only to children but also to the parent or carer. Inclusivity and diversity are also important. Where books feature children, priority will be given to those featuring boys and girls, with a variety of abilities, and from different ethnic backgrounds. A further consideration is that there are multiple books in the bags, and therefore can form a complementary set, working for varying levels of ability and interests. This should also acknowledge that children will have had different experiences with books, and therefore what might appeal to some three-year-olds might be too challenging, long, or unappealing to others.

The book selection process begins with an annual visit by Scottish Book Trust to a range of publishers. Information and selection criteria are sent in advance of the meetings, allowing for an open dialogue in which Scottish Book Trust is able to provide feedback, and elicit submissions, of books considered suitable for the Bookbug Bags. Publishers are welcome to submit their own book selection, but working with them to tailor and elicit submissions helps Scottish Book Trust streamline shortlisting and guide submissions toward books that are suitable based on format, content, and projected cost. After the submission period is closed, a team from Scottish Book Trust decides on a shortlist. The length of this list varies depending on the number of submissions in each category and their overall suitability for the Bookbug Bags.

Once the short list is agreed upon, a book selection panel is convened by Scottish Book Trust. This panel typically includes representation from key early years partners, including libraries, health, education, and the third sector. Membership of the panel changes yearly, though ensuring a range of professional backgrounds is a priority. In advance of the meeting, panel members are given the entire short list to "try out" in different settings, and where possible, collect feedback from parents, carers, and children. Panel members are also encouraged to report on more than feedback from parents, by considering the voices of children, even those who are very young. A key element of "trying out" books is thus watching children's reactions, and noting the ways in which they inspire interaction between adults and children. With feedback collected, the panel members discuss, debate and ultimately vote on their favorite books. As might be expected, this discussion is always lively and often involves compromise among members to ensure that the books chosen are appealing to a broad range of families.

Scottish Book Trust has, in the past, had the opportunity to work with publishers to make minor modifications to texts or illustrations before inclusion in the Bookbug Bag. Such decisions have been made to better align the message being conveyed by the book with national government policies around health or to promote inclusivity and diversity. Examples have included removing a baby bottle, changing an image of a sleeping baby on its front to be sleeping on its back, or removing a dummy (pacifier) from an illustration. These modifications were all initiated by Scottish Book Trust to fit National Health Service (NHS) Scotland guidance, with the aim of ensuring that images do not contradict core messages given to families by other professionals, such as health visitors. In these cases, the books were not changed to be specific tools for teaching or influencing but rather subtly modified so as to embolden the messages being promoted by gifting partners. As in the past,[40] these examples reveal the social and cultural construction of children's literature, whereby Scottish Book Trust and its partners not only determine the suitability of books for different ages and stages but also have the opportunity to affirm societal norms and behaviors associated with early years and childhood.

HOW CHILDREN AND THEIR
FAMILIES SHOULD READ

We now move beyond the book and the other materials to consider another aspect of the parent-child-book triad—that is the act of gifting the Bookbug Bag by a professional to a family. Such a professional, for example, a health visitor, can gift a Bookbug Bag, but no matter how good the books are, or how high quality, it cannot be assumed that the family will look at the contents, let alone make use of them. Moreover, it cannot be assumed that parents and carers who use the bags do so in a way that maximizes their benefits. This follows Makin, who suggests that there is a "danger that parents and early childhood educators may accept the importance of reading to children but do so in ways that may have less than optimal results."[41]

Scottish Book Trust recognizes that the gifting process is critical in mediating the ways families share books and maximizing the benefits to children. However, it is emphasized that the act of gifting should not involve telling parents and carers what to do, or how "best" to read to their children (or indeed, parent their child). For Scottish Book Trust, the organizational aim is that Bookbug Bags are gifted with a clear and simple message about the importance of early booksharing. At the same time, this interaction should recognize context, the child's agency, and the quality of the relationship and interactional style. In other words, families should be supported, but in a way that allows them to develop an approach that reflects their family's own preferences, abilities, and characteristics.

To do this, Scottish Book Trust has developed a range of resources to support practitioners responsible for gifting Bookbug Bags locally. This includes an extensive and ongoing training program for those gifting bags and delivering sessions, as well as "gifting advice" which describes good gifting practices and further information on the program. A large part of the "message" that practitioners are being asked to mediate to families relates to the various benefits of sharing books, songs, and rhymes (as described in the earlier section). Practitioners also receive guidance on mediating how children and their families should read. These, as summarized below, focus as much on interactional patterns as the process of reading:

- Gifting should begin as early as possible, and families encouraged to read to their babies.
- There is no "right" or "wrong" way to read to your child.
- Reading a book from start to finish is not essential.
- Encourage the use of song, pictures, and "talk" when reading.
- Start with a child's interests and travel with them.

• Reading is not just about books, but about all types of reading matter—be it cereal boxes, leaflets, magazines, or books.

Good practice also states that practitioners gifting bags should, wherever possible, take the contents out of the bag, show it to families, and demonstrate or "model" booksharing. This is encouraged so that parents have a chance to witness how their baby responds to books and so that practitioners can use this to facilitate a discussion. Bookbug Sessions operate on much the same ethos. These group sessions allow practitioners to "model" songs and booksharing to parent, carers, and children.

We can also see a strong focus on children's agency in the program, especially in the bags for children ages three and over. An activity book in the Explorer Bag aims to encourage children's active participation in reading using simple questions and prompts parents and carers to support "talk" about the book, and children to express their own views about what they liked, or did not like, about a particular story. Similarly, Bookbug Sessions are designed as child-centered and participative, combining opportunities for physical closeness between carer and child, as well as self-expression, confidence, and sociality.

THE MEDIATING EFFECTS OF BOOKBUG IN PRACTICE

Practitioners' Reactions

We have outlined Scottish Book Trust's *intended* approach to mediating children's reading via a network of local partners. But how do the practitioners working with families respond to the bags, and to their role mediating Scottish Book Trust's message? A focal point for the evaluation was the extent to which Bookbug practice—that is distributing bags to families or running sessions—was being successfully embedded into everyday working practices. This was important since Bookbug is, ultimately, delivered voluntarily through a network of local practitioners working in health care, nurseries, and other early years setting, libraries, and specialist family support services. For Scottish Book Trust, the objective is for the Bookbug program, in all its forms, to be a resource which adds value and complements practitioners' core duties. It should not be an additional burden to practitioner's already overstretched workloads.

The results of the evaluation revealed that overwhelmingly the Bookbug program was understood by practitioners, and regarded as complementary their existing duties. Not only this, Bookbug was described as having a positive impact on their organization, their own role, and on the people they worked with. For example, of the 627 practitioners participating in the survey almost all (99%) agreed that Bookbug was beneficial to their organization, with the majority stating that it impacted positively on the knowledge of the workforce, on levels of collaborative and cross-sectoral working, and on their ability to work as part of their community. Notably, 76% felt that it provided a "resource" through which to engage with families, while a similar proportion (73%) stated that Bookbug helped them reach families considered to be "disadvantaged."

Practitioners working with Bookbug were highly supportive of Bookbug. This support was strongly associated with the concept of quality of the program's training, printed materials, resources for sessions, and digital materials. However, the most frequently discussed aspect of quality was the bags and their contents, mentioned by almost all practitioners involved in gifting. Particular emphasis was given to the quality of the book selection, which was variously described as age appropriate, insightful, easy to read, and enjoyable:

> *[The books] are excellent choices and both kids and parents respond immediately and positively to the quality of the chosen titles. I think they are getting better and better over time. (library, survey respondent)*

> *The current selection of books for this year is of a very high quality in terms of genre, illustrations and story content. I think this will be very motivating for children. (early years, survey respondent)*

Practitioners' comments about the bag were largely shaped by their experience of how families react to the bag. Practitioners universally agreed that families respond positively to the bag. In parallel with parent responses, a particular comment was in relation to children's reaction to the bags, with several describing the way a child's face "lights up" on receiving their gift from Bookbug. The combination of the quality of the bags, and the positive reaction of families, resulted in practitioners describing Bookbug Bags as a resource which they were proud of and motivated to gift:

> *[I love] the fantastic selection of books. Wonderful to be able to give these books out and to demonstrate for parents how babies' eyes pop out of their heads when you hold a gorgeous colorful book for them to see. (early years, survey respondent)*

Practitioners also repeatedly referred to Bookbug Bags as a "tool" that helped to enable and nurture quality family reading practices. It was noted, for example, that the Bookbug approach allows practitioners to model dialogic reading practices. These acknowledge the importance of talk surrounding the booksharing experience, helping to shift the focus away from more simplistic measures such as reading frequency or "successfully" reading a book from start to finish which parents and carers cited as being a source of stress. Instead, practitioners valued the attention given to the quality of family interaction with books and songs, the diversity of these interactions, and the opportunities these presented in terms of attachment and reading for pleasure.

Practitioners gifting bags also emphasized that offering free, high-quality resources can help to establish a relationship with a family. This was particularly the case for families distrustful of professional interventions. Critically, the bag was referred to as a "springboard" upon which discussions about bonding, brain development, attachment, and literacy could be framed, and which provides the opportunity to move onto more challenging conversations around wider support issues.

> It is just a great tool for engaging with families, not just on reading, but on other issues and just getting to know them. (Bookbug coordinator, case study)

Mirroring the vision of Scottish Book Trust staff, practitioners valued Bookbug's flexible approach and use of role modeling to demonstrate booksharing. This was highlighted as significant in supporting and enabling families, rather than reproaching or blaming them:

> Sometimes you don't want to be in a position where you are treating parents as stupid or telling them what they don't know. Role modelling means I'm not saying it directly, "this is how you read to your child." (nursery, case study)

Bookbug Sessions were also praised by practitioners for offering multiple benefits to parents and children, including increased knowledge of songs and rhymes; improved speech and language skills; understanding of social cooperation; supporting social networks and friendship. One of the most frequently highlighted views was the way Bookbug Sessions can build on benefits provided by Bookbug Bags by incorporating creativity, physical movement, and play into families' experiences of sharing books, songs, and rhymes:

> Those who access the Bookbug Sessions gain huge benefits, but those who just receive the bags but do not attend any song and rhyme sessions have a much diminished benefit. (early years, survey respondent)

Families' Reactions

The reactions of families to the bags were largely in line with those of practitioners, with open responses from both the survey and face-to-face interviews being overwhelmingly positive. Parents regarded them as a free gift and, overall, as something they were grateful to receive. Chiming with practitioners' comments, parents interviewed stated that the quality of the bags made them more likely to use them, and perhaps at an earlier age than they intended to start reading. Several also spoke about the bags making them feel valued and respected as parents. One of the most significant reported effects of the Bookbug Bags related to the age at which parents introduce books to their children. Research has shown that a parent's beliefs and experiences play an important role in determining behavior.[42] This can influence or shape assumptions, even among parents who enjoy and value reading. This was reflected in a recent report from Book Trust in England which found evidence of assumptions that it is not practical or helpful to read to babies until they can sit unaided and vocalize responses.[43] Scottish Book Trust's gifting messages, and the resources in the bag, seek to introduce the idea that babies have the capacity to enjoy books from birth. As well as free, age-appropriate books, a free calendar provides parents with information on how to read to babies, on what books are suitable and on suggested new authors.

Our survey of parents and carers who had recently received the Bookbug Bag for babies found that almost a fifth (18%) did not read to their child before getting their bag. We looked further at the demographic of the 18% of parents and carers who did not read with their baby at the point when they received their bag. A relationship by age, indices of multiple deprivation, and English as an additional language was identified, although given the limitations of the survey it is not possible to state the statistical significance of this finding. We are unable to attribute a causal relationship between the gifting of the Bookbug Bags and changes to reading practices, as families are being exposed to a range of interventions and activities which can shape behavior. However, qualitative interviews sought to interrogate parental reactions to the bags and perception of impact. Parents and carers widely reported Scottish Book Trust's message about early reading practices as having a tangible impact upon their attitudes and knowledge:

A lot of the things I may not have thought of doing . . . I would never have thought about getting wee books, because I would have thought "well, she can't read," so I would say it's a great benefit to myself and to her. (parent, interview)

I don't think I would have known what kind of books to buy for a newborn, I don't think I would have thought of buying something like that but when we got

*given the books I was more sort of inclined to use them, you know . . . reading
at an early age is still relevant, kind of thing. (parent, interview)*

There is also evidence in the interview data that for parents more generally,
Bookbug Bags had a cumulative influence on the way in which they read with
their children. Parents talked about spending more time reading with their
children, talking about the story and the pictures, and making up games as
a consequence of receiving their Bookbug Bag. Notably, receiving multiple
bags over time was thought to provide a regular prompt, nudge, or reminder
to engage in reading and singing whenever possible. This was especially
significant for parents and carers who were "time poor" as a consequence
of changing family structures (e.g., where there was no extended family to
provide child care) and working patterns:

*I am pretty sure that the free books is what makes me read now. I wouldn't be
reading to my kids if it wasn't for these books. (parent, case study)*

*These things are good to remind you to do it . . . like in theory I should know
what I'm doing because this is number two, but getting books does make you
think "oh yeah, I should actually be reading to her and not just to her sister."
(parent, telephone interview)*

Relative to the children's developmental stage, one of the key differences
identified in parents' accounts of the Explorer Bag was a focus on their
child's reaction, rather than their own. These accounts described children's
excitement about receiving the bag, and children's perception of the bag as
a gift to them. Children, as such, were seen as having a sense of ownership
over the bag, and parents felt that this was very positive:

*It's something that's theirs as well, you now, it's theirs to keep so they look
after it [. . .] you know, to be careful with them and not tear books and things.
(parent, telephone interview)*

*She's been enjoying it because it's like a gift for her, she's been quite excited
about that. (parent, telephone interview)*

Several parents described the way that their children had taken an active
role in exploring and using the contents of the bag, for example, by taking
everything out:

*It was him that opened it up and rummaged through, he gave me the booklets
and the crayons and said, "mummy you hold that," while he automatically*

flicked through every single book he was given, 'cos I think there were three books in it. (parent, telephone interview)

Everything got torn out of it and all the books had to get read instantaneously one after the other. (parent, telephone interview)

Families reported similar reactions to Bookbug Sessions, with parents reporting ways in which Bookbug Sessions contributed to their child's learning and development. Most obviously, parents reported that they had learned new songs which they continued to sing at home. Parents also believed that Bookbug Sessions helped to develop their child's speech and language, specifically citing the activity as helping them learn new words and phrases and, in turn, applying new learning to other aspects of life (e.g., through play):

I came because he didn't have many words, I've been coming for a year now and I can see the difference in his language, he is mouthing out the words of the songs and he is using words he has never used before. (parent, case study)

Some parents felt that going along to Bookbug Sessions increased their confidence in singing at home with their babies and children and that observing their children's positive response to singing and rhyming has encouraged them to do it more often:

When we go home and sing the songs in the car she knows them and knows all the actions. (parent, telephone interview)

BOOKBUG AS MEDIATOR: LIMITS AND CHALLENGES

This chapter has demonstrated the positive impact of the Bookbug program on families' reading behaviors in Scotland. As noted earlier, the Bookbug program is an example of "targeted" or "proportionate" universalism. A concept normally used in relation to health equity, this is an approach which balances universal service delivery with targeted interventions proportionate to the needs and levels of disadvantage of a population. In the case of Bookbug, bags and sessions are always free, and available to everyone, regardless of age, ability, health, gender, gender identity, ethnicity, religion or belief, and sexual orientation. Bookbug, we found, can have a positive impact on all families: not just those who might be judged "in need" should the program be means tested. For many of the parents we spoke to—including those who already described themselves as placing a high value on reading—Bookbug played a key part in reminding them of the importance of reading and singing to their children and prompting them to dedicate time to do this. The outreach program, in turn, provides a means through which to support groups identified as facing barriers to accessing the Bookbug program (e.g., young parents, fathers, or families where English is a second language). Additional services, such as the training of outreach workers in local communities, the delivery of sessions in Gaelic, dedicated titles for children with ASN, and translated information about Bookbug, support this work.

That everyone gets the same physical resources, combined with relational support, is important. Universality removes stigma and allows families to benefit from the program in their own way, whether as a reminder of the importance of reading, new knowledge about the benefits of booksharing, new songs or authors or new friends and communities of interest formed at Bookbug Sessions. Practitioner training and the outreach service, in turn, provides proportionate, targeted support to those most in need. This targeted universalism enables Bookbug to successfully reach the majority of the population, while at the same time equipping practitioners with the skills to engage with families facing barriers to learning in the home.

Targeted universal provision, of course, does not equate to equal access or equal benefits. Positively, the survey revealed high levels of awareness of Bookbug Sessions. However, young parents and carers, those living in more deprived areas and those for whom English was an additional language, were less likely to have heard of Bookbug Sessions. A similar finding was found in relation to reading at home. A total of 18% of families stated that they were not reading to their babies at the point the Bookbug Bag was gifting. Examination of these respondents again found younger parents, parents living in deprived areas, and families with English as an additional language overrepresented. Given the survey was self-selecting, and likely to be a more affluent sample, it is a reasonable expectation that were this survey issued to the general population, these inequities would be more pronounced. Within the case study research, we found many positive examples of Bookbug being a tool for recognizing diverse and exploring culturally relevant literacies. For example, some families with English as an additional language described Bookbug sessions were useful for learning English. Other Bookbug groups encouraged parents to share songs from their own culture and language. There were others, however, who felt unable to attend Bookbug since they felt their English was "not good enough." At a local level, practitioners identified a lack of information on the needs of families for whom English was an additional language, citing resources and staffing as the core reason specialist provision being expanded.

Intersecting with this point, the evaluation also identified the conditions in which Bookbug operates most effectively in mediating children's reading. Locally, impact was highest where there was strong strategic commitment;

visible and adequately resourced local programming; and a supported, trained, and motivated community of Bookbug practitioners. Risks, conversely, occurred when Bookbug was under-resourced locally, which placed practitioner's core duties, and their ability to prioritize Bookbug activities, under pressure. This hints at a regular theme in the evaluation literature, namely interconnectedness between the booksharing intervention and wider early years and family literacy services, and with the community.[44] Cuts to community and family support services and libraries threaten effectiveness, a point that practitioners keenly expressed throughout the evaluation:

> *I think that the Bookbug programme is fantastic and I am so pleased to be involved. There are challenges including staffing capacity issues and storage capacity issues. In our current economic times staffing capacity issues are no surprise but we must press on to do our best in the circumstances. (Bookbug coordinator, survey respondent)*

Although the social consequences of recession and welfare cuts in Scotland seemed to have the greatest impact, it was in relation to supporting those families facing inequalities in the home learning environment. Practitioners, for instance, stressed the disproportionate effect that cuts to public services in the UK have had on their ability to deliver sustainable outreach, and in particular to those most in need of Bookbug's benefits. Many, especially those working in library services, felt constrained by what they could provide to more disadvantaged families, and were keenly aware that more could be done to bridge the divide.

CONCLUSION

We conclude by reflecting on the role that Bookbug plays in mediating families' relationship to children's reading. Mediation, we suggest, represents some kind of "intervention" in a process or relationship, with the possible impact being positive or negative. In the case of Bookbug, it mediates children's reading by providing families with physical resources for sharing books in the home learning environment. However, Bookbug's mediating role goes far beyond the provision of resources "in-hand." This chapter has demonstrated a clear ethos at the heart of the program and that is to ensure that every child has access to books and is supported to develop a love of stories. Most crucial is the approach Bookbug takes to achieving this since it does not seek to impose a particular or "correct" approach to children's reading. Rather it seeks to support families across Scotland to develop reading practices that suit their own household circumstances.

Providing free, universally gifted Bookbug Bags is an instrumental part in achieving this vision. The bags are gifted universally recognizing that all families can benefit from, and provide, effective home literacy practices such as the sharing of stories, songs, and rhymes. The message of importance of sharing stories cannot be separated from ensuring families have the physical tools required to do this.

The outreach program ensures that professionals are sensitive to, and aware of, the additional support that some families require to engage in the universal program. The books and resources in the Bookbug Bags are intended as tools to support professionals to discuss the benefits of book sharing with families. Crucially, as evidenced throughout this chapter, Bookbug does have the potential to support positive family reading practices, encouraging families to engage in reading for the first time, and to read when they had not planned or intended to. This is especially critical to those who are affected by systemic patterns of inequality.

Looking forward, there is cause for concern. Across the UK, austerity measures following the 2008–2009 recession have resulted in successive cuts to local government spending.[45] While statutory social care services have been protected to an extent, spending on universal services, including public libraries, community centers, and youth and children's centers, has been significantly reduced.[46] Evidence on the impact of austerity has shown that the most marginalized people, and the most marginalized places, are among those most affected by the cuts. The cost of COVID-19 to the UK's public finances is likely to result in an even deeper recession, and to place universal public services under even greater pressure.

The investment and value given to Bookbug in this challenging social and economic context is significant. It is a national program, with universal reach, and one which continues to respond to the changing social and economic context in which it operates. Practitioners' willingness to deliver the program, and their recognition of its contribution to tackling inequalities in the home learning environment, speaks volumes. While Bookbug cannot be a panacea for social inequalities, the program does represent a national commitment to equalizing children's literacy beginnings. As we look forward to challenging economic times, it is important that free, universal services are protected. Bookbug and its role in supporting children's emergent literacy is the perfect place to start.

NOTES

1. Scottish Book Trust is a national charity based in Edinburgh, Scotland, promoting literature, reading, and writing in Scotland. It works with and for a range of

audiences, including babies and parents (through the Bookbug program), children and young people, teachers and learning professionals, writers and publishers. In addition to Bookbug, the charity runs other government programs for primary age schoolchildren, program for adult learners, as well as program for writer development and author events. For more information about Scottish Book Trust, visit their website scottishbooktrust.com. Accessed January 28, 2022.

2. Emma Davidson, Christina McMellon, Laura Airey and Helen Berry, *Evaluating the Impact of Bookbug Bags and Sessions in Scotland* (Edinburgh: Scottish Book Trust, 2018).

3. Davidson, McMellon, Airey and Berry, *Evaluating the Impact of Bookbug Bags*.

4. See, for example, John Mayne, "Contribution Analysis: An Approach to Exploring Cause and Effect," *The Institutional Learning and Change (ILAC) Briefing* 16 (2008), http://betterevaluation.org/sites/default/files/ILAC_Brief16_Contribution_Analysis.pdf.

5. Barbara Riley, Alison Kernoghan, Lisa Stockton, Steve Montague, Jennifer Yessis and Cameron D. Willis, "Using Contribution Analysis to Evaluate the Impacts of Research on Policy: Getting to 'Good Enough,'" *Research Evaluation* 27, no. 1 (2017): 16–27.

6. See, for example, Adriana G. Bus, Marinus H. van Ijzendoorn and Anthony D. Pellegrini, "Joint Book Reading Makes for Success in Learning to Read: A Meta-Analysis on Intergenerational Transmission of Literacy," *Review of Educational Research* 65, no. 1 (1995): 1–21; Michelle Hood, Elizabeth Conlon and Glenda Andrews, "Preschool Home Literacy Practices and Children's Literacy Development: A Longitudinal Analysis," *Journal of Educational Psychology* 100, no. 2 (2008): 252–71; Monique Sénéchal and Jo-Anne LeFevre, "Continuity and Change in the Home Literacy Environment as Predictors of Growth in Vocabulary and Reading," *Child Development* 85, no. 4 (2014): 1552–68; Paul Bradshaw, Tom King, Line Knudsen, James Law and Clare Sharp, *Language Development and Enjoyment of Reading: Impacts of Early Parent-Child Activities in Two Growing up in Scotland Cohorts* (Edinburgh: The Scottish Government: Children and Families Analysis, 2016).

7. Patricia K. Kuhl, "Early Language Learning and Literacy: Neuroscience Implications for Education," *Mind, Brain and Education: The Official Journal of the International Mind, Brain, and Education Society* 5, no. 3 (2011): 128–42.

8. Graver J. Whitehurst and Christopher J. Lonigan, "Child Development and Emergent Literacy," *Child Development* 69, no. 3 (1998): 848–72; Sara E. Rimm-Kaufman and Robert C. Pianta, "An Ecological Perspective on the Transition to Kindergarten: A Theoretical Framework to Guide Empirical Research," *Journal of Applied Developmental Psychology* 21, no. 5 (2000): 491–511; Jennifer Buckingham, Kevin Wheldall and Robyn Beaman-Wheldall, "Why Poor Children Are More Likely to Become Poor Readers: The School Years," *Australian Journal of Education* 57, no. 3 (2013): 190–213.

9. See, for example, Betty Hart and Todd R. Risley, "The Early Catastrophe," *American Educator* 27, no. 4 (2003): 6–9.

10. See, for example, Barbara D. DeBaryshe, Janeen C. Binder and Martha Jane Buell, "Mothers' Implicit Theories of Early Literacy Instruction: Implications for Children's Reading and Writing," *Early Child Development and Care* 160, no. 1 (2000): 119–31.

11. Annemarie H. Hindman, Carol M. Connor, Abigail M. Jewkes and Frederick J. Morrison, "Untangling the Effects of Shared Book Reading: Multiple Factors and Their Associations with Preschool Literacy Outcomes," *Early Childhood Research Quarterly* 23, no. 3 (2008): 330–50; Monique Sénéchal and Laura Young, "The Effect of Family Literacy Interventions on Children's Acquisition of Reading from Kindergarten to Grade 3: A Meta-Analytic Review," *Review of Educational Research* 78, no. 4 (2008): 880–907; Jenny Spratt and Kate Philip, *An Appraisal of Bookstart in Sighthill* (Edinburgh: Bookstart, 2007); What Works Clearinghouse, *Fast Forward Language: English Language Learners* (US Department of Education, Institute of Education Sciences, 2006), https://files.eric.ed.gov/fulltext/ED540656.pdf.

12. Suzanne E. Mol and Adriana G. Bus, "To Read or Not to Read: A Meta-Analysis of Print Exposure from Infancy to Early Adulthood," *Psychological Bulletin* 137, no. 2 (2011): 267–96.

13. Kathy Sylva, Edward Melhuish, Pam Sammons, Iram Siraj-Blatchford and Brenda Taggart, *The Effective Provision of Pre-School Education Project: Final Report: A Longitudinal Study Funded by the Dfes 1997–2004* (London: Institute of Education, University of London/Department for Education and Skills/Sure Start, 2004).

14. Scott D. Gest, Nicole R. Freeman, Celene E. Domitrovich and Janet A. Welsh, "Shared Book Reading and Children's Language Comprehension Skills: The Moderating Role of Parental Discipline Practices," *Early Childhood Research Quarterly* 19, no. 2 (2004): 319–36.

15. Bradshaw, King, Knudsen, Law and Sharp, *Language Development and Enjoyment of Reading.*

16. Sheffield Hallam, *The Contribution of Early Years Bookgifting Programmes to Literacy Attainment: A Literature Review* (Sheffield: Sheffield Hallam University, 2014), https://www.booktrust.org.uk/globalassets/resources/research/final-bookgifting-lit-review.pdf.

17. Laurie Makin, "Literacy 8–12 Months: What Are Babies Learning?" *Early Years* 26, no. 3 (2007): 269–77, 269; Guy Claxton and Margaret Carr, "A Framework for Teaching Learning: The Dynamics of Disposition," *Early Years* 24, no. 1 (2004): 87–97.

18. Jane Torr, "The Pleasure of Recognition: Intertextuality in the Talk of Preschoolers during Shared Reading with Mothers and Teachers," *Early Years* 27, no. 1 (2007): 77–91.

19. Nicholas Dowdall, Peter J. Cooper, Mark Tomlinson, Sarah Skeen, Frances Gardner and Lynne Murray, "The Benefits of Early Book Sharing for Child Cognitive and Socio-Emotional Development in South Africa: Study Protocol for a Randomised Controlled Trial," *Trials* 18, no. 1 (2017): 1–13, 3.

20. Fiona M. Collins and Cathy Svensson, "If I Had a Magic Wand I'd Magic Her Out of the Book: The Rich Literacy Practices of Competent Early Readers," *Early Years* 28, no. 1 (2008): 81–91.

21. Sheffield Hallam, *The Contribution of Early Years Bookgifting*, 7.

22. Anne van Kleeck, "Research on Book Sharing: Another Critical Look," in *On Reading Books to Children: Parents and Teachers*, eds. Anne van Kleeck, Steven A. Stahl and Eurydice B. Bauer (New York: Routledge, 2003), 271–320.

23. Makin, *Literacy 8–12 Months*, 276.

24. Evelyn Arizpe and Morag Styles, *Children Reading Picturebooks: Interpreting Visual Texts* (Oxford: Routledge, 2016), 9, 86.

25. van Kleeck, "Research on Book Sharing," 280; see also Charles A. Elster, "Influences of Text and Pictures on Shared and Emergent Readings," *Research in the Teaching of English* 32, no. 1 (1998): 43–78, 4.

26. Research Centre for Children, Families and Communities, *The Role of the Bookstart Baby Gifting Process in Supporting Shared Reading* (Canterbury: Canterbury Christ Church University, 2016), 6.

27. Kimberly G. Noble, Martha J. Farah and Bruce D. McCandliss, "Socioeconomic Background Modulates Cognition-Achievement Relationships in Reading," *Cognitive Development* 21, no. 3 (2006): 349–68.

28. See, for example, Seung-Hee Son and Frederick J. Morrison, "The Nature and Impact of Changes in Home Learning Environment on Development of Language and Academic Skills in Preschool Children," *Developmental Psychology* 46, no. 5 (2010): 1103–18; Jacob E. Cheadle, "Educational Investment, Family Context, and Children's Math and Reading Growth from Kindergarten through the Third Grade," *Sociology of Education* 81, no. 1 (2008): 1–31; Hyunjoon Park, "Home Literacy Environments and Children's Reading Performance: A Comparative Study of 25 Countries," *Educational Research and Evaluation* 14, no. 6 (2008): 489–505; Whitehurst and Lonigan, "Child Development and Emergent Literacy."

29. Cheadle, "Educational Investment," 25.

30. Ann Phoenix and Fatima Husain, *Parenting and Ethnicity* (York: Joseph Rowntree Foundation, 2007).

31. Office of National Statistics, "Child Poverty and Education Outcomes by Ethnicity," 2007, https://www.ons.gov.uk/economy/nationalaccounts/uksectoraccounts/compendium/economicreview/february2020/childpovertyandeducationoutcomesbyethnicity.

32. Lorraine Dearden, Luke Sibieta and Kathy Sylva, "The Socio-Economic Gradient in Early Child Outcomes: Evidence from the Millennium Cohort Study," *Longitudinal and Life Course Studies* 2, no. 1 (2011): 19–40.

33. See, for example, Edward Melhuish, "Why Children, Parents and Home Learning Are Important," in *Early Childhood Matters: Evidence from the Effective Pre-School and Primary Education Project*, eds. Kathy Sylva, Edward Melhuish, Pam Sammons, Iram Siraj-Blatchford and Brenda Taggart (Abingdon: Routledge, 2010): 44–69; also Sylva et al., *The Effective Provision of Pre-School Education*; and Mary Bailey, Colin Harrison and Greg Brooks, "The Boots Books for Babies Project:

Impact on Library Registrations and Book Loans," *Journal of Early Childhood Literacy* 2, no. 1 (2002): 45–63.

34. Dimitra Hartas, "Families' Social Backgrounds Matter: Socio-Economic Factors, Home Learning and Young Children's Language, Literacy and Social Outcomes," *British Educational Research Journal* 37, no. 6 (2011): 893–914.

35. Lyn Tett and Jim Crowther, "Families at a Disadvantage: Class, Culture and Literacies," *British Educational Research Journal* 24, no. 4 (1998): 449–60, 457.

36. See, for example, Michael Marmot, *Fair Society, Healthy Lives: The Marmot Review* (London: University College London, 2010).

37. The outreach service was evaluated by Blake Stevenson, *Bookbug for the Home–Outreach Programme: Year 3/4 Evaluation* (Edinburgh: Scottish Book Trust, 2016).

38. In Scotland every family has a named health visitor who will visit them until the child is five, when they go to school. The health visitor has a proactive and health promoting role and plays vital role in supporting children and families in the early years of a child's life.

39. Isabel Karremann, "Mediating Identities in Eighteenth-Century England," in *Mediating Identities in Eighteenth-Century England: Public Negotiations, Literary Discourses, Topography*, eds. Isabel Karremann and Anja Müller (London: Routledge, 2011), 1–16.

40. Karremann, "Mediating Identities in Eighteenth-Century England."

41. Makin, "Literacy 8–12 Months," 275.

42. Barbara DeBaryshe and Janeen Binder, "Development of an Instrument for Measuring Parental Beliefs about Reading Aloud to Young Children," *Perceptual and Motor Skills* 78, no. 3 (1994): 1303–11.

43. Research Centre for Children, Families and Communities, *The Role of the Bookstart Baby Gifting Process*.

44. See for example, Margaret Hines and Greg Brooks, *Sheffield Babies Love Books: An Evaluation of the Sheffield Bookstart Project* (Sheffield: City of Sheffield, 2005) and Blake Stevenson, *Bookbug for the Home–Outreach Programme*.

45. National Audit Office, *Financial Sustainability of Local Authorities* (London: NAO, 2018).

46. Mia Gray and Anna Barford, "The Depth of the Cuts: The Uneven Geography of Local Government Austerity," *Cambridge Journal of Regions, Economy and Society* 11 (2018): 541–63.

Part III

TEXTUAL AND MATERIAL
STRATEGIES

Chapter 5

Reading Information

Using Graphic Language to Enhance Engagement with Children's Books

Sue Walker

The middle decades of the twentieth century saw changes in the appearance and content of children's information books. Also known as textbooks, topic books, nonfiction texts, or expository texts,[1] these books underwent a general transition involving a shift from black-and-white text and image to full-color page layouts featuring text and image that depicted everyday scenes familiar to children. This transition was the result of revisions to educational policy and developments in type and printing technology. Any discussion of book design in the mid-twentieth century should be seen in the broader context of book publishing and design in Britain after World War II, the best summary of which is Paul Stiff's 2009 essay "Austerity, Optimism: Modern Typography in Britain after the War."[2] Stiff notes that "learning through vision" was "a recurring thread in the cultural wing of reconstruction," a development also seen in nonfiction publishing for children where images began to assume greater prominence and relevance. However, this chapter is less about the publishing and cultural context of these books than the verbal and graphic attributes that mediate between text and young readers.

In designing information books for children there are three broad areas of decision-making: structure and articulation of content, use of illustrations, and typography. In each of these areas there are many ways to mediate between reader and text, though in practice there are constraints that limit the options available. Such constraints include cost of production, advances in typesetting and printing technology, and existing printing practices and conventions. This chapter draws attention to the development of the "integrated page," a term that refers to the interplay and connectivity of text and image as a means of articulating content. The chapter traces the move away from printer-driven conventions to show how designer-led approaches came to determine a book's use of text and image. As such, this study is not concerned with "picture books," nor does it explore the interconnections among layout, typography, and meaning.[3] Rather, in the pages that follow I offer an overview of design elements in selected English information books for children, exploring how these have developed over the past century. While the graphic features of such books initially followed conventional printing practices, technological advances enabled designers to make use of interventions such as close integration of text and image across a double-page spread, the use of color to articulate meaning, and the use of typography to meet the reading needs of children. As we shall see, such features of book design were used to mediate the reading experience of young readers in largely positive ways by encouraging engagement with and understanding of nonfiction texts. Though this chapter focuses on the role of visual organization as a mediating force, it is unfortunate that the constraints of publishing have made it impossible for me to include the substantial number of illustrations needed to fully explain the points I make. Rather than providing a selection of images, I have chosen not to include any visual examples so as to avoid prioritizing some publications over others. Reader, I offer my apologies for inadequate mediation, and when appropriate, I have included references to websites and other printed sources where the images are available.

INFORMATION BOOKS FOR CHILDREN

While there is variety within the broad category of information books, this chapter limits its discussion to texts with the following characteristics.[4] The information books I explore are factual in content, focused on either a narrow topic (such as "squirrels") or a broader theme (such as "medieval history"). As such, these books may include different linguistic styles including both narrative and non-narrative writing, and they are also illustrated with pictorial or schematic images. In the early years of the twentieth century there was a steady increase in the number of information books available for use in schools, but most of these were produced for older children.[5] Useful sources to locate books such as those discussed in this chapter are educational publishers' catalogs, such as those produced by Blackie, Nelson, Collins, Schofield and Sims, Evans, and Chambers in the 1940s and 1950s; and Kathleen Lines's *Four to Fourteen: A Library of Books for Children* (Cambridge: National Book League, 1950, 1956) includes sections entitled "Information Picture Books," "Animal Picture Books," as well as sections covering science, history, and geography. By the 1920s and

1930s more information books were available for home and school reading, the quality improved, and some books were produced with thought for the needs of younger readers. The books I discuss were designed for young people at the beginning of primary school to the early years of secondary education, and these texts were meant to be read either independently or with an adult.

DESIGNING INFORMATION BOOKS FOR CHILDREN

Designing books for children is challenging; it involves sensitivity to their needs and expectations as well as consideration of the variety of ways in which their books are read and used, whether by children on their own, with an adult, or in a group. This challenge has been nicely put by the book designer Jost Hochuli:

> It is different for school children who read, not because they want to, but because they must. This demands an especially attractive typography that pulls the reader in. For this one should draw on the whole repertoire of form and, if necessary, colour: type (graded in hierarchies), image, areas of the grid, lines, rules, spaces. And all these elements in tune with each other and consistently applied, so that the different levels of the text can be perceived and distinguished at one glance: general text, centrepieces, text to be learnt and remembered, commentary, exercises.[6]

Hochuli hints at the repertoire or "tool box" that designers have to engage children with text.

Designers consider how text and illustrations are organized in chapters, spreads, or pages, how different kinds of verbal and graphic content can be organized to suit the needs of readers, and how readers can be supported to find their way around a book and its component parts. Illustrations to describe or explain are key attributes of information books, and designers have a role to play in engaging readers through the positional and functional relationship between text and image. As noted by Evelyn Goldsmith:

> Pictures in educational materials perform many different functions, from teaching infants the symbolic nature of pictures themselves, to describing the spatial characteristics of, say, some organic or mechanical object. Many of these functions cannot be adequately or economically performed verbally, and in these cases the need for illustration is self-evident; but it sometimes happens that pictures play a more peripheral role: breaking up the text to make a spread look more accessible . . .[7]

Goldsmith goes on to define "design factors" relevant to decision-making about the use of illustrations; to this end, she shows how variables, such as age of the reader, density of ideas, and subject matter potentially influence design choices that affect the visual organization of text and image on a page or double-page spread.

Illustrations might be in the form of line or shaded drawings, photographs, maps or plans, diagrams or charts, and these may be positioned on the same page or spread as the text that relates to them, or these may appear elsewhere in the book. Decisions then need to be made as to the placement of an illustration in relationship to the text: Should the illustration go above or below the text to which it refers? Should the text wrap around the illustration or be positioned alongside it? Illustrations may be squared up or boxed; bled off the page on one or more edges; vignetted or cut out; or perhaps organized as a series of plates. Decisions about the placement of illustrations by anyone involved in making the book—printer, designer, publisher—are influenced by other aspects of book design that help readers engage with the text. Such considerations include the organization of "information units" that bring together text and images on particular themes or topics: chapter or section; double-page spread; or the page. And pages are designed to support different kinds of content including main text, supplementary text, headings, captions, and exercises. Other tools that help readers find their way around a book or navigate a text include contents pages, indexes, levels of headings, page numbers, running heads, use of key words in text, and differentiation of text components.

The considerations and options listed here relate to ways that book designers organize not only the structure and articulation of content but also the use of illustrations. Other decisions are concerned with typography—the use of type and spacing to articulate structure and meaning and to make text legible and are discussed later in this chapter. Book design also tends to be shrouded in convention that often dictates the visual organization of text and image. Depending on when books were produced, decisions about visual organization were made by printers, publishers, or designers, with each group applying their own different rules and considerations. In the middle decades of the twentieth century, however, we begin to see how the appearance of information books for children was affected by collaborative and design-driven decisions made with the needs of younger readers in mind. However, at this time few research studies were available to designers that provided evidence about what might work for children (though there were recommendations for typeface and typography in books for children).[8] With regard to the use of illustrations in books for young children, working in the 1950s, psychologist Margaret Vernon noted the motivational value of pictures in books for children, depending on their age and other factors. More recent research has focused on the relevance and importance of the information content of pictures in this context.[9]

For the information books under discussion here, the position of illustrations in relation to the text is a key issue, and design decisions were affected by the production process. The means of production play a key role in determining the extent to which illustrations can be aligned with text.[10] And in the mid-twentieth century new processes (such as autolithography) as well as traditional ones opened up possibilities for picture placement and for use of color. A compelling summary of available processes with examples of each is John Lewis's *A Handbook of Type and Illustration*, published by Faber & Faber in 1956.[11] While young readers in the 1940s, 1950s, and 1960s were familiar with colored illustrations in books for learning to read, many of the information books that were available for reading were usually printed in black only.

THE PREVALENCE OF MONOCHROME

Many information books for children in the first half of the twentieth century were illustrated with black-and-white line drawings and photographs printed as half-tones. This is likely to have been regarded as cost-efficient by printers and publishers, and educationists were probably aware of this constraint. For example, in 1926 James Kerr made the following observation about suitable types of illustrations: "Line illustrations are preferable to half-tone work both from visual and educational considerations. Black and white is the only kind necessary for ordinary school purposes."[12] The 1928 Hadow report, *Books in Public Elementary Schools* produced by the Board of Education in the UK, went further in suggesting that "many of the illustrations in current use, particularly in books for older children, are unnecessarily elaborate, and, especially if they are coloured, increase the cost of production without proportionately adding to the usefulness of the book."[13] This report reinforced the use of black-and-white illustrations by drawing attention to high-quality reproductions of illustrated manuscripts and photographs of both ancient monuments and objects in museums and galleries. These images were found in existing publications produced by entities such as the Science Museum, the Wallace Collection, the Museum of Practical Geology, and the Tate Gallery. This advice was certainly acted upon by some publishers. *The Story of Prehistoric and Roman Britain*, one of the books from the "Told in Pictures" series, published by the Manchester publishers, Sankey, Hudson & Co in the 1930s, is one example. This book, as stated on the title page, comprised "over 550 illustrations depicting the history of Britain in its earliest days" with the following acknowledgment: "The antiquities illustrated are reproduced by kind permission of the Trustees of the British Museum."[14] Most of the book was organized in double-page spreads containing small black-and-white illustrations, which resulted in crowded pages that do not seem at all engaging for children. On the other hand, the "Pictorial History" series published by Schofield and Sims in the late 1930s, which also used images derived from historical sources, gave some thought to the ways that teachers might use the book with their pupils, as in this extract from the introduction to *A First Course in History*. *Book 1*:

> Each STORY LESSON is explained by a picture, which the teacher may use as a subject of conversation, introducing as far as possible the words of the text, and so helping the pupils to read and understand the words of the Lesson to follow.[15]

This approach to the organization of the material in the book, along with a relatively large serifed typeface, suggests that there had been some consideration of the reading requirements of a younger audience. While visually rather uninspiring, books such as these were produced with a particular rationale, in this case in response to a specific recommendation.

Even without the use of curated museum images, books produced for use in schools about history, geography, science, and nature were usually printed in black-and-white throughout (sometimes with occasional color plates), and this approach to the presentation of information continued until well into the 1950s. A typical example is E. M. Stephenson's "Nature at Work" series, published by A. & C. Black in the early 1940s: *Book 1* of the primary series was organized in short sections of two or three pages illustrated with black-and-white line drawings and half-tones (photographs), with related captions, and sometimes with labels to point to particular parts of an illustration.[16] Six color plates were tipped in in relation to relevant content throughout the book. The "Naturecraft" readers, by Percival Westell, published in the 1940s by McDougall's Educational Company Ltd., is another typical series. *Book II, In City, Field and Farm*, for example, was organized in short chapters, with a large number of black-and-white photographs, some of which were almost full-page and bled-off at top and sides.[17] Bleeding off (taking images right to the edge of the paper) would have been regarded as a modern trend. There was little attempt to engage young readers, though there was some recognition that the graphic attributes of text may be important in this respect. For example, in 1950, Beatrice Warde, publicity manager at Monotype, commented that "Nobody ever sees a schoolbook" except "negligible, compelled readers" who are "forced to gaze, intently and receptively [on schoolbooks], not just for one afternoon, but for the best part of a year." She made this observation as a means of initiating a discussion about the benefits of using well-designed (Monotype) typefaces for children's reading.[18] Even though such books were visually uninspiring, these texts sometimes showed extensive picture research and featured text written in a clear and straightforward way—elements that would have been appreciated by teachers and children. An example for older primary school children is R. J. Unstead's "Looking at History" series, published by A & C Black, a work that ran into numerous editions until the 1970s. *Book 4, Queen Anne to Queen Elizabeth II* (1957) comprised 112 pages, printed black-and-white throughout with four tipped-in color plates printed on the same stock as the rest of the book.[19] The text was organized in two columns with line drawings and half-tones interspersed throughout. The illustrations relate to the text that refers to them, and the text is edited so that each page ends with a full point. It is altogether a book that has been designed with some consideration for the reader and how it might be used, which may be one reason for its popularity as a classroom text. The approach taken to the Unstead book shows that even within the constraints of economical black-and-white printing, the visual organization of text and pictures can effectively take account of how books might be used and read. The sparing use of color was not at all unusual in this kind of book, influenced by the printing process and educational reports.

RAISING THE IMPORTANCE OF THE VISUAL AND THE EVERYDAY

As well as supporting the use of black-and-white pictures, from the late 1920s reports about education in schools had commented on how pictures might be better used in books, responding in some cases to the impact that the process of printing potentially had on the placement of illustrations in a book. The way a book was printed, for example, determined whether color appeared on alternate spreads and whether colored plates were interspersed throughout the book or put in a section in the middle or at the end of the book. The 1928 Hadow Report drew attention to "the fact that they [illustrations] are often unsuitably placed in relation to the part of the text which they are intended to elucidate."[20] This remark appears to support the view that the relationship between text and image was perceived as being important, and one of the changes in information books for young people in the middle decades of the twentieth century was the closer integration of text and image, a development that became possible with lithographic printing.

Interest in the use of pictures for motivation and learning coincided with a move toward an educational environment in schools that was receptive to a child-centered approach. Education reports encouraged engagement with everyday life. The 1930 Hadow Report *The Primary School*, for example, proposed lessons "providing fields of new and interesting experience to be explored" that appealed to "the sympathy, social spirit and imagination of the children."[21] The 1937 *Handbook of Suggestions for the Consideration of Teachers and Others Concerned in the Work of Public Elementary Schools* proposed that childhood should not exist in isolation but be "linked with home and an ever-widening environment with family and ancestry, with friends and the people of his own country, and with mankind at large."[22] It encouraged children, through their learning, to relate to other people and their communities, and it promoted comparison and contrast as mechanisms for learning. There was an increased focus on children's lives and their environment, and this in turn affected the language used in information books as well as their visual appearance.

The word "everyday" began to appear in titles such as "The Everyday Books" published by J. M. Dent in the early 1940s and "Our Everyday World" from Oxford University Press from 1949 onwards. The Longmans "Things We Use Series" included titles such as *A Packet of Tea*, *A Loaf of Bread*, and *A Tin of Milk*. Even books for very young children, such as the series, "Betty's Geography Lessons," published by George Gill & Sons in the 1930s, described on the back cover as "a new geography series for six-year olds" included such titles as *Bread and Butter* and *Oranges and Lemons* that related to an everyday environment that would be familiar to many young children. The book entitled *Rice Pudding* (n.d., *c.* 1930) exemplifies the approach taken in the series and began with the words, "Mother, must I eat this rice pudding? I like jam tart much better than rice pudding."[23] The book then moved on to feature "mother" explaining where rice came from and how it was grown and transported to England. This focus on the everyday offered considerable scope for illustration of recognizable objects and situations, and these featured in many children's information books in the mid-twentieth-century UK, resulting in a degree of familiarity that encouraged readers' engagement.

The use of photographs of young people engaged in activities became a popular way of relating young readers to the text and that helped to reinforce the notion of the everyday as well as engaging children through the realism that can be achieved through photography. This practice was well-established in Europe as noted by Kimberley Reynolds who draws attention to John Heartfield's photographs that show "real children working together and enjoying each other's different family lives" in Alex Wedding's *Eddie and the Gipsy* (London: Martin Laurence, 1935).[24] In the 1940s and 1950s art-directed photographs gave children or animals roles as central characters in an activity or event. "The photographic books" by Ruth Bakewell and David Fletcher, published by Oliver and Boyd (c. 1954), featured a little girl called Helen in books including *At the Zoo: What Is It? What Are We Making?* and

Helen and Her Dog. These small-format square books included a bled-off, black-and-white photograph on every page or spread, accompanied by a sentence or in some cases a longer narrative text.[25] Animals featured in a series published by Hamish Hamilton in the 1950s with photographs by Ylla and text by Paulette Falconnet. Described by Katherine Lines as an "introduction for five-year-olds to nature books," *Two Little Bears* (London: Hamish Hamilton, 1954) is based around a series of remarkable photographs of bear cubs swimming and climbing outdoors.[26]

The 1937 *Handbook* had further advised, echoing the earlier Hadow report, that attention should be paid to illustrations readily available through museums and galleries.[27] But it went on to recognize that there were different ways of presenting information visually. The *Handbook* referred to time charts as an excellent way to clearly delineate for children the dates and the duration of time periods. It drew attention to a Historical Association pamphlet, *Time Charts* by Helen Madeley, first published in 1921 and reprinted throughout the 1920s and 1930s.[28] This little book made the case for charts not only by promoting them as a means of expressing information concisely and comparatively but by stressing that charts encourage children to learn for themselves, enabling them to relate historical events to their own experience. The book offered practical advice about how to make three types of time chart—rectangular or chessboard charts, circular or viewpoint charts, and longitudinal or timeline charts—and it suggested that this last group were the chart of the future. The book showed examples of charts made by teachers and pupils, suggesting how others might make and use similar visual designs. While the charts that are illustrated are naïve in design terms, they nevertheless were indicative of an interest among teachers in introducing children to forms of visual presentation. And certainly, during the 1940s many information books included charts, diagrams, and other forms of schematic presentation.

Offering a splendid example of what Otto Neurath called "education by the eye," one such book that prioritized different kinds of images was *The Changing Shape of Things* (London: John Murray, 1947).[29] The author, John Redmayne, explained in the foreword that "the whole argument of this book has been put into pictures." Calling it "an essay in visual presentation," he aimed for the book to "arouse an interest in the design of everyday things."[30] The forty-eight-page text, described by Katherine Lines as "one of a stimulating, original modern series,"[31] comprised spreads that illustrated a particular topic with photographs and line drawings that dominate the text. In the book there are different image types: half-tone images of objects, people, landscapes, and architectural drawings; line drawings and shaded line drawings, all black-and-white. The designerly intervention is most evident in how the images are used within the spreads of the book. In a spread devoted to suspension bridges, for example, there are squared-up half-tones in different sizes, creating a dynamic layout that both explains and intrigues. For example, in detailing how the Forth Bridge was constructed, the book includes a small image of three schematic figures along with the following text: "It is as if three giants stood in the river with their arms outstretched clasping each other's hands."[32] Every spread in the book is designed differently, giving predominance to the illustrations and highlighting how they can be used to get ideas across. The typography in this book, however, is inconsistent from page to page, with considerable variation in the space between the lines. This issue was improved on in later, related books produced by Redmayne, which continued to emphasize the visual in the presentation of information. Stating on its title page that the book is "designed and edited" by Redmayne, *Transport by Land* (London: John Murray, 1948) is more ordered, with the text presented in a two-column grid toward the bottom of each page.[33] The use of the term "designed" is an early acknowledgment of this activity, and, given Redmayne's commitment to visual presentation, this designation recognizes the skills needed for text/picture integration that is both visually pleasing and pedagogically effective. In addition to photographs and line drawings, *Transport by Land* also features maps and schematic, Isotype-influenced images.[34] The book makes use of a second color to add interest to the drawings and to denote different kinds of information in the maps and diagrams. Redmayne's books deployed the double-page spread as an "information unit" that contained both text and pictures about a particular topic. This approach to book design means that from the outset there must be consideration of how verbal and graphic information will be structured. By the 1940s, several publishers in the UK were using the double-page spread as a way of organizing information in their books.

USING THE DOUBLE-PAGE SPREAD
AND MORE COLOR

The use of color in information books became more prevalent from the 1940s and was a feature that some publishers promoted in their marketing. "Color for the children," "simple and vivid in color," and "rich color" were phrases used by Max Parrish in their publicity materials in the 1950s and 1960s to draw attention to Marie Neurath's nonfiction children's books. Young readers at the time would have been accustomed to seeing colored illustrations in their reading books; educational publishers perhaps found that the use of color was not only cost-effective due to large print runs but essential for remaining competitive in the children's book market.[35]

Growth in the use of visually exciting and colorful children's books was influenced in part by children's book publishing in the United States and in Europe, notably the Maud and Miska Petersham books and the Père Castor books. Text on the back of the dust jacket of *Scaf the Seal* (c. 1938) explains the rationale behind the Père Castor "Wild Animal Books" drawing attention to qualities that were beginning to be recognized by others:

> Prolonged and serious nature study lies behind these stories; realistic and unsentimental but not crude; seeming to be really imagined from inside the animal's skin. The educational value of the books is great, but do they look like "school" books.
>
> The text is delicious in its freshness; the plot moves grippingly through the seasons with the development of each animal's life, and Miss Fyleman has just caught the delicate gaiety of the original.
>
> And have you seen Rojan's lithographs, accurate and controlled, but ablaze with fearless colour.[36]

Noel Carrington was inspired to launch Puffin Picture books, which relied on autolithography, a process through which illustrators drew directly onto stone or plastic plate.[37] Offering scope for creativity and imagination, this method resulted in visually exciting, colorful spreads where illustrations enhanced and described the textual content. Overall, autolithography inspired innovative approaches to the visual organization of text and image within a double-page spread, as described by Paul Stiff in relation to S. R. Badmin's *Village and Town* (London: Penguin Books, 1942):

> Pictures are on the same page as the text, not separated as "plates." The pictures are not enclosed within rectangular boundaries. The argument is developed through topics? "The first houses," "What they built with," "The new style," and so on assigned a page each, more or less. In this sense, the book plan is radical: design derives from the artifact rather than being led by conventional norms of serial text composition. In simple terms, topic boundaries coincide with page breaks and, in other titles in the series, with double-page spreads.[38]

There are many visually exciting examples of double-page spreads in Puffin books from the 1940s and 1950s, some of which are illustrated in Phil Baines's *Puffin by Design: 70 Years of Imagination 1940–2010* (London: Penguin Books, 2010).[39] Notable examples include spreads from *A History of the Countryside* (Harmondsworth: Penguin Books, 1944), *About a Motor Car* (Harmondsworth: Penguin Books, 1946), and *Building a House* (Harmondsworth: Penguin Books, 1949).

Oxford University Press was another publisher that followed this approach in their books for young people. A fine example of illustrator-led picture-text integration was *The Map That Came to Life* (Oxford: Oxford University Press, 1948).[40] In this book, John and Joanna go to stay on their Uncle George's farm where they and the farm dog, Rover, learn the mapping conventions used on Ordnance Survey maps. Each double-page spread includes a small section of an OS map. The map is then interpreted pictorially to fill the entire spread, with bled-off edges. The text in one, two, or three columns is placed in different positions on each spread, so that the relationship between the map section and the image is shown. The result is a visually stimulating and colorful book with the same components presented on each spread in a different way (see website with spreads from the complete book[41]). To set this visual approach in context, it is interesting to compare it with a book on a similar topic, published around ten years earlier. *The Magic Map: An Introduction to the Fascination of Maps* (Exeter: Wheaton, 1935) tells the story of Kathleen and John, who travel to the country to stay with their Uncle Harry.[42] Uncle Harry insists that they must learn to read maps before they are allowed out on their own to explore. While the narrative relates directly to the visual material, the book is very conventional in design terms. It is organized in short sections, each with a heading; the text is set justified to a full column width resulting in very long and uninviting lines of prose. Colored, but mostly schematic, illustrations are placed within the text in various ways. Nevertheless, the book remained popular as evidenced by the following description from Wheaton's 1957 catalog: "Universally recognised as by far the best of its kind, this book has already sold over 100,000 copies. Attractively produced, it has over 30 illustrations and maps in FULL COLOUR."[43]

Another design-led solution that prioritized the double-page spread, integration of verbal and visual content, and use of color was the innovative "Visual History of Mankind" series initiated by Otto and Marie Neurath in the late 1940s, and published by Max Parrish. This series aimed to engage young people with histories of everyday life through contrast and comparison (rather than history through the lives of kings and queens and battles).[44] The distinctive and innovative design attributes of this series can be seen not only in its meaningful and consistent application of color, but in its use of charts that clearly communicated information through various forms including timelines, before and after scenarios and pictorial lists. Each topic in "The Visual History of Mankind" is presented as a double-page spread, with a series of questions down the outside edge of each page. These questions direct young readers to look closely at the content of the charts to find out the answers, and they also encourage engagement with visual attributes of the charts by asking, for example, what colors stand for in a particular image. Marie Neurath and her colleagues at the Isotype Institute in London went on to produce over eighty books for young people between the end of the 1940s and the 1970s in series such as "The Wonder World of Nature" and "Wonders of the Modern World."[45] The illustrations in the Isotype books were designed to explain and to engage; great care was taken to ensure that the illustrations were scientifically accurate and that the language used was easy for children to understand; each double spread went through numerous iterations before being printed. What Marie Neurath achieved through the transformation of often complicated scientific principles to understandable and engaging images is a powerful example of design as mediation between text and reader. Marie Neurath was keen to draw on children's experience in her design solutions. In relation to a spread from the *First book* of "Visual Science" (London: Max Parrish, 1950) that explains floating and sinking she wrote:

> Floating in water, or feeling oneself lighter in water, are part of children's experience. We can go on to ask: which things sink, which are suspended, which float on top? And we can go onto make a visual statement which makes use of a simplified balance to tell "lighter" and "heavier than water" and "of the same weight" . . . Such statements take less space visually than verbally, and certainly require less effort to be understood.[46]

Some of the Isotype children's books were designed for younger readers. In a spread from *The Wonder World of Birds* (London: Max Parrish, 1953), the recto compares four different beaks, each with three lines of supporting text that explains the use of each beak. The facing page shows birds using their beaks in different ways, again with supporting, explanatory text. The heading "Beaks which are Slender or Strong, or Sharp" explains clearly what the double-page spread portrays. "Ball rolling beetles" from *The Wonder World of Insects* (London: Max Parrish, 1953) is an example of repeated base images often used by Marie Neurath. In this case the repeated elements are the male and female beetles (in brown and dark blue), and the yellow ball containing the egg. The pictures can be read independently of the text, which provides more detail. (See website showing examples of Marie Neurath's science books for children.[47])

Ladybird Books, published by Wills and Hepworth, introduced nonfiction texts in the 1950s. After publishing its "Nature" series in 1953 (the first book was *British Birds and Their Nests*), Ladybird went on to produce many more nonfiction series which found a place in school and county libraries.[48] In Ladybird books, the organization of text and illustration was determined by the way the books were printed, resulting in text on one side of the double-page spread and illustration on the other. In design terms, the consistent vertical orientation constrained the format that illustrators worked within, and this layout worked well for trees and figures as seen in texts such as Charles Tunnicliffe's *What to Look for in Winter* (Loughborough: Wills & Hepworth, 1959), where trees and plants are frequently used as a vertical element within the composition and to frame the picture.[49]

The use of the double-page spread to align text and images relevant to a particular topic became a typical graphic characteristic of information books from the 1950s onward, though many of these publications lacked the enticing use of color seen in Puffin, Isotype, and Ladybird books. As an example, in "Kingsway Pictorial Science," a popular series for older children, published by Evans in 1952, each spread comprised a series of hand-drawn illustrations that continued across both pages.[50] The two-column text referred to the illustrations placed directly above, and it also included other contextual illustrations. A "topic per spread" approach was also taken in "A visual geography of the world" (Educational Publishing Company Limited, 1957), where text and explanatory diagrams appeared on one page and a map-based illustration on the other, and where hand-lettering introduced a distinctive visual element.[51] In both these examples, letterforms and typography guided readers through the information presented by incorporating more than one level of heading, using captions and articulating key words within the text—methods that became commonplace in information books from the 1950s onwards. The double-page spread also provided teachers with a way of organizing their lessons assuming that each member of the class could open the book at the spread needed for the set text. The use of the double-page spread in defining the structure of a book became so widespread that it was referred to as a "tyranny" by Edward Blishen, author, teacher, and critic.[52] However, as evident in the books selected for the 1966 "Textbook Design Exhibition" organized by the National Book League, there are many innovative design solutions that chose not to prioritize the double-page spread. One of the jurors for this exhibition, the educational publisher Kenneth Pinnock drew attention to the impact of technology:

> Printing by offset lithography has become the rule rather than the exception for many classes of educational book. This has given designers greater freedom in making layouts than they previously had. Quite commonly nowadays, educational books are made up page by page in the publisher's office, instead of being assembled at the printers. Text and illustrations can now be adjusted with relative ease, so that they are blended into a harmonious whole in a way that was rarely achieved using metal type and blocks.[53]

While offset lithography enabled close alignment of text and image, information books for children in the first half of the twentieth century tended to follow conventional typesetting practices with little or no accommodation for young readers.

TYPOGRAPHY

However, as noted previously, typesetting is bound in the conventions of craft tradition, and for many kinds of printed books, typesetters used their training to make decisions about a range of issues including hyphenation, use of vertical space, and treatment of headings. So, typically, information books for young people were typeset in small seriffed typefaces, with justified setting and centered headings. As a result, such books featured text-heavy pages with black-and-white illustrations or photographs, divided into chapters or sections with page breaks determined by the fit of type onto the page. However, there were exceptions to this format, and even in the 1920s and 1930s, one can find examples showing how typography is used to differentiate kinds of text. *How You Began: A Child's Introduction to Biology* (London: Gerald Howe Ltd, 1928) engaged its young readership by distinguishing between two narratives. The first, where the text is set to the full width of the page, describes how a child grows; the second narrative, where the text is indented with a printer's flower in the margin, discusses "the slow way all the animals of the earth have grown."[54] The author suggests that if the young reader is tired of reading about how humans develop and grow, they might find it fun to read through the other parts about animals. Another reader-friendly approach is shown in *Living things for lively youngsters* (Cassell, 1933) which, although set in a small seriffed typeface, has generous spacing between the lines and sufficient space around the text to make it inviting to read.[55] The text is justified, but the short sentences that start on a new line give the visual impression of unjustified (ragged right) typesetting, which suggests a degree of informality. Some pages in this book that contain more text were typeset with a closer line feed. The technique of varying line feed was used by printers to fit text within a page even though typographic consistency from page to page is beneficial to readers. The topic of each double-page spread is clearly signaled by a heading in centered, large capital letters; this designation is reinforced by a similarly worded heading above the illustrations on the facing page. Throughout the book, each topic is illustrated with line drawings, and the handwritten captions provide another level of reader engagement. Both the above examples are in black-and-white only and show how even within such limits typography can play a part in mediating between the intended reader and the text.

From the 1930s there are examples of information books for younger readers that followed recommendations about typeface, type size, and spacing as seen in reports such as those produced by the British Association for the Advancement of Science in 1913 and by the publishers Ginn in 1935.[56] These guidelines were primarily aimed at books for teaching reading, but some reading schemes included nonfiction texts about crafts, nature, geography, and so on. "Evans' Activity Readers" (London: Evans Brothers) produced in the 1940s is one such example. This was a series that with titles such as *Washing* and *Out to Play* reflected the everyday activities that children would be familiar with. The books were typeset in a large size (18 point) Gill Sans, which took some heed of the recommendation that children needed larger type sizes than adults; however, the tight line spacing and justified setting resulted in word spaces that varied from line to line, an outcome that indicates a limited understanding of the relationship between type size and space between the lines.

Some publishers introduced alternative forms of "a" and "g" as a way of engaging young readers by making an association between handwritten letterforms that children would have been familiar with and that some teachers and publishers were keen to promote. "Betty's Geography Lessons" (London: George Gill & Sons, n.d., c. 1930s) introduced Gill Sans alternative forms of "a" and "g," which were known as "rounded" or "single-story" characters that children would have encountered in their handwriting teaching. J. M. Dent's "The everyday Books" (London, 1942) were set in a large serif typeface with generous space between the lines and a small amount of text relative to the page size. Oxford University Press in "Our Everyday World Series" (Oxford, 1950) used Gill Sans, a sanserif typeface that was popular in reading schemes at the time. However, despite these typeface choices, the text was justified (which results in variable word spacing from line to line), and there was very little space between the lines.

Originating in the mid-nineteenth century, the use of bold type in information books became a standard way of drawing readers' attention to key words in the text.[57] In addition to bold type, there were other options designers could use for emphasis and signposting such as color, change of typeface, underlining, and capital letters. While a specific design choice may be based on convention (as with bold type for key words), it may also be determined by the other typographic elements used to make information accessible; these include headings, subheadings, captions, and explanatory text. Nicola Robson, in her survey of the graphic aspects of over 150 information books published between 1900 and 1990, found that headings were differentiated using type size, bold, italic, typeface, capitalization, color, underlining, reversing out, and decoration; in many cases, she also noted that these treatments were combined.[58] As these examples show, there are many possible combinations of graphic differentiation, along with multiple options for varying horizontal and vertical space. Designers therefore have many choices available when it comes to articulating just one element of a page that helps readers negotiate a text.[59]

CONCLUDING REMARKS

This chapter has offered a glimpse into the graphic characteristics of some of the information books that young people may have encountered at school or at home in the middle decades of the twentieth century. It has identified just some of the ways that printers, designers, and authors have tried to engage their young audiences, through illustration, picture-text interaction, and typography. As we have seen, design can play a significant role in mediating between the text and young readers, and designers use various tools to make clear the structure of a text; to make text easy to read; and to engage and motivate readers. Because children in the mid-twentieth century were very rarely asked about the books they read (an omission still in place today), it is difficult to ascertain the extent to which such design interventions worked. In the past, the success of an information book was measured solely by print runs, number of editions, published reviews, and inclusion in books of recommendation such Kathleen Lines' *Four to Fourteen: A Library of Books for Children* (Cambridge: Cambridge University Press, 1950 and 1956). Those who made design decisions probably did not consult research recommending the best practices for children's books. Rather, the final product was shaped by book design conventions, financial constraints, and available technological resources for presenting text and images to suit the needs of readers.[60]

The mid-twentieth century saw closer integration of text and image, and the use of more visually exciting and child-centric content. The work produced by Noel Carrington, Marie Neurath, and Paul Redmayne stands out as examples of good design, but there are many other information books in this same category that are not associated with a particular author's or designer's name. Children in schools are likely to have benefited from increased focus on explaining the content of books more clearly. To this end, information books increasingly made use of the following design strategies: consistency of color to denote meaning; different levels of headings to structure the text; boxes, color, and tints to differentiate kinds of text or information; lists and tables to present some kinds of conceptual material; and captions and labels to add supplementary explanatory text. By the 1960s many of these methods became typical features in the information books used in schools, books in which text and pictures were closely aligned and sometimes intertwined.

NOTES

1. See Margaret Meek, "The Critical Challenge of the World in Books for Children," *Children's Literature in Education* 26, no. 1 (1995): 5–23; Margery Fisher, *Matters of Fact: Aspects of Non-Fiction for Children* (Leicester: Brockhampton Press, 1972); Margaret Mallett, *Making Facts Matter: Reading Non-Fiction 5–11* (London: Paul Chapman, 1992).

2. In Paul Stiff, ed., *Modern Typography in Britain: Graphic Design, Politics and Society, Typography papers 8* (London: Hyphen Press, 2009), 5–68.

3. This topic in recent years has attracted the interest of scholars in genre, social semiotics, and multi-modality. See, for example, John Bateman, Janina Wildfeuer and Tuomo Hiippala, *Multimodality: Foundations, Research and Analysis, a Problem-Oriented Introduction* (Berlin: De Gruyter, 2017), and specifically in relation to information books, Jeff Bezemer and Gunther Kress, "Visualizing English: A Social Semiotic History of a School Subject," *Visual Communication* 8, no. 3 (2009): 247–62, and Judy Delin, John Bateman and Patrick Allen, "A Model of Genre in Document Layout," *Information Design Journal* 11, no. 1 (2002): 54–66.

4. After Nicola Robson, "Information Books for Children: Their Visual Anatomy and Evolution (1960 to 2005)" (unpublished PhD thesis, Department of Typography & Graphic Communication, University of Reading, 2007), 5–6.

5. Alec Ellis, *A History of Children's Reading and Literature* (Oxford: Pergamon Press, 1968), 123.

6. Jost Hochuli and Robin Kinross, *Designing Books: Practice and Theory* (London: Hyphen Press, 1996), 76.

7. Evelyn Goldsmith, "Learning from Illustrations: Factors in the Design of Illustrated Educational Books for Middle School Children," *Word and Image* 2, no. 2 (1986): 111–21, 111.

8. As summarized in Sue Walker, *Book Design for Children's Reading: Typography, Pictures, Print* (London: St Bride Library, 2013), 23–27.

9. See Magdalen D. Vernon, "The Value of Pictorial Illustration," *The Journal of Educational Psychology* 23, no. 1 (1954): 180–87; Magdalen D. Vernon, "The Instruction of Children by Pictorial Illustration," *The Journal of Educational Psychology* 24 (1953): 171–79 and discussion in Lynne Watts and John Nisbet, *Legibility in Children's Books: A Review of Research* (Slough: NFER Publishing Company, 1974), 70ff. More recent research, such as that by Joan Peeck, for example, continued this work drawing attention to the different functions of picture/text interaction in non-fiction texts, such as to enhance or complement meaning. See Joan Peeck, "Increasing Picture Effects in Learning from Illustrated Text," *Learning and Instruction* 3, no. 3 (1993): 227–38; Maria Nikolajeva and Carole Scott, *How Picture Books Work* (London: Psychology Press, 2001). Martinez and Harmon, who investigated picture/text relationship in developing literary elements found younger children relied on pictures for critical information about plot, character, setting and mood in a story and although this research involved fictional, text it suggests that the position of pictures in relation to the text may affect the ease with which children pick up information that enhances their understanding: Miriam

Martinez and Janis M. Harmon, "Picture/Text Relationships: An Investigation of Literary Elements in Picture Books," *Literacy Research and Instruction* 51, no. 4 (2012): 323–43.

10. See Michael Twyman, "The Emergence of the Graphic Book in the 19th Century," in *A Millennium of the Book: Production, Design and Illustration in Manuscript and Print, 900–1900,* eds. Robin Myers and Michael Harris (Winchester: St Paul's Bibliographies, 1994), 135–80.

11. John Lewis, *A Handbook of Type and Illustration* (London: Faber & Faber, 1956).

12. James Kerr, *The Fundamentals of School Health* (London: Allen and Unwin, 1926), 556–57.

13. Board of Education, *Report of the Consultative Committee on Books in Public Elementary Schools* (London: HMSO, 1928), 22.

14. C. W. Airne, *The Story of Roman and Pre-Roman Britain.* "Told in Pictures" (Manchester: Sankey, Hudson & Co., c. 1930).

15. H. E. Hounsell and James Hilton, "Pictorial History" *A First Course in History Book 1* (Huddersfield: Schofield & Sims, 1937), ii.

16. E. M. Stephenson, "Nature at Work," *Primary Series, Book 1* (London: A&C Black, c. 1940).

17. Percival Westell, "Naturecraft Readers." *Book II, In City, Field and Farm* (Edinburgh: McDougall's Educational Co., c. 1940).

18. Beatrice Warde, "Improving the Compulsory Book," *The Penrose Annual* 44 (1950): 37–40, 37.

19. R. J. Unstead, "Looking at History" *Book 4, Queen Anne to Queen Elizabeth II* (London: A&C Black, 1957).

20. Board of Education, *Report of the Consultative Committee on Books*, 22.

21. Board of Education, *Report of the Consultative Committee on the Primary School* (London: HMSO, 1931), xvii–xviii.

22. Board of Education, *Handbook of Suggestions for the Consideration of Teachers and Others Involved in the Work of Public Elementary Schools* (London: HMSO, 1937), 112.

23. Harriett M. T. Carnell, *Rice Pudding.* "Betty's Geography Lessons" (London: George Gill & Sons, c. 1930), [1]

24. Kimberley Reynolds, *Left Out: The Forgotten Tradition of Radical Publishing for Children in Britain 1910–1949* (Oxford: Oxford University Press, 2016), 33.

25. See Walker, *Book Design.* See, for example, Ruth Bakewell and David Fletcher, *Helen and Her Dog. The Photographic Books* (Edinburgh: Oliver and Boyd, c. 1954). The "Growing and Reading" series, published by Macmillan in 1956, is another example of the use of black-and-white photography in this way. By the 1960s photographs, often in color, were used in children's reading schemes to add authenticity to classroom activities; examples include "Dominoes" by Oliver & Boyd and "Through the rainbow" by Schofield & Sims. See Walker, *Book Design.*

26. Katherine Lines, *Four to Fourteen. A Library of Books for Children* (Cambridge: National Book League, 1956), 20; Ylla and Paulette Falconnet, *Two Little Bears* (London: Hamish Hamilton, 1954).

27. The Historical Association was mentioned as an "excellent" source and the *Handbook* refers to pamphlet no. 82 (p. 31) which is *A List of Illustrations for Use in History Teaching in Schools*, ed. Miss D. Dymond, M.A. (1930).

28. H. M. Madeley, *Time Charts,* pamphlet no. 50 (London: The Historical Association, 1921) (reprinted 1923, 1929, 1938; 2nd edn., 1948).

29. See Otto Neurath, *International Picture Language* (London: Kegan Paul, Trench, Trubner & Co., Ltd, 1936), 22.

30. John Redmayne, *The Changing Shape of Things* (London: John Murray, 1947), 5.

31. Lines, *Four to Fourteen*, 138.

32. Redmayne, *Changing Shape of Things*, 17.

33. John Redmayne, *Transport by Land* (London: John Murray, 1948).

34. "Isotype (International System of TYPographic Picture Education) was a method for assembling, configuring and disseminating information and statistics through pictorial means. Its initiator, Otto Neurath, described it as a 'language-like technique' characterised by consistency in the use of graphic elements. The basic elements are pictograms—simplified pictures of people or things, designed to function as repeatable units. From its beginnings in Vienna of the 1920s, Isotype spread to the Netherlands, Britain, the Soviet Union, the United States and elsewhere. Its potential for communicating with people of all ages and nationalities was explored in a wide range of projects and publications through the 1960s." Definition from "Isotype Revisited," www.isotyperevisited.org (accessed November 2020).

35. See, for example, in images in the timeline of children's reading books in Walker, *Book Design for Children's Reading*, 124ff.

36. Lida, *Scaf the Seal*, trans. Rose Fyleman (London: George Allen and Unwin, c.1938), back of dust jacket.

37. See Michael Twyman, *A History of Chromolithography: Printed Colour for All* (London: British Library, 2013), 303–308; and Ian Rogerson, *Noel Carrington and His Puffin Picture Books*, exhibition catalog (Manchester: Manchester Polytechnic Library, 1992). Phil Baines, *Puffin by Design: 70 Years of Imagination 1940–2010* (London: Penguin Books, 2010) is illustrated with examples of covers and spreads of the early Puffins.

38. Paul Stiff, "Showing a New World in 1942: The Gentle Modernity of Puffin Picture Books," *Design Issues* 23, no. 4 (Autumn 2007): 22–38, 26.

39. Phil Baines, *Puffin by Design: 70 Years of Imagination 1940–2010* (London: Penguin Books, 2010).

40. H. J. Deverson, *The Map that Came to Life* (Oxford: Oxford University Press, 1948).

41. "The Visual Telling of Stories" shows a full scan of *The Map that Came to Life*, http://www.fulltable.com/VTS/aoi/l/lampitt/map.htm, accessed November 2020.

42. C. Midgley, *The Magic Map: An Introduction to the Fascination of Maps* (Exeter: Wheaton, 1935).

43. *Catalogue of School Books for Primary Schools* (Exeter: Wheaton, 1957). The catalog draws attention to the companion book *Look at the Map* (1939) and, for older children, *The Map Unfolds* (1954).

44. The making of this series has been discussed in detail in Sue Walker, "Explaining History to Children: Otto and Marie Neurath's Work on the 'Visual History of Mankind,'" *Journal of Design History* 24, no. 4 (2012): 345–62. Color illustrations of spreads from the "Visual history" can be seen in this paper.

45. For a detailed illustrated account of this work, see Sue Walker, "Graphic Explanation for Children, 1944–1971," in *Isotype. Design and Contexts 1925–1971*, eds. Christopher Burke, Eric Kindel and Sue Walker (London: Hyphen Press, 2013), 390–437.

46. Marie Neurath, "Report on the Last Years of Isotype Work," *Synthese* 8, no. 1/2 (1950–51): 22–27, 25.

47. Marie Neurath: Picturing Science, https://www.marieneurath.org/.

48. Lorraine Johnson and Brian Alderson, *The Ladybird Story: Children's Books for Everyone* (London: The British Library, 2014), 69ff.

49. Charles Tunnicliffe, *What to Look for in Winter* (Loughborough: Wills & Hepworth, 1959). The "People at work" series illustrated by John Berry in the 1950s and 1960s is another Ladybird Books example of how the vertical page format is used to good advantage.

50. See, for example, Harold Webb, "Kingsway Pictorial Science" *Book 3* (London: Evans Brothers Limited, 1950).

51. See, for example, T. S. Patchett, "A Visual Geography of the World" *Book 1 Africa and Australasia* (London: Educational Publishing Company, 1950).

52. Cited in Johnson and Alderson, *Ladybird*, 78.

53. National Book League, *Textbook Design Exhibition. Catalogue of an Exhibition of Books Published between May 1962 and May 1965 and Chosen for the National Book League by G. Fielden Hughes, Ruari McLean and Kenneth Pinnock* (London: National Book League, 1966).

54. Amabel Williams-Ellis, *How You Began: A Child's Introduction to Biology* (London: Gerald Howe Ltd, 1928), 16.

55. T. J. S. Rowland, *Living Things for Lively Youngsters* (London: Cassell, 1933).

56. British Association for the Advancement of Science, *Report on the Influence of Schoolbooks upon Eyesight* (London: John Murray, 1913); Robert D. Morss, "The Neglected Schoolbook," *Monotype Recorder* 34, no. 2 (1935): 3–13.

57. See Michael Twyman, "The Bold Idea: The Use of Bold-Looking Types in the Nineteenth Century," *Journal of the Printing Historical Society* 22 (1993): 107–43.

58. Nicola Robson, "Information Books for Children," 74.

59. See, for example, in relation to headings, James Hartley and Mark Trueman, "A Research Strategy for Designers: The Role of Headings," *Instructional Science* 14, no. 2 (1985): 99–155 and Michael Twyman, "Typography without Words," *Visible Language* 15, no. 1 (181): 5–12.

60. Sue Walker, Alison Black, Ann Bessemans, Kevin Bormans, Maarten Renckens and Mark Barratt, "Designing Digital Texts for Beginner Readers; Performance, Practice and Process," in *Learning to Read in a Digital World*, eds. Mirit Barzillai, Jenny Thomson, Sascha Schroeder and Paul van den Broek (Amsterdam: John Benjamins Publishing Company, 2018), 31–56.

Chapter 6

Mediating with Metafiction

Rethinking What Counts *about Reading with Parents, Using Picturebooks*

Jennifer Farrar

As their children's first teachers,[1] parents both consciously and unconsciously mediate their young offspring's knowledge of *what counts* about literacy during the act of shared reading. On one level, this can be done through the selection of specific types of texts or particular authors over others; on another, by the literacies normatively practiced and the socially and culturally constructed ideas about reading that give shape to the "ways with words" that ultimately emerge and are prized as valuable.[2]

Drawing on the findings of a doctoral study that inquired into the assumptions about reading made visible when a group of parents and their young children were confronted by the disruptive and playful demands of metafiction in picturebooks, this chapter describes how some adult readers were provoked into a heightened, reflective awareness of their mediatory influence over the reading process or were prompted to adapt and change their reading practices.

By visualizing readers' responses to the picturebooks as individual expressions of their *literate habitus*,[3] that is, as representations of the "durable and transposable, structuring and structured" forces that mold how and why we approach literacy practices in the ways that we do,[4] I aim to highlight the practices that emerged as most dominant between the adults and the children and consider what they might suggest about the normative literacies practiced by this particular set of twenty-first-century readers. Extending this further, I also draw attention to the intergenerational gaps in normative reading practices that were made visible by the disruptive effects of metafiction and consider their implications for teaching, research, and the future nature of home-school relationships.

PARENTS AS MEDIATORS

For the purposes of this chapter, parents are positioned as *mediators* in order to acknowledge the active, go-between nature of their role during shared reading,[5] especially when it takes place with young children who may not yet be able to decode all of the words they encounter in printed texts. As this suggests, the term "mediator" is used here to indicate the nature of the complicated and multilayered relationship or transaction that takes place between the parent, the text, and the child reader, rather than being rooted in the word's more negative-sounding connotations that include dispute resolution and arbitration (although it is recognized that reading a book with a small child can indeed require minor acts of dispute resolution by adult co-readers).[6]

As Gee observed, the theoretical "social turn" of the late twentieth century recognized literacy as socially constructed and inherently ideological, rather than natural or, to use Street's term, autonomous.[7] Contemporaneous work by family literacy scholars led to a far wider acknowledgement of the home as a valid and powerful context for learning.[8] The home has subsequently and increasingly become valued as space in which the process of primary socialization is initiated and developed.[9] Such theories were made visible by Heath's seminal work into the literate lives of American families within different communities and social classes, which revealed how a family's literacy practices could have a profoundly shaping effect on an individual child's trajectory through the school system, depending on the level of conflict or accord that existed between the practices prized in school and those promoted at home.[10] When viewed through a Bourdieusian lens, Heath's work clearly illustrates how the *habitus* acquired in the family—Bourdieu's term for the complex network of micro and macro influences and understandings that give shape to an individual's network of dispositions in relation to the field or context[11]—is of fundamental significance to the structuring of the school experience and beyond. More specifically, it is possible to see how lessons about reading can be mediated and learned, both consciously and unconsciously, through the literacies practiced by families in their homes and by the ways that "life is lived,"[12] thus leading to the construction and evolution of an individual's *literate habitus*.[13] This can be discerned through the literacies selected, valued, and encouraged by families, which will vary according to cultural and social factors, not least the deep-rooted influence of schooled approaches to reading and writing.

Framed by these sociological understandings, the concept of family literacy has itself evolved in recent decades away from narrow, school-focused interventions designed to teach parents how "best" to support their children's learning, into a broader exploratory set of approaches that aim to discover "what children know about literacy and how it is intrinsically informed by their social and cultural upbringing" rather than "whether or how well they can read or write."[14] Such a shift places far greater emphasis on context and ecology rather than skills and proficiency. For researchers working with families today, there is therefore a greater methodological and ethical responsibility to seek out ways of "using and valuing what families already know in order to teach them what they do not know" through collaboration rather than imposition or assumption, a subtle balance that Brooks and Hannon have warned can so easily go awry.[15] This heightened sense of responsibility had a profound impact on my methodology, as I discuss in a later section.

READING ALONE

When considered against this backdrop, it is clear that an adult's role in the shared reading process is one that involves far more than simply reading some words out loud while turning a page. As Luke has noted, "when we teach the word, we also disburse a way of reading the world, with all of its wrinkles of power and politics,"[16] a comment that not only has clear implications for those employed to teach reading in schools but also, by extension, for parent co-readers.

To further unpack the mediational role of the more experienced reader in the shared reading process, it is first necessary to consider what happens when an individual reader engages with a text. According to Rosenblatt's highly influential theory of reader response, reading is "a transactional process that goes on between a particular reader and a particular text at a particular time, and under particular circumstances," one that involves the "unique reservoir of public and private significances."[17] This can also be understood as the social, cultural, and individual "funds of knowledge" that readers always bring with them to the act of reading.[18]

Citing William James, Rosenblatt portrays what happens during reading as involving a process of "selective attention," in which readers make automatic, split-second decisions about the specific aspects of a text to dwell on—or ignore—as a result of the "complex, to-and-fro, self-correcting transaction" that takes place between the reader and the printed symbols on a page.[19] As Bourdieu might have observed, and here I conject, this transaction between reader, text, and context can be understood as being "constitutive of the dynamic of a relationship between individuals and the social conditions—both material and ideational—which surround them."[20] Therefore, by acknowledging how habitus operates at the very heart of every reading transaction, both shaping and being shaped by the field and context, it becomes possible to recognize the socially constructed nature of the reading self that emerges.[21]

READING TOGETHER

When experienced as a shared process between an adult and child, the reading transaction becomes more complicated still, with the adult reader's assumptions and socially constructed understandings of *what counts* about reading and interpretation of the subject matter brought into direct interplay with the child's emerging literate habitus and practices in ways that vary according to the relationship between participants, not to mention the impact of forms of capital, context and field. What this suggests is that shared reading can also be understood as a process of intergenerational mediation, an experience during which assumptions and ideas about literacy can be transmitted from one generation to the next. Building on the work of Heath, Anderson et al. have noted that children learn how to engage with texts and what is considered to be important about literacy through the sorts of textual interactions modeled or offered by their parents, including the types of questions asked, the level of support provided and the adjustments made to encourage new or extended learning.[22] By extension, children also learn about literacy from the assumptions that adult readers bring with them to the shared reading experience about other aspects of literacy, such as genre and mode, or "how books work," or preconceived ideas about the relationship between words and pictures, as well as perceptions about the suitability of certain text types over others. The highly subjective and sociocultural nature of such understandings means that a considerable range of interpretation and reception can be possible within even the most homogenous groups of parents and young readers,[23] as this study has also found.

While the points raised in the previous paragraph highlight the important role that adults play in scaffolding children's learning, it is crucial to recognize that the flow of learning is not necessarily unidirectional from the parent to the child in such situations. As I begin to discuss later on in this chapter, it is equally possible for parents' understandings about literacy to be influenced by their children's insights or to be altered by the experience of sharing a book, especially those that are particularly "troublesome" in their form and format.[24] Before that, it is necessary to establish a more specific context for the study described here by outlining some of the key assumptions about reading and picturebooks that provide its frame.

WORDS AND PICTURES—OR PICTURES AND WORDS?

Thanks to rapid developments in communicative practices and technologies, traditional assumptions about the "division of labour" between words and pictures have been challenged in recent decades, with writing seen to be losing some of its unquestioned dominance in an increasingly visual world.[25] The rising prominence and sophistication of the visual mode in our daily lives have led to scholarly calls for a greater recognition of visual literacy (a relatively new field) in classrooms, given its crucial role in developing creative and critical thinking.[26] According to Bearne and Kress, acknowledging the shifting relations between images and words has raised some profound cultural questions and challenges, including what reading is; what the functions of writing are; how we are to think about language and its relation to thinking, to imagination, to creativity.[27]

As interesting as they are, such questions may seem curious to adults outside of literacy scholarship, given that so many people have been schooled into privileging images over words by education systems that have traditionally considered pictures as far less intellectually challenging than words.[28] Writing in the 1980s, Meek described how whole generations of adult readers have been trained to "skip and scan" over images in order to get at the more serious and meaningful message carried by the printed text.[29] According to Kress, adults' literacy practices are limited by their knowledge of social and cultural norms and regulations, which can compel them to equate language with writing, perhaps because it seems to be the most culturally conventional, or common sense, approach.[30] At the opposite extreme are young children who are said to use "whatever is to hand that is apt for the purpose,"[31] an approach that in comparison is unbridled by convention and replete with creative possibility. A result of such well-entrenched power dynamics between adults and children, words and pictures, is the existence of the "rather simplistic correlation between 'looking at pictures' and a deficiency in literacy," and the related assumption "that only those who are unable to read the words have a need for illustration."[32]

As Millard and Marsh's points help to suggest, this long-standing underestimation of the visual mode in pedagogic terms is now somewhat at odds with the recent boom in communicative technologies that expose readers to a bewildering array of sophisticated, multimodal texts that can challenge and subvert normative assumptions about literacy, or how texts *should* work. But it is important to note this experience will not be the same for all. For younger readers who have been born into a world that is increasingly "dominated by the logic of display," the changing dynamic between words and pictures may seem "utterly unremarkable" simply because it is what they have always known.[33] Yet for others, such as their parents and teachers from generations who have been schooled in a world "dominated by the logic of narrative, of structures, of events sequenced in time,"[34] the sense of change and dislocation may seem more acute and running counter to *what counts* to them about reading. While this logic cannot be applied wholesale to every reader, what it begins to indicate in broad, theoretical terms is the presence of an intergenerational *gap* or a sense of a mismatch between some taken-for-granted expectations about the role of words and pictures among differently aged readers that may become visible through the process of adult-to-child mediation. Nikolajeva has expressed the tensions between words and pictures as a "dilemma" faced by readers,[35] a term that also helpfully suggests the decision-making processes involved when faced with the challenge of responding to both modes at once. Building on Nikolajeva's term, the notion of a dilemma can be extended to the process of mediated reading as it occurs between adults and young children, which, as discussed earlier, often involves a child being read *to* by an adult. Considering this gap or tension leads to a number of questions. Do older, adult readers, who have been schooled into placing greater emphasis on written language, privilege the verbal over the visual? More specifically, how do adult readers mediate texts that *force* them to pay attention to both the words and pictures to younger readers and what factors influence these mediation strategies? Would a greater awareness of the "dilemma" help to improve or enhance the experience of reading for both adults and children?

In the next section, I explain why metafictive picturebooks can make ideal vehicles for exploring—and exploiting—this textual gap, dilemma, or tension, and why they may prove helpful when addressing the questions about twenty-first-century literacy practices raised earlier.

PICTUREBOOKS, METAFICTION, AND THEIR AFFORDANCES

According to Lewis, what gives picturebooks their power is the "mutual interanimation" of the words and the pictures;[36] in other words, it is the "synergy" that exists between the two modes.[37] Unlike illustrated texts, in which pictures can often play a supportive or reflective role to the words, the "intrinsically plural nature" of a picturebook challenges readers to extract and assemble meaning from *across* both modes without necessarily privileging one over the other.[38] As Grenby and Reynolds have noted, it is necessary for picturebook readers to engage with both the words and the pictures if an "interdependent and a satisfying understanding of the text" is to be achieved, with the implication being that an *unsatisfactory* reading may result if both modes are not acknowledged.[39] Sipe agrees that it is the tension or relationship between the different "characters" of words and pictures that gives picturebooks so much of their potential.[40] He points to the predominantly temporal, linear nature of words and contrasts it with the tendency of images to create a "diffuse network" of responses in a reader's mind that is inherently spatial in character.[41] Consequently, the written text carries a forward momentum that encourages readers to progress in one direction, while the spatial aspect of the pictures can create a desire to "gaze . . . dwell . . . contemplate," acting as a sort of narrative brake or pause button.[42] When combined, both modes promote a "recursive and reflective" reading style that is quite unlike the traditional linear approach described in the previous section.[43]

Yet the inclination to make meaning through a combination of both modes may not occur *naturally* to those readers who have been trained to "skip and scan," simply because it falls outside of their normative practice.[44] This disinclination toward images may be confirmed and compounded by socially constructed assumptions, already referred to earlier, that earmark picturebooks as texts that should be read aloud by proficient, adult literate readers while less proficient and preliterate readers follow along using the pictures.

Previous research by McClay has attempted to explore how separate groups of teachers and their pupils made meaning from the complexities of the same picturebook.[45] Using David Macaulay's *Black and White*, a text that was also one of the four used in this doctoral study, McClay found that the younger readers responded with positivity and flexibility to the book's challenging form and format by devising sets of reading strategies to help them cope with—and enjoy—the text's metafictive complexities.[46] Yet many of the teachers voiced dislike for the text and struggled to make meaning individually or as a group.[47] Several adult readers claimed that their reading had been "seriously impeded" by others' attempts to impose alternative reading strategies upon them, something they actively resisted.[48] In addition, some teacher readers assumed that because they had found the text inaccessible, their pupils would automatically struggle too, although the children had independently demonstrated that this was not the case.[49] McClay's study is significant not simply because it illustrates the mismatch between adult expectations and young readers' capabilities, but also because it shows how reading as an act of conscious and unconscious mediation can be made visible through an individual's reflections on their encounter with a challenging or complex text.

METAFICTION

Much of the complexity of Macaulay's *Black and White*, mentioned earlier, derives from its metafictive characteristics. Broadly speaking, metafiction can be understood as a set of literary techniques that disrupt and "problematise the mimetic illusion" of fiction, thus interrupting and challenging readers' normative expectations of how a text *ought to* work and by exposing a text's artifice, fictionality and constructedness.[50] Commonly recognized metafictive devices can include nontraditional ways of using narrative, character, and setting: plot lines become multiple and subject to fragmentation or frequent dispute; conventional page boundaries are broken by narrators who directly address the reader or interrupt other characters; and any sense of "narrative logic and consistency" is surrendered to playfully carnivalesque displays that can be characterized by excess, inversion, and indeterminacy.[51] In picturebooks, the disruptive, ludic effects of metafiction can be effectively harnessed by authors who choose to toy with the dynamic between words and pictures by offering multiple, often contradictory, pathways through stories that subvert expectations about which mode should carry the "right" version of events—the words or the pictures? The disruptiveness of metafiction may register all the more acutely to parent readers of picturebooks, perhaps because such texts are commonly so associated with the preliterate stage and are therefore assumed to pose nothing other than a straightforward, comfortable read.

By interrupting such assumptions and by refusing to permit readers access to the vicarious, or lived-through story experience they may have been anticipating,[52] metafiction can create a sense of distance between a reader and a text that can be critical in its impact. As Mackey has suggested, the effect of such an unexpected or surprising gap may be to heighten an individual reader's awareness of "how the processes of fiction are operating as they read."[53] When experienced within a shared reading context, it may be that the disruption is also sufficient to draw attention to the "force of the [literate] habitus" and its role within the mediation process.[54]

THE STUDY: METHODOLOGY AND METHODS

The larger study referred to here took place over several months in 2014 in a western suburb of Edinburgh, Scotland, involving a group of eight parents, their children (ages between 4.5 and 6 years) and four metafictive picturebooks, which are briefly described here. Comprised of two distinct yet intertwined parts, the project revolved around the intergenerational readers' responses to the picturebooks that were sent home from school "cold" on a fortnightly basis; that is, they were issued without any scaffolding or guidance on how to read, or what to look out for while reading. Participant families were recruited via letters sent out to all children in separate Primary 1 and Primary 2 classes, the youngest years of primary schooling. First of all, I discussed the books inside the school with the children but outside of their usual classroom contexts and without their teachers. Motivated by a methodological desire to let the children generate themes and ideas, I used literature circles to promote pupil dialogue, interruptions, and digressions, and also hoped this would enable me to decenter myself as the teacher-like figure "in charge" of the reading process. [55]

In the second part, I met with the children's parents in a range of settings that best suited their individual routines and circumstances. Inspired by Moles's use of walking as method—a practice also known as bimbling[56]—I offered the parents less formal, more fluid ways of talking about the books in order to unsettle the power structures created by our dual roles as researcher and researched.[57] I talked about the books while walking to collect children at the end of the school day with one mother. With another, our discussions took place in the local play-park while our children clambered and dangled around us. Conversations took place by the school gates; on the way to playgroup after the morning drop-off, and even amid the turbulence of the playground after school. With several parents, for whom bimbling was not an option, our discussions took place by telephone in the evening, once the children were in bed and more time was available.

After transcription, all conversations were analyzed using a theoretical framework comprised of Freebody and Luke's Four Resources Model and Serafini's expanded version of the Four Resources, an approach that was inspired by Ryan and Anstey's exploration of primary school pupils' reading identities.[58] In Ryan and Anstey's study, participants' responses were analyzed according to the reading resources they drew on "naturally" when making meaning from a picturebook, a word I understood as referring to the responses readers considered "right" or most appropriate to their own context.[59] Building on this, and in order to further foreground the socially constructed decisions that all readers make while reading, I also interpreted the "nature" or content of readers' responses as representative expressions of their literate habitus to the demands of this study.[60]

THE PICTUREBOOKS

The four metafictive picturebooks selected for this study were sent home in an order that reflected my interpretation of their increasing complexity. The texts were ordered as follows: *The Bravest Ever Bear* by Allan Ahlberg and Paul Howard; *No Bears* by Meg McKinlay and Leila Rudge; *The Three Pigs* by David Wiesner; and *Black and White* by David Macaulay.[61] A brief summary of each picturebook follows here:

The Bravest Ever Bear contains a sequence of interrupted and fractured narratives caused by a succession of disgruntled characters who usurp the dominant story in order to tell their own in ways that suit them. Two fonts carry the written text: a larger typeface representing the dominant narrative voice is a serif font that suggests this voice is linked to well-established traditions of print and storytelling. The smaller one, which initially carries the Bear's voice, is sans serif, printed in bold and is suggestive of a more vernacular, conversational style. The function of this font, or voice, is meta-fictive in that it is used by the majority of the characters, including the Bear and the Princess, to interrupt, challenge and subvert the version of reality that is presented by the more imposing-looking "narrative" serif font. However, the divide between imposing and imposed upon is not as clear-cut as this account might suggest because the dominant voice also has a metafictive function. Indeed, the story delivered by the dominant narrative voice is far from traditional and toys with the idea of "what counts" as a story. The first story, "The Bear," consists of only two sentences: "Once upon a time there was a bear. The End," causing the Bear to exclaim in disbelief: "What's going on?" By the seventh "chapter," the Bear, who has by now become thoroughly irritated with the disruptive, nonconventional approach of the dominant voice, peels back the white page of the "book" to reveal a back office, where he settles at a desk among piles of crumpled-up paper to work on the version of the story *he* thinks should be told. This sequence of editing and rewriting is repeated by several characters during the course of the story, such as the Princess and some typical "baddie" characters, including a wolf and a troll. By highlighting the possibility of different versions and by playing with readers' expectations of narrative conventions, the text can be seen to invite subsequent retellings that reflect alternative and perhaps marginalized voices.

In *No Bears*, Ruby the (rather unkind) narrator attempts to tell a totally bear-free story. She is surreptitiously interrupted and contradicted by a paral-lel visual (and entirely wordless) narrative, in which a benevolent-looking bear manages to save the day—and Ruby. The written story is about a prin-cess (Ruby), who is kidnapped by a monster but saved from a tragic end by her faithful fairy godmother. After throwing a party to celebrate her fairy god-mother's courage and loyalty, Ruby's story ends "happily ever after." Yet the visual narrative carries an alternative plotline that contests the certainty and dominance exuded by Ruby's text. Unseen by Ruby, a benevolent-looking yet marginalized Bear is present on almost every page, despite Ruby's deter-mination to create a bear-free book.

The book ends ambiguously with the narrator failing to recognize the bear's valuable contribution although the visual text makes the injustice clear. While Ruby concludes her narrative with a confident-sounding "happily ever after," the Bear's unhappy, wordless outcome jars with the reader, creating a sense of injustice that is exacerbated by the fairy godmother's dejected expression as she is helped to recognize her role in the proceedings. Therefore, for a full meaning to emerge, *No Bears* requires its readers to interpret the gaps and silences that exist between the contradictory verbal and visual narratives and to weave them together into a meaningful whole. Through an appreciation of the interplay of the modes, or the counterpoint between the verbal and visual perspectives,[62] it is possible for readers to appreciate the extent of Ruby's complicity in the Bear's unhappy, isolated predicament.

Although *The Three Pigs* begins relatively conventionally, the metafictive aspects of Wiesner's text soon become apparent when the pigs are unexpectedly and delightfully blown out of the story by the wolf's huffing and puffing, setting them all off on a chaotic, nonlinear adventure into other stories. The traditional version of *The Three Pigs* is interrupted in terms of its plot (the pigs turn the wolf's page into a paper airplane, visit both a nursery rhyme and a fantasy story about knights and dragons before returning to their own transformed tale) and also in terms of the devices that are used to tell the story. Like *No Bears*, there are points when the words and images contradict one another; there are competing narrative threads and visual styles as the pigs try out different genres for size, and the majority of the action takes place in the usually innocuous white space that surrounds the story frames the pigs have now evacuated. As a result, the limits or boundaries of stories are made visible as we watch the pigs decide which story worlds to enter—or leave—and then witness as they reassemble and re-enter the panels of their original narrative once they feel it is safe to return home. This time, of course, they do so complete with a wolf-deterrent in the shape of a powerful dragon.

Macaulay's award-winning picturebook *Black and White* begins by warning readers that it may (or may not) contain more than one story. Each double-page spread is divided into quadrants, each carrying a narrative thread that varies in subject matter, visual style or grammar, font, and narrative perspective. Individual readers need to decide how to read the text (all four boxes at once, left to right, or one box at a time) and have to determine whether the stories are separate entities or all part of a single story. What makes Macaulay's approach so metafictive is that it makes explicit some of the readerly decisions that underpin the processes of reading and meaning-making, but which often remain invisible. By constructing the text as a challenge or a puzzle for readers to work through, Macaulay positions his audience as coauthors while also challenging perceptions about how books are read. There are multiple ways of reading this book, presenting readers with a level of ambiguity not found in the other picturebooks used in this project.

For reasons of space, it is not possible to discuss every participant's response to the books. In order to explore the role of adults as mediators of their child's reading, the next section will instead track the responses of two parents (one father and one mother) as they read their way through the four picturebooks. Given the individualized nature of our conversations, the amount of time spent discussing each text varied from person to person, but the overall intention is to provide an overview of how adults responded to the disruptive nature of the texts' metafictive aspects.

Michelle

Michelle, who joined the project along with Matthew, her six-year-old son, had recently started to work as a learning or classroom assistant in a primary school, where she supported children in activities across the curriculum that included reading. Declaring herself to be an avid reader, she belittled her own reading choices as limited to "just chick lit," a comment that suggested her anxieties about reading as a form of social capital. With an older son also at primary school, Michelle brought a range of parental, professional, and personal knowledge about reading to the study. From her responses to the first book, *The Bravest Ever Bear*, it was clear that the metafictive devices employed by this text clashed with her usual approach to reading with her sons:

> *It wasn't what I was used to. It took a couple of times to get into it. The first time I was reading it, I was like, "oh right, okay, okay." And then it would stop and the Bear would start writing his own story and I was like, "we are going to have to read this again!"* (Michelle)

As "It wasn't what I was used to" suggests, the "stop-start" structure of *The Bravest Ever Bear*'s narrative had an impact on Michelle's experience of reading it aloud. She explained: "I'm used to books that just sort of flow," a comment that politely implied a preference for books with structures less disjointed and approaches a bit less "weird." The sorts of books she said they preferred included titles by the popular children's author Julia Donaldson, as well as texts from an "at home" version of the Oxford Reading Tree, a basal reading scheme used in many UK primary schools to teach reading. According to Michelle, "We just go through Biff and Chip[63]—I've got my own Biff and Chip, outwith the school's—so we go through them." As a staged, school-approved approach to reading, the stories included within such schemes tend to adhere to traditional narrative conventions, usually privileging the status of words over images. By replicating a similar pattern of ordered progression through the books at home, Michelle indicated that her literate habitus was primarily aligned herself with the dominant literacy practices advocated by schools and reinforced by so many other outlets.

More details about Michelle's reading preferences emerged during our discussion of *No Bears*, which she seemed to regard as a welcome improvement on the first book. "It was more my sort of thing. I like surprises and tricks and treats," she explained, referring to the running joke of the banished yet visible bear at work in the book's margins. Interested to know how Michelle had mediated the complex interplay between words and images in *No Bears*,

I asked how they had read the book at home. In response, Michelle sketched out a typical reading scene, complete with mime:

Michelle: What we always do is that I will read the book first and then when he is reading the book he always starts talking. He'll start [points as if at illustrations on a page] *and I'll say no, no wait until after and we'll discuss it . . .*
Jennifer: Do you stop him?
Michelle: Yes, so I stop him! But he carries on anyway!

By beginning her commentary with "what we always do," Michelle conveyed the sense of a habitual routine, a tried-and-tested approach to reading books of this type. As she depicted with some humor, Michelle's approach seemed to be aimed at preventing lengthy digressions into the visual realm, once again illustrating her intention to put words first:

Once I've finished the book, I'll go back in. In general, I try not to discuss it till afterwards because it will take us an hour to read a Biff and Chip book just because he wants to talk about it: "There's a book! And there's the sunglasses!" And I am like, "Can we just read the book? Can we just read the book?"
(Michelle)

In a sense, the (comic) exasperation of Michelle's repeated exclamation "can we just read the book?" animates theoretical claims that adults are schooled into automatically privileging words over images,[64] although clearly the converse is also possible. By drawing attention to Matthew's interest in the images and her *own* emphatic intention to focus on the written text ("Can we just read the book?"), Michelle's response once again revealed the proximity of her literate habitus to the print-bound nature of dominant schooled literacies. Her use of pronouns in this extract can also be seen as indicative of the power dynamics at work in the reading process. While reading started out as a shared act ("What *we* do . . ."), her rapid switch to individual pronouns ("I" and "he") highlighted the sense of a divide between her own focus on words and Matthew's interest in images, an intergenerational split that echoes the pedagogic shift between the verbal and visual modes.

As discussed earlier, the long-standing marginalization of visual literacies in classrooms could make a child's interest in images seem like an off-task pursuit, a distraction from the more urgent task of achieving fluency with the written word. These ideas were fleshed out further with Michelle as our conversation about *No Bears* continued:

Jennifer: So, reading for you is very much about the words, with the pictures secondary?

Michelle: Yes.

Jennifer: And is that reflected in the books you read with Matthew?

Michelle: . . . It's not always going to be picturebooks so [I say] let's concentrate on the story first and then we can go back and look at them. Because when they get older, there's not going to be pictures anymore.

Jennifer: What about movies and the telly and adverts? They are pictures and we need to read them . . .

Michelle: Yeah, but when you are reading a book. . . . What I try to say is that the pictures are sort of secondary, so read the words and understand what they mean. And then go back to the pictures if you don't understand, you can maybe get a little bit more. But to me, reading is reading.

As "it's not always going to be picturebooks" indicates, Michelle's practice as an adult mediator of reading was influenced by her concerns for her son's future, suggesting her overarching interest in aligning the family's reading practices with the professional competences traditionally associated with scholastic success. Consequently, the literacies she privileged were expressions of her literate habitus, such as her focus on the written text ("let's concentrate on the story first and then we can go back and look") and her very definite equation of reading with words, not pictures: "To me, reading is reading."

Despite Michelle's stated enjoyment of *No Bears*, it was not clear from our conversation that she had actually recognized the subtle dynamic or interplay between the images and the words in this book. In fact, her emphatic defense of words in the extract earlier could be interpreted as an indication that Michelle had maintained her usual focus on words over images while reading, despite the book's metafictive efforts to disrupt this. Yet her initial response to the contradictory modes at work in the next book, *The Three Pigs*, made it abundantly clear that she had noticed something different was at work in this picturebook. She admitted:

At first, I thought, "Oh! I can't even read these words!" . . . I got about two pages in and I thought, "okay! I see what's happening now." So I had to discuss that with him, whereas normally I wouldn't but I had to discuss it. (Michelle; her emphasis)

As her emphatic and quite indignant use of "had" seems to signify, Michelle had been compelled to read the book to Matthew in a different way in order to ensure that a clear meaning emerged. As a result, she had to forego her usual mediational practice of leaving any discussion until after the first read-through. Having already altered her approach in order to make meaning from this third book, Michelle noted even more radical differences during her reading of *Black and White*, the fourth and arguably most challenging book of the series. "It was weird," she remarked. "But I really enjoyed it. It really made me really think. You really had to think, 'hold on, there's four different stories and do you read across the way or down the way—what do you do? Does it matter?'"

By repeatedly emphasizing how this book had made her "think," Michelle drew attention to her own awareness of the cognitive, decision-making processes she had engaged in while puzzling her way through *Black and White*. This could suggest that her transactions with the devices used in this text had provoked some heightened meta-level understandings linked to her role as a reader and within the shared reading process. Indeed, some of Michelle's comments about the text showed evidence of an awareness of reading as not only a product or outcome but also as a process:[65]

> *Michelle: It engages your brain, that's the first thing I would say about it. It's very, very different.*
> *Jennifer: Yeah, do you think it's about anything? Does it have a point?*
> *Michelle: No, it's not got a point. It's just very cleverly made. . . . See at first, I was thinking they were four different stories, but half way through I was thinking this isn't four different stories, this is one story but it is all interlinked in different wee ways.*

As this brief exchange shows, Michelle's focus seemed to be on *how* she had read, rather than *what* she had read, as shown by her definite statement: "No, it's not got a point," which suggested she had not considered (or had possibly ruled out) the idea of any moral or authorial intention. To Michelle, this was a book that "engaged her brain," in part because of its challenging form and format and also because of its difference from the books she usually read at home with her sons. In this instance, the process of reading seemed to have become slightly more significant than the product or narrative outcome. In fact, it seemed that reading *Black and White* with Matthew had once again caused Michelle to adjust her own practice of read-through first and discussion later, which, as described in previous paragraphs, she had been reluctant to deviate from. However, in this book she found that talking about the text was unavoidable on the way through: "I had to explain a lot of things to him. . . . If I had just read it through and not talked about the pictures at all there is no way he would have got anything."

As this last comment shows, reading *Black and White* caused Michelle to extend her reading to account for both images and words, when her previous firmly stated preference had been to focus on the words exclusively. This change in emphasis was clearly visible in her recount of one of the most confusing spreads in the text—when fragments of torn-up mail are mixed with drifting pages from some railway passengers' newspapers and fall together as the snowflakes that envelop the toy train a young boy plays with:

> *Like for instance the snow. We were like, "oh, it's snowing" and turned the page and then I was thinking, "is that snow?" and then we turned another page and then I said, "no, I think that's newspaper." So it was like you were getting it just before [it happened]. It was like a page turner.* (Michelle)

Spurred onwards by the "drama of the turning page," Michelle's comment showed how the changing interplay between images and words had impacted on what she chose to look at and discuss with Matthew.[66] Yet such alterations were also stimulated by her perception of changes to her son's responses as a co-reader during *Black and White*:

> *Normally with the books that we read, I have to keep on saying, "shhh! Shhhh! Let me read but we'll talk about that afterwards! We'll read the page first!" But he was more quiet this time; he was listening to it all, whereas normally he is interrupting me and talking and saying "look at this and this!"* (Michelle)

As this overview indicates, the disruptive effects of metafiction seemed to force Michelle to alter aspects of her fairly well-entrenched reading practices, including her habit of discouraging any discussion of the plot or pictures until at least the second read-through. The increased flexibility of the reading practices that emerged seemed more responsive to the demands of the story and the needs of her co-reader, Matthew. While there was some implicit recognition that change had taken place, it was not entirely clear whether Michelle had explicitly reflected on why such changes had occurred and what they might indicate about her own assumptions about literacy. This outcome is in contrast to Brendan, the next parent to be described, whose experience of metafiction led to a more obvious reflection-led process of inquiry and change.

Brendan

With a professional background in engineering and commerce, Brendan joined the project with Eva, his daughter who, at 4.5 years old was the young- est participant. As he revealed during our conversations, his own childhood reading habit had disappeared at the end of secondary school, something he attributed to the "double . . . and treble analysis" that took place in his English lessons. As a university student, reading became purely functional and done on a *needs must* basis. Now, as a father, he had rediscovered his love of read- ing and described himself to be a fan of both shared and individual reading for pleasure. Consequently, Brendan came to the project with a range of personal and professional experiences of reading that suggested his literate habitus was less closely aligned to that of the school's than Michelle's. When asked what he had made of *The Bravest Ever Bear*, Brendan's response was quite practically focused on the strategies he had used to make meaning:

> *Once you got the concept, you were fine. You ended up using the ends* [of the separate stories]. *Like, normally you would read through a book and say "what do you think?" That sort of thing.* [Here] *you were reading a passage and then discussing the passage, as opposed to what you would normally do in a book, when you could go through five pages of Kipper and all the rest, and you wouldn't have an opportune moment to stop. It broke it up in such a way that there . . . was more interaction between us.* (Brendan)

Just as Michelle had discovered, the "concepts" found in *The Bravest Ever Bear* provoked Brendan to adopt different tactics while reading, such as more frequent pauses to discuss the narratives as they cropped up ("using the ends"), rather than ploughing on towards a summative discussion at the end. While there is perhaps nothing so very remarkable in pausing to discuss a book more frequently, it is nevertheless interesting that Brendan decided to articulate this fact, perhaps because it seemed different to his usual practice, as confirmed by his use of "normally you would read through" and "what you would normally do." In this way, Brendan's observations illustrated some of the heightened reader engagement that metafiction is said to demand,[67] by challenging readers to assemble meaning in new ways from unconventional narrative patterns and unruly narrative voices.

Unlike Michelle, Brendan seemed to enjoy the nonlinear and chaotic narrative of *The Bravest Ever Bear*, yet this positive start did not extend to the multimodal complexities found in *No Bears*, the second book:

> *I found it . . . a bit too clever for its own good. I may well end up patronising my daughter here, but I feel the need to spot or highlight things. And I'll be honest, the first time I read "No Bears," I didn't even notice the bear was in the story.* (Brendan)

As "too clever for its own good" suggests, Brendan's resistance stemmed from the fact that the book had "tried too hard," a comment that conveys the idea that *No Bears* had somehow failed to meet up to his expectations of what a children's book *should* be or do. Bound up with this was the sense that the book had denied him one of his expert functions as an adult co-reader—to spot or highlight things—causing him to feel tricked or even upstaged by the operations of the metafictive devices in the book: "I didn't even notice the bear was in the story."

Brendan's extended commentary revealed that several read-throughs had been necessary to make sense of *No Bears,* an acknowledgment of the challenge this book's unconventional format had posed to his credentials as the adult reader in charge, by forcing him to re-read, re-register and possibly reconsider the possibility that a more complex relationship *could* exist between the words and the pictures. As a result, Brendan seemed to recognize that both images and words had to be consulted for a coherent meaning to emerge:

> *It wouldn't have been that good a story until you start going in and notice the wand's being put in the paint pot and the bear is not actually in the story and you can see the bear has done something with the shoelaces. . . . Two or three reads and you are finding new things yourself.* (Brendan)

While *No Bears* had provoked some irritation and frustration, *The Three Pigs* represented even more of a break from the norm for Brendan. "We haven't seen anything like this ever," he remarked, "it's a completely new concept, not just in reading but in all things." Similarly to *No Bears,* the challenge of reading this book aloud caused Brendan to reflect again on his role in the reading process:

> *You want to try to explain, but I'm opening up page two, the pigs have already been blown out of the page and the story doesn't match what's going on. It's not quite knowing what I need to say, as far as I am concerned.* (Brendan)

As seen earlier, a sense of his frustration at these disruptions was conveyed by his repeated use of the word "explain" ("I feel the need to explain"; "I want to try to explain"; "how do I explain?"), thus emphasizing the destabilizing effect that engaging with this text had on his assumptions, both inwardly as a reader but also outwardly, as someone who had to process the words and images and then mediate or project these understandings onto another.

Interpreting Brendan's comments on this book helped to reveal the multiple facets and forces at work within his response—each influenced and tugged at by separate, yet also interlinked, aspects of his "identity in practice" or literate habitus.[68] Following Pahl's suggestion, it helped to imagine the habitus as "semiotic sediment,"[69] a phrase that encapsulates how habitual meaning-making practices can be "stirred up" as a consequence of change, before settling down again into taken-for-granted, more solidified ways of being and taking—with the prospect of more sedimentary swirling and reconfiguration always a possibility. Perhaps as a consequence of his own negative experiences of reading at secondary school and his subsequent rediscovery of reading for pleasure, Brendan could identify where his reading habits—or literate habitus—had already been reconfigured, something that also suggested his confidence as a reader. Given the increasingly reflective and evaluative nature of Brendan's responses to metafiction in *The Three Pigs*, I wondered if reading and talking about the book within the context of the project had caused some more sedimentary swirling to occur. Indeed, several comments suggested that Brendan had "grasped the force of the habitus" while reading and talking about *The Three Pigs*.[70] In other words, the act of discussing how he had struggled to make meaning from a text that had deliberately defied his notion of logic seemed to enable Brendan to become more aware of the "possibilities and constraints" that his normative assumptions imposed on shared reading with Eve.[71] This awareness was especially visible in off-the-cuff remarks such as: "You know, maybe it's an issue with me being an adult" and *"It could just be me* and I should just let her get on with it," with the words in italics indicating Brendan's growing recognition that his status as an adult and his personal taste in books could both have a mediational and shaping effect on how he read with Eve.

An effect of his increasingly reflective approach became apparent close to the start of our conversation about *Black and White*, the final text, when Brendan revealed that he had deliberately changed his stance as a co-reader in order to approach this book with Eve. This was not something we had discussed in advance.

Brendan: After the chat we had last time, I took a step back, just to sort of see how Eve reacted to it really.
Jennifer: Oh that's interesting. Why did you do that?
Brendan: It was just from talking to you. I was thinking, "how much am I steering?" I thought I would try to . . . leave pauses and see what happens. Just be a little less guiding . . . rather than putting my ideas on her, just trying to give her the opportunity.

When pushed to provide a little more detail on the changes to his approach, he said: "I was consciously not putting ideas in her head. It was more of a pull than a push, if you see what I mean? I was trying to extract information from her, rather than impact my views."

As these comments make clear, participating in the study and engaging with the complex texts had prompted Brendan to consider the ideological implications of his role in the shared reading process, including how much he might "steer" his daughter's responses while reading. His deliberate selection of directional language—"pulling," "extracting," "pushing," and "impacting"—also illustrated his recognition of the opposing forces that can shape the "ways with words" at work during something as "simple" as sharing a story at home.[72] Indeed, it is interesting to speculate whether Brendan's decision to remove himself from a more explicitly mediational role during the shared reading of the final text was rooted in his own resistance to the highly controlled and analytical reading practices he experienced as a learner or his desire to encourage his daughter to read widely and for pleasure.

Although they had previously sent the sediment of Brendan's literate habitus into a swirl of resistance, the metafictive texts seemed also to have taught him some valuable lessons about reading as a mediated activity. By using the disruptive potential of metafiction for his own parental, pedagogic purposes in the latter stages of the project ("I thought I would try to . . . leave pauses and see what happens"), Brendan demonstrated that he had consciously improvised at the level of habitus by experimenting with and reconfiguring his normative assumptions about how to read with his daughter.

CONCLUSION

When considered together, it seems that Michelle and Brendan had quite different experiences of the books and apparently quite different sets of understandings to take away from the project. Given the highly subjective nature of reader response, such diversity is not only to be expected but is to be welcomed. Yet despite the sense of difference, there are also points in common that relate to the role of parents as mediators of their children's reading. Through the experience of resistance as a reader response to these deliberately disruptive texts, both Brendan and Michelle were able to describe aspects of their practice that changed. For Michelle, this involved a shift away from quite a rigid approach to shared reading to one that seemed more responsive to the multimodal demands of contemporary texts. For Brendan, the change seemed more epistemological in nature and linked to his heightened awareness of how his own thinking, or "behind the scenes reasoning processes" had an impact on his daughter's reading experiences too.[73]

According to Meek, adults do not often tend to "inspect what they do" when they read, meaning that "*how* we read isn't part of the consciousness we bring to texts."[74] In other words, adult readers are seen to be less likely to engage in meta-level insights about language in use while reading, unless such practices already have a specific role in their daily lives. Yet through their engagement with—and resistance to—the metafictive aspects of the picturebooks in this project, it seemed that adult readers could be cajoled into a more conscious and, in Brendan's case, more deliberate awareness of *how* they read, and what should and could take place when books are shared at home. Given that the responses to metafiction discussed here were made without explicit instruction or scaffolding, it is interesting to consider what else might be possible from these exciting, playful, heterodox texts were such structures sensitively applied. For this reason, perhaps metafictive picture-books can be considered as *training grounds*,[75] as informal teaching spaces in which readers from across the generational divide can learn challenging new lessons about literacy (and beyond) through the experience of making meaning from the complex interrelations between words and pictures.

As suggested in the introduction, focusing on the readers' responses to metafiction also enabled me to consider the ideas about literacy that registered as most dominant. As literary "radioactive isotopes," the "signals" emitted by the metafictive devices indicated that these adult readers had been discombobulated by the metafictive picturebooks' disruption of their usual approach to reading at home.[76] The surprise and resistance with which the parents responded to the texts also suggest that there is a need for concepts such as multiliteracies and visual and critical literacies to be given higher profiles both inside and outside of the classrooms,[77] especially since so many of them have come to greater prominence in recent decades, in part thanks to recent and rapid developments in communicative technologies. In order to do that, it seems vital to find ways of working that do not subordinate parental knowledge to that of the school's and value all literacies practiced. Therefore, if we are to prepare all of our learners to become mediators of twenty-first-century literacies, it seems clear that we need to continue to find new ways for families, schools, and researchers to develop and mediate shared sets of understandings together.

NOTES

1. Angela Bonci, *A Research Review: The Importance of Families and the Home Environment* (London: National Literacy Trust, 2011), 2.

2. Shirley Brice Heath, *Ways with Words* (Cambridge: Cambridge University Press, 1983).

3. Vicky Carrington and Allan Luke, "Literacy and Bourdieu's Sociological Theory: A Reframing," *Language and Education* 11, no. 2 (1997): 96–112, 100.

4. Pierre Bourdieu, *Outline of a Theory of Practice* (Cambridge: Cambridge University Press, 1977), 72.

5. The word "parent" is used here to represent the actual status of the more experienced adult co-readers in this research projects, although it is recognized that family groupings are far from uniform.

6. Louise M. Rosenblatt, "The Aesthetic Transaction," *Journal of Aesthetic Education* 20, no. 4 (1986): 122–28.

7. James P. Gee, "The New Literacy Studies and the 'Social Turn,'" opinion paper (Washington, DC: Institute of Education Sciences (ERIC), 1998),

Jamespaulgee (website), accessed 13 May 2019, http://jamespaulgee.com/pdfs/
The%20New%20Literacy%20Studies%20and%20the%20Social%20Turn.pdf; Brian
Street, *Literacy in Theory and Practice* (Cambridge: Cambridge University Press,
1984).

8. Barbara Tizard and Martin Hughes, *Young Children Learning: Talking and
Thinking at Home and at School* (London: Fontana Press, 1986), 249.

9. Kenneth Hemmerechts, Orhan Agirdag and Dimokritos Kavadias, "The
Relationship between Parental Literacy Involvement, Socio-Economic Status and
Reading Literacy," *Educational Review* 69, no. 1 (2017): 85–101, 85.

10. Shirley Brice Heath, "What No Bedtime Story Means: Narrative Skills at
Home and School," *Language in Society* 2 (1982): 49–76, 50.

11. Bourdieu, *Outline of a Theory*, 72.

12. Kate Pahl, "Habitus in the Home: Texts and Practices in Families," *Ways of
Knowing Journal* 2, no. 1 (2002): 45–53, 48.

13. Carrington and Luke, "Literacy and Bourdieu," 100.

14. Flora Rodriguez-Brown, "Family Literacy: A Current View of Research on
Parents and Children Learning Together," in *Handbook of Reading Research Volume
IV*, eds. Michael Kamil, David Pearson, Elizabeth Moje Birr and Peter Afflerback
(London: Routledge, 2011), 726–53, 734.

15. Greg Brooks and Peter Hannon, "Research Issues in Family Literacy," in
Sage Handbook of Early Childhood Literacy, eds. Jackie Larson and Jackie Marsh
(London: SAGE Publications, 2013), 194–206, 196.

16. Allan Luke, *Reading and Critical Literacy: Redefining the Great Debate*
[conference paper] presented at the 18th New Zealand Conference on Reading,
Wellington, NZ, 1992, 7.

17. Rosenblatt, "The Aesthetic Transaction," 123.

18. Norma Gonzalez, Luis Moll and Cathy Amanti, eds., *Funds of Knowledge:
Theorizing Practices in Households, Communities and Classrooms* (Mahwah, NJ:
Lawrence Erlbaum, 2005).

19. Rosenblatt, "The Aesthetic Transaction," 123.

20. Michael Grenfell, *Pierre Bourdieu: Education and Training* (London:
Continuum Books, 2007), 59.

21. Steph Lawler, "Rules of Engagement: Habitus, Power and Resistance,"
Sociological Review 52, no. 2 (2004): 110–28, 111.

22. Ann Anderson, Jim Anderson, Jacqueline Lynch, Jon Shapiro and Ji Eun Kim,
"Extra-Textual Talk in Shared Book Reading: A Focus on Questioning," *Early Child
Development and Care* 182, no. 9 (2012): 1139–54, 1149.

23. John Shapiro, Jim Anderson and Ann Anderson, "Diversity in Parental
Storybook Reading," *Early Child Development and Care* 127–128 (1997): 47–59.

24. Glynis Cousin, "Exploring Threshold Concepts for Linking Teaching and
Research," (conference paper, The International Colloquium: International Policies
and Practices for Academic Enquiry, Winchester, 2007), accessed January 2021,
https://www.ee.ucl.ac.uk/~mflanaga/Glynis_Cousin_Exploring_.pdf, "Threshold
Concepts: Undergraduate Teaching, Postgraduate Training, Professional Development
and School Education: A Short Introduction and a Bibliography from 2003 to 2018,"
accessed January 2021, https://www.ee.ucl.ac.uk/~mflanaga/thresholds.html.

25. Eve Bearne and Gunther Kress, "Editorial," *Reading* 35, no. 3 (2001): 89–93, 91.

26. For discussions about visual literacy's importance, see Frank Serafini, "Paths to Interpretation: Developing Students' Interpretive Repertoires," *Language and Literacy* 17, no. 3 (2015): 118–33; Evelyn Arizpe and Morag Styles, *Children Reading Pictures: Interpreting Visual Texts* (Hoboken, NJ: Taylor and Francis, 2016).

27. Bearne and Kress, "Editorial," 89.

28. Maria Nikolajeva, "Reading Other People's Minds through Word and Image," *Children's Literature in Education* 43 (2012): 273–29, 278.

29. Margaret Meek, *How Texts Teach What Readers Learn* (Stroud: Thimble Press, 1988), 19.

30. Gunther Kress, "Perspectives on Making Meaning: The Differential Principles and Means of Adults and Children," in *Handbook of Early Childhood Literacy*, eds. Nigel Hall, Jackie Larson and Jackie Marsh (London: SAGE, 2003), 154–66, 155.

31. Kress, "Perspectives on Making Meaning."

32. Elaine Millard and Jackie Marsh, "Sending Minnie the Minx Home: Comics and Reading Choices," *Cambridge Journal of Education* 31, no. 1 (2001): 25–38, 27.

33. Bearne and Kress, "Editorial," 91.

34. Bearne and Kress, "Editorial," 91.

35. Maria Nikolajeva, "Verbal and Visual Literacy: The Role of Picturebooks in the Reading Experience of Young Children," in *Handbook of Early Childhood Literacy*, eds. Nigel Hall, Jackie Larson and Jackie Marsh (London: SAGE, 2003), 235–48, 238.

36. David Lewis, *Reading Contemporary Picturebooks* (London: Routledge Farmer, 2001), 36.

37. Lawrence Sipe, "How Picture Books Work: A Semiotically Framed Theory of Text-Picture Relationships," *Children's Literature in Education* 29, no. 2 (1998): 97–108, 98.

38. David Lewis, "The Constructedness of Texts: Picture Books and the Metafictive," *Signal* 62 (1990): 131–46, 141.

39. Matthew Grenby and Kimberley Reynolds, *Children's Literature Studies: A Research Handbook* (Hampshire: Palgrave Macmillan, 2011), 211.

40. Sipe, "How Picture Books Work," 100.

41. Sipe, "How Picture Books Work," 101.

42. Sipe, "How Picture Books Work," 101.

43. Sipe, "How Picture Books Work," 98.

44. Meek, *How Texts Teach*.

45. Jill McClay, "'Wait a Second . . .': Negotiating Complex Narratives in Black and White," *Children's Literature in Education* 31, no. 2 (2000): 91–106.

46. David Macaulay, *Black and White* (Boston, MA: Houghton Mifflin Harcourt, 1991).

47. McClay, "'Wait a Second . . . ,'" 97, 101.

48. McClay, "'Wait a Second . . . ,'" 103.

49. McClay, "'Wait a Second . . . ,'" 101.

50. Ann Grieve, "Metafictional Play in Children's Fiction," *Papers* 8, no. 3 (1998): 5–15, 5.

51. Lewis, *The Constructedness of Texts*, 144.

52. Lawrence Sipe and Caroline McGuire, "The Stinky Cheese Man and Other Fairly Postmodern Picture Books for Children," in *Shattering the Looking Glass: Challenge, Risk and Controversy in Children's Literature*, ed. Susan Lehr (Norwood, MA: Christopher-Gordon Publishers, 2008), 273–88, 284.

53. Margaret Mackey, "Metafiction for Beginners: Allan Ahlberg's *Ten in a Bed*," *Children's Literature in Education* 21, no. 3 (1990): 179–87, 179.

54. Bridget Fowler, *Reading Bourdieu on Society and Culture* (Keele: Blackwell Publishing/The Sociological Review, 2000), 1.

55. See Kathy Short, "Researching Intertextuality within Collaborative Classroom Learning Environments," *Linguistics and Education* 4, no. 3–4 (1992): 313–33; and Mariana Souto-Manning, "Negotiating Culturally Responsive Pedagogy through Multicultural Children's Literature: Towards Critical Democratic Literacy Practices in a First Grade Classroom," *Journal of Early Childhood Literacy* 9, no. 1 (2009): 50–74.

56. Kate Moles, "A Walk in Thirdspace: Place, Methods and Walking," *Sociological Research Online* 13, no. 4 (2008), http://www.socresonline.org.uk/13/4 /2.html.

57. Alison Phipps, "Intercultural Ethics: Questions of Methods and Intercultural Communication," *Language and Intercultural Communication* 13, no. 1 (2013): 10–26, 18.

58. Peter Freebody and Allan Luke, "Literacies Programs: Debates and Demands in Cultural Context," *Prospect: An Australian Journal of TESOL* 5, no. 3 (1990): 7–16; Frank Serafini, "Expanding the Four Resources Model: Reading Visual and Multi-Modal Texts," *Pedagogies: An International Journal* 7, no. 2 (2012): 150–64; Mary Ryan and Michele Anstey, "Identity and Text: Developing Self-Conscious Readers," *Australian Journal of Language and Literacy* 26, no. 1 (2003): 9–22.

59. Ryan and Anstey, "Identity and Text," 13.

60. Carrington and Luke, "Literacy and Bourdieu," 100.

61. Allan Ahlberg and Paul Howard, *The Bravest Ever Bear* (London: Walker Books, 1999); Meg McKinley and Leila Rudge, *No Bears* (London: Walker Books, 2013); David Wiesner, *The Three Pigs* (Boston, MA: Houghton Mifflin Harcourt, 2001); David Macaulay, *Black and White* (Boston, MA: Houghton Mifflin Harcourt, 1991).

62. Maria Nikolajeva and Carole Scott, "The Dynamics of Picturebook Communication," *Children's Literature in Education* 31, no. 4 (2000): 225–39, 232.

63. Biff and Chip are the names of two main characters in the Oxford Reading Tree basal program.

64. For discussion of the tensions between words and pictures, see Meek, *How Texts Teach* as well as Kress, *Perspectives on Meaning Making* and Nikolajeva, *Visual and Verbal Literacy.*

65. Vivienne Smith, *Making Reading Mean* (Royston, Herts: UKLA, 2005), 22.

66. Barbara Bader as cited by Lewis, *Reading Contemporary Picturebooks*, 1.

67. For discussions of metafiction, see Sylvia Pantaleo, "Young Children Interpret the Metafictive in Anthony Browne's *Voices in the Park*," *Journal of Early*

Childhood Literacy 4, no. 2 (2004): 211–33, and Bette Goldstone, "The Postmodern Picture Book: A New Subgenre," *Language Arts* 81, no. 3 (2004): 196–204.

68. Pahl, "Habitus in the Home," 48.

69. Pahl, "Habitus in the Home," 48.

70. Fowler, *Reading Bourdieu*, 1.

71. Diane Reay, "'It's All Becoming a Habitus': Beyond the Habitual Use of Habitus in Educational Research," *British Journal of Sociology in Education* 25, no. 4 (2004): 431–44, 433.

72. Heath, *Ways with Words.*

73. Sipe and McGuire, "The Stinky Cheese Man," 286.

74. Meek, *How Texts Teach,* 36.

75. Maria Nikolajeva, "Picturebooks and Emotional Literacy," *The Reading Teacher* 67, no. 4 (2013): 249–54, 254.

76. Gee, "The New Literacy Studies," 24.

77. New London Group, "A Pedagogy of Multiliteracies: Designing Social Futures," *Harvard Educational Review* 66, no. 1 (1996): 60–92.

Part IV

TEXTS, WORLDS, AND MEDIATION

Chapter 7

Mediating the Act of Reading through Picturebooks and Fictional Readers

Evelyn Arizpe

The ways in which acts of reading are represented, and books are culturally situated within books, reveal a great deal about a given society's expectations and beliefs about literacy practices. Within children's literature in the Western world, there is a long history of characters who are readers or who have become readers by the end of the book, deriving benefit and pleasure in the process. Most of these texts emphasize the message that the act of reading is a significant and esteemed activity. They also tend to stress the importance of books in the traditional codex form and endorse them as powerful objects, whether it be as tools for social mobility, as cultural capital, or as magical artifacts. Therefore, it is perhaps not surprising that given the anxieties around the perceived decrease in children's reading and the pervasiveness of digital technology (along with fears about the "death" of the printed book), the turn of the century has been marked by the production of contemporary children's literature, and particularly books aimed at emerging readers, that directly and heavily emphasizes the value of reading and books.

This emphasis can be seen in the plethora of picturebooks in English that have been published since 2000 which are about readers, reading, and the printed book. Yet, as Jessica Pressman points out, the "aesthetic of bookishness" is not new and "the fetishized focus on textuality and the book-bound reading object" has historically been a response to the feared "death of the book."[1] However, she observes that in (adult) novels published since 2000, there is a different "tone and ambition" that emerges from the novel's constant innovation "in relation to its contemporary environment of popular culture and media, [and] so too do these novels expose how the literary book needs the threat of its demise as stimulus for its defense."[2] I would argue that this defense also applies to children's fiction, where it comes across with even more urgency and employs the medium that most appeals to those who must be converted into readers as soon as possible and that is unique in its double impact: the picturebook.

Following the well-established tradition of children's fiction, picturebooks about readers and reading are vehicles for the cultural assumptions and ideological aspirations that reflect the desires adults project upon childhood. Claudia Nelson has accurately noted that these texts represent what adults wish childhood reading to be.[3] As a result, there is often an idealized celebration of the act of reading print in these picturebooks, which leaves the reader in no doubt that books are worthy and captivating and that reading them is not only necessary but also fun.[4] Erika Hateley sums up the impact this is meant to have on the construction of the child's subjectivity:

> Children's literature predominantly seeks to convey a positive understanding of reading, modelling for the implied child reader an idealised reading experience that shapes the self and improves the subject's relation to the world.[5]

With characters that children can relate to, images that even very young children can understand, and affordances that draw attention to the book and the act of reading itself, picturebooks are perfect intermediaries between emerging readers and the world of books and reading. In addition, these texts can help develop critical literacy skills as they encourage reflection on what it means to be literate. Finally, they ostensibly leave the "modeling" to fictional child readers (sometimes in the guise of animals) who teach their peers how books should be treated, read, and enjoyed. This allows for the child characters' agency, as adults can "hide behind the bookshelves" and only appear when required, but it also supports real readers who may not have parents or carers that can perform this mediating role.

Picturebooks are not the only form of children's literature that provides a reflection on reading. Recent young adult (YA) fiction also often deals with issues around the control of reading, censorship, and/or "dangerous" books,[6] although fictional readers have been appearing in children's and YA literature for many decades and their metafictive devices have drawn the attention of scholars such as Claudia Nelson, Poushali Bhaudry, and Joe Sutliff Sanders.[7] These devices are usually intended to help create an awareness of how books and fiction work and at the same time are a sophisticated form of play. Nelson notes that metafictional texts tend to feature messages about the pleasures of narrative in general: "Among their defining traits is a shared emphasis on the delight associated with immersing oneself in story, a delight that the complexity of their construction seeks to replicate for the reader."[8] While the narratives in most metafictive picturebooks are necessarily shorter and tend to address less challenging topics, the visual possibilities create other complexities that show that the relationship between children and books is not always straightforward, and they raise equally complex philosophical questions to do with reality and fiction.

In this chapter, I will argue that the act of reading printed books, as visually represented by fictional readers in picturebooks, is a form of mediating that ideal vision that adults have of a reader's engagement with the codex in childhood. Although other scholars have drawn attention to aspects of the role of reading, books, and metafiction in picturebooks (Frank Serafini; Rebecca-Anne Do Rozario; Nina Goga; Erika Hateley and Morag Styles and Mary Anne Wolpert), they all refer to a limited range of texts.[9] Through an analysis of a corpus of picturebooks in English published since 2000, this chapter extends the critical exploration of the phenomenon of fictional readers and reading in picturebooks within the literary field, focusing on the following common traits: the book as object, the physical performance of reading, the social and affective act of reading, book culture (vs. popular or digital culture), and intertextuality.[10] These traits call attention to significant changes in traditional images of the reader (in Western culture) in terms of personal qualities as well as to the associated cultural practices and the social consequences of the act of reading. As a result of their affordances, some of these picturebooks are also becoming essential intermediaries between the changing status of the book in its historical codex format and the younger "digital" generations.

THE LEGACY OF HISTORICAL PERCEPTIONS OF READING

Underlying the invitation to children to imagine themselves as readers who enjoy stories, make friends, and explore real and fantastical worlds are perceptions of the act of reading that are rooted in history. They subscribe to different but related aspirations of Western society in the construction of childhood and are not only deeply embedded in the cultural imaginary but also in the socioeconomic context. The most prominent vision draws on the "romance of reading" narrative that emerges from Romantic conceptions of childhood and tends to be imbued with nostalgia. The representations of reading in children's literature are also related to moral values that tend to position readers and the act of reading as virtuous, with characters who are morally "good" engaging in this positive activity. Vivienne Smith and I have argued that in contemporary texts that celebrate reading, what seems to be happening is "a re-manifestation of the romantic ideal of childhood" where electronic literacy is seen "as a threat to the innocence of the child" and thus, "the book itself, the artefact not the content, has become a symbol for what we want childhood to be."[11] This vision is linked to the contemporary belief that children who were not read to when they were very young or do not read are somehow missing out on childhood itself. While this belief can be contested, it can have profound consequences for a child's education given the book-centric notions that persist in schools and other educational and cultural spaces, along with particular expectations, such as bedtime stories or visits to the library, of literacy-related behaviors.[12]

The "romantic" vision of a child absorbed in a book (text and/or pictures) is not without its contradictions, as it can also imply that a child is out of reach, "escaping" into another world and perhaps becoming "lost" in it. Historically, fictional young female readers who ignore the advice of their elders in terms of the content of their books and the amount of time spent on them suffer for this, as in the famous examples of *The Female Quixote* by Charlotte Lennox (1752) or *Northanger Abbey* by Jane Austen (1817). There is also the issue of content, with censorship occurring at many different levels and applied to wildly differing topics (from gothic novels to Disney princesses or LGBTQ themes). Underlying most contradictions, however, is a historic tension between the need for literacy for educational empowerment and a suspicion on the part of the establishment of what this empowerment might lead to in social, cultural, and ideological terms.

This leads to a second perception of the act of reading which has a more pressing agenda: the production of a (emerging) literate subject and the learning of "ways of taking from books" that are valued in society.[13] Literacy learning is linked to the function that schools, libraries, and bookshops play in education and in narratives of social mobility and cultural capital. In the UK, these narratives can be traced back to the first appearance of fictional readers in books intended for children in the eighteenth century. Patricia Crain confirms that this perception of the act of reading was present in early children's books, which presented the pragmatic benefit of learning to read and write, not only for the character but for society and the economy, such as *The History of Little Goody Two Shoes* published by John Newbery in 1765.[14] In this text, there is a personal benefit in that Goody not only becomes a rich lady due to her learning and virtue, but also, as Crain shows, derived from the text is an economic benefit to the developing print marketplace and the world of commerce in general.[15] Publishers benefited from new ideas about childhood which encouraged education and reading as well as from the growth of the middle class which meant that parents could afford to buy books for their children.[16]

Valuing and treating books properly was a part of this literary and cultural education, and children's relationship to these material artifacts was important because these were commodities they could consider their own.[17] Many of these early books depict children as active readers having conversations around books and playing games or creating performances based on their reading, and we know from historical accounts that children of the educated classes would have done the same as their fictional counterparts.[18] Grenby notes that publishers were creating books that were both playful and aesthetically appealing, for example, in terms of format and illustration, with the result that "the pleasures of children's literature could be more material than textual."[19]

By the beginning of the twenty-first century we have a wealth of children's literature that offers a variety of topics, formats, aesthetic modes, and reading experiences, but we also have serious competition for readers' time in the form of electronic gadgets that offer an overwhelming choice of different activities, many of which still involve reading but in diverse ways. Margaret Mackey speculates that because children now meet printed books as "one option out of many," the "bookness" of the book has become more visible and authors and illustrators have consciously played on this change by inviting readers to note the elements that make a book a book, from its physical construction to its aesthetic possibilities.[20] In other words, this trend responds to the need to introduce, or even reintroduce, the elements of a printed book to children. Based on the historical link noted by David Lewis between the development of the early picturebook and that of the trade of games and toys,[21] Hateley observes that the development of computer games and other forms of interactive reading and playing in the twenty-first century is linked to the publication of picturebooks on "metareading." She defines "metareading" as "reading about reading" and argues that it "invites young readers to identify with the 'right' kind of reading, not only in terms of content but also of medium";[22] however, she notes that not all books about books are books about reading and what it signifies.[23] Do Rozario similarly argues that the representations of books in books, where they are valued as material objects, are deliberate and a result of "a publishing environment increasingly looking toward the e-book and the dematerialization of text and illustration."[24] She concludes that "it is the ability to synthesize this materiality with narrative itself that distinguishes picturebooks."[25] From the perspectives of Mackey, Hateley, and Do Rozario, picturebooks thus have a significant role to play in mediating the change between "old" and "new" technologies and the perceptions that accompany this change.

"BIBLIOPHILIC PICTUREBOOKS"

Erica Hateley (2013) uses the term "bibliophilic picturebooks" to refer to picturebooks that profess and encourage a love of books. It is ironic that the visual has become one of the main modes for impressing on the reader the importance of reading given that, before the digital turn, there was an anxiety that the "visual turn" and the move from the "dominance of writing" to the "dominance of image" in books for children (among other cultural artifacts) would have an adverse effect on readers.[26] However, it is not just the visual but the overall affordances of the picturebook that means it has become one of the main literary artifacts for exploring the "bookness" of books. Mackey notes that the features of postmodern picturebooks, which include metafiction, fragmentation, and a mixing of genres, "virtually put readers *inside* book systems" and that "to read these books coherently, it is necessary to know these systems and to bring their possibilities and constraints into play."[27] Morag Styles and Maryanne Wolpert also consider play and performance in a selection of postmodern picturebooks,[28] looking at the how the "invitations, challenges and affordances" of key texts "have shaped new understandings of what we mean by reading, what this means for readers."[29] This chapter extends the work of Mackey and Styles and Wolpert by expanding the corpus and building on the idea of how picturebooks have been "shaping" new understandings of reading and how fictional characters mediate the act of reading to those beginning their reading lives.

The corpus for this project comprises thirty-six picturebooks published in the United Kingdom or the United States between 2000 and 2018[30] that have readers, reading, and/or books at the core of the story and which are easily available through bookshops or online purchase.[31] The focus on fictional readers means that fictionalized biography and realistic stories about characters who acquire literacy skills (such as those explored by Kuhlman and Lickteig or Mathis and Patterson) were excluded.[32] Initially only picturebooks with the words "reading," "book," or "library" were included, resulting in a selection of thirty-two books. However, four other books have also been included despite not meeting the title criteria, because readers, reading, and/or books are at their core and some of their features proved significant for this study: *Wolves* and *Again!* by Emily Gravett and *Look!* by Jeff Mack are classic metafictive stories about reading, with paratextual features referring to books and libraries; and *Detective Dog* by Julia Donaldson (illustrated by Sara Ogilvie) was included because it is the only picturebook that shows a classroom and a teacher. The resulting corpus includes well-established author/illustrators as well as newcomers to the publishing field. Inevitably, the collection is incomplete because it was not possible to identify and locate every single picturebook related to the topic and because it was not possible to set a rigid line in terms of quantifying their representations of reading.[33] In any case, the objective of the project was not to create an exhaustive list but to widen the range of picturebooks that have been the object of other studies and to consider publications from the beginning of the twenty-first century. Each picturebook was coded according to a series of basic questions around who reads, what, where, and with whom, which were extended to more complex questions around the purpose and consequences of reading and the literary and visual devices most commonly used to represent the reader, the book, and the act of reading.

No matter their focus, all these picturebooks celebrate reading (whether it is fiction or nonfiction) and imply that books are enjoyable, especially when they are linked to play and shared with others. Some of the common patterns that surfaced have to do with the positioning of the intended audience as emerging readers. This positioning includes knowledge about the "bookness" of books, about intertextuality, about libraries and bookshops, what each of these spaces offers and how to behave within them. Out of the thirty-six picturebooks, twenty-two have elements of metafiction and make use of metalepsis to emphasize the parallels between the story and the book held in the readers' hands and to increase readers' understanding of how books and fiction work. Intertextual links to fairy tales are another commonality. All the books are set within a Western cultural background; the majority of the human children represented are white and none suggest that any of the fictional readers live in poverty.[34]

It would seem that, overall, the intention of contemporary authors and illustrators is to merge "romantic" and "pragmatic" notions into that "idealized reading experience" for the child,[35] where reading is not only linked to the emotions, the imagination, and virtue but also to a skill that allows access to knowledge and increases intellectual prowess. Both images and text mediate this ideal notion in a way that suggests that children who are engaged with books are clever and are also having fun, usually with their peers. Yet, a closer examination of this idealization, reveals, five notable gaps or absences in this picturebook corpus. They are briefly noted here because of their significance, but I will discuss them in more depth later in the chapter.

The first of these gaps is the presence of adults as mediators. Despite the fact that with a few exceptions these picturebooks will mostly be read *to* children *by* adults—most of whom are librarians—it is fictional children that encourage reading or teach other fictional children or anthropomorphic animals about books. Linked to this need for a mediating fictional reader is the lack of images of solitary readers absorbed in a book.[36] Even when a reader is shown to have their nose (or snout) in a book, they tend to be surrounded by other readers, either children or animals, but not adults. The third absence is perhaps more striking: that of the school or classroom and of teachers while, on the other hand, libraries are common settings (perhaps as a reaction to library closures). A fourth absence has to do with the lack of ephemeral texts from popular culture texts. Finally, also striking, is the conspicuous absence of digital devices.[37]

Along with revealing absences, the analysis of the corpus identified the ways in which these picturebooks are positioning books and reading as a social and shared pleasure and as potential transformative tools. However, before entering into the discussion of how this positioning is done, it is worth referring to Robin Bernstein's argument that however much children's literature is considered a potential model or tool "to achieve a special effect highly desired—by adults,"[38] there are cases where this effect cannot be achieved without the child's participation. Bernstein examines the case of the "going-to-bed-books," but this can also be applied to "get reading" books. Forcing someone to get in bed or to read may be possible, but forcing someone to sleep or to read for pleasure is not. Nor is it possible, as parents and teachers well know, to force a child to become a reader. Extrapolating from Bernstein's argument, "get-reading-books," just like "going-to-bed-books," reveal the limit of adult power and other methods must be employed so that these textual "tools" achieve their goal. In the case of the picturebook, it is the persuasive use of its affordances that can help the adult to get a child to read and enjoy it. Therefore, by examining the affordances, it is possible to identify the ways in which adults, particularly those with vested interests such as authors, illustrators, and publishers, use these affordances to attempt to shape the relationship between children and books.

PICTUREBOOK AFFORDANCES

The features that allow the picturebook to carry out this mediating role so effectively emerge from the distinctive characteristic of this genre: the crucial interaction between words and images. From the title to the back cover, both words and images must work together with the reader to construct the narrative; if the reader can dispense with one or the other, then the work cannot be defined as a picturebook.[39]

The overall design of a picturebook presents its creators with the opportunity to use the peritext in ways that would be more difficult in a purely text-based narrative. The size and shape of some hardcover versions of books in my corpus draw attention to the book as an object. Dust-jackets, textured hardcovers, endpapers, back covers, dedications, gutter, and even publishing information can be used to call attention to books as objects and reading. For example, in *The Red Book* attention is focused on the object of reading starting from the moment the reader looks at the cover where the lack of a title on the dustjacket, along with its red color and the image of a child running with a red book under their arm, refers to the book which held by the "real" reader. In *Look!*, the title page double spread includes a realistic library card with a due date of 2050, a broken book spine and a rather crumpled page on which an endearing gorilla gazes directly at the book in his hand. The endpapers of *This Is Not a Picture Book!* contain words telling the book's story, although in the front endpapers the letters of each word are not in the right order, making the reader sympathize with the duckling's struggle to read a book with no pictures. Several books have more than one title page, and some front or back covers make use of *mise en abyme* such as in *Who's Afraid of the Big Bad Book?* and *Charlie Cook's Favourite Book.*

Supported by a range of bright colors and large fonts, the covers of these picturebooks present the most immediate appeal to potential readers. They tend to immediately signal what they will be about through the title and the cover image. *Look!* and *This Is Not a Picture Book!* draw attention to visual reading and, as it does in another six titles, the exclamation mark denotes a demand or strong emotions. It is notable that the word "read" only appears in one title (*Bears Don't Read!*), perhaps to avoid any associations with educational demands. With few exceptions, there is usually an image of a book on the cover and they tend to be held by one or more characters. The immediate suggestion of a link between books and shared happiness is obvious in that although among the thirty-six book covers, only one character, Red Reading Hood, is actually looking down at the book; all the rest look at another character or out at the reader. In addition, of the characters who are holding books, all look content or are smiling, with two exceptions: Ralfy, the Rabbit Burglar (*Wanted!*), who has been caught stealing books, and the duckling who is upset because the book has no pictures (*This Is Not a Picture Book!*).

Presenting a character on the cover holding a book calls to mind stereotypes about readers; usually, that they are "different" in some way and this is confirmed by most of the stories. As the title suggests, in *Bears Don't Read!* George is first misunderstood by other bears because he seems to want more from life than they do and later by all adults except Emily's mother when he becomes interested in learning to read. Like George, readers (or would-be readers) are often isolated at the beginning of the story (interestingly, they tend to be animals rather than children), but by the end they are surrounded by friends who also love reading. Overall, there seems to be a move away from using eyeglasses to indicate that a character is a reader; only two of the protagonist (child) readers wear them: Princess Marta in *Prince Ribbet* and Peter, the owner of Nell, the Detective Dog. The suggested link between glasses and cleverness remains, but this does not mark characters who wear glasses out as "different" to their peers. This differs from Serafini's findings in his picturebook analysis, which suggested that reader characters who wear glasses and are often "closeted bookworms" cannot be "normal" and engage in activities such as sport or watching television.[40] Whether this is because Serafini was analyzing books from before 2000 and the more recent corpus represents a new trend is a hypothesis that would require further exploration.

Running through the design, images, and text of the books in the corpus are the twin threads of humor and playfulness, both physical and imaginative.[41]

Humor ranges from slapstick to parodies of existing book titles (a nod to the adult reader). For example, in the most complex text within this corpus, *Wild about Books*, where animals take to reading (and later, writing), the author uses animal characteristics and book types to raise a laugh:

Giraffes wanted tall books and crickets craved small books,
While geckos could only read stick-to-the-wall books.
The pandas demanded more books in Chinese.
Molly filled their requests, always eager to please.
She even found waterproof books for the otter,
Who never went swimming without Harry Potter.[42]

Other books mentioned in the text or which appear in the images are *Uncle Vanya, Candide,* and *The Grass [sic] Menagerie* all read by llamas "while eating their llunches [sic]." Giraffes read about basketball, crocodiles read *Peter Pan*, raccoons read "Trash," and baby bunnies read *Goodnight Moon.* This type of textual and visual intertextuality will be discussed in more detail here, but *Wild about Books* is an example of how messages about reading can be supported through the amalgamation of images and words.

Playfulness is linked to the two most commonly used literary features in this corpus: metafiction and visual metalepsis. In particular, visual play on the book the reader is holding in their hands and the boundaries between story-worlds invite the imagination to take a more active role. This role involves the construction of the narrative, but it also leads to a reflection on how stories are constructed and the reading process itself. The majority of these picturebooks highlight the nature of the book as a material object, made of sheets of paper that are bound together and which exist alongside other objects in children's every-day lives that can be played with, broken, or ignored and which occupy specific spaces in room, bookshelves, the floor, or tables. Through their metafictive and metaleptic devices picturebooks make us question the ontological status of read-ers and of the object they have in their hands; they problematize and challenge the relationship between the imaginary, the fictional and the real and what we do as readers not only around the act of reading but also during the act of reading.

Authors and illustrators invest books with lives of their own or imagine lives going on inside the books themselves, even when there are no readers to open the books. The book characters perform metaleptic jumps, looking for a different or better story to "move into," as in *Otto the Book Bear*, or moving by mistake as Bella and Ben do in *We're in the Wrong Book!* (they find themselves in different genres including a sticker book and a fairy tale story app). If, rather than a character coming out of a book, the fictional reader somehow ends up in the book they are reading, they not only impact on the narrative but also cause a physical change in the images through this intrusion: in *Interrupting Chicken*, the little chicken "interrupts" the fairy tales being read to her by her Papa in order to ensure the safety of characters such as Hansel and Gretel, thus changing the well-known endings. In *Who's Afraid of the Big Bad Book*, Herb causes mayhem for characters, words, and pictures in the books he is reading but manages to put things as right as he can before returning to his own storyworld.

Visual metalepsis is a main feature in these picturebooks as it allows characters from different storyworlds or diegetic levels to be seen in the same space.[43] We often see both the diegetic narrative and the extradiegetic narrative on the same spread, as in *Interrupting Chicken* or in Emily Gravett's picturebooks, especially in *Again!* and *Wolves*, where we can see both the reader reading in the foreground and what the reader is reading (or looking at) in the background. *Mise en abyme* confuses reality and fiction in *Baxter's Book*, when it is revealed that the "special book" Baxter longs for is the book that real readers already have in their hands (and a careful reader will note that even as Baxter is looking for ways to "be in a book," his Owl friend is already reading *Baxter's Book*). The coupling of different diegetic planes works not only to make a point about the connection between fiction and reality during the act of reading but also signals the multiple possibilities of humor and book-play a picturebook can offer a perceptive viewer, preparing them for more complex textual literary metafiction. Together with the other affordances of the picturebook, it also prepares them for understanding the "bookness of books" as it calls attention to the book as visual and narrative object.

THE BOOK AS MATERIAL OBJECT

In these picturebooks, books appear as physical artifacts that invite contemplation and are mainly associated with pleasure and play. These associations can be found in a picturebook intended for the very young, *Books Always Everywhere*, which reflects the theories of educators and psychologists who stress not only the emotional importance of sharing books with babies but also the cognitive and aesthetic importance of the physical exploration of books at these early developmental stages.[44] Even more than the illustrations, the simple but effective rhythm and rhyme of the text and the coupling of the repeated word "book" with nouns, verbs, and adjectives convey the materiality and potential for engagement with this object: "Book build/ Book mat/ Book chair/ Book hat."[45] In the rest of the picturebooks, the focus is on moving from the book as a toy to play with, toward other pleasures related to books, such as sitting comfortably and quietly close to a friend and carefully turning the pages. In fact, readers are clearly encouraged to treat books with care, such as in *Look!*, where the gorilla learns the consequences of trying to juggle books. There is no suggestion in any of the picturebooks that books are too valuable to play with; they are mostly "treated casually," as Nina Goga found in her analysis of the placement of books in Scandinavian picturebooks. Her finding can also be applied to this corpus: books "are there to be used, to be read, to be held in and to be part of daily life."[46]

It is access to as many books as possible in order to read them rather than to possess them that is shown to matter in these picturebooks, reflecting an awareness of the socioeconomic and cultural implications of this access. While bookshops appear in three of them (both the ones in *Baxter's Book* and *Maisy Goes to the Bookshop* present enticing book displays), the only instance of a character buying a book and a reference to paying money is in the Maisy book. There are few overt mentions, among these thirty-six books, of the pleasure of book ownership, and even when Maisy does buy a book, it is to give as a gift. Baxter leaves the bookshop with a load of books, but he is so happy that he does not even notice a few have fallen off his cart. Taking other people's books, however, is frowned upon even if it is done because the thief loves reading and they did not mean to "keep" them as in the cases of the Snatchabook; Ted, in *The Detective Dog*, and Ralfy in *Wanted!*. The Snatchabook has no mother or father to read to him, Ted was just "borrowing" them, and Ralfy explains, "I just can't get enough books." This is the opportunity for characters (especially Ted, who comes across as a rather scruffy adult without much education) and readers to learn that there are public places called libraries where reading is "free."

Excessive consumption of books is also not recommended, a point made literally and humorously by Oliver Jeffers in *The Incredible Book Eating Boy*, where the character eventually learns it is better to read books than to eat them. Jeffers places the intended reader as a book lover who knows better than Henry: "Henry loved books. But not like you and I love books, no. Not quite. . . ."[47] Jeffers also shows that by eating books, Henry is being selfish because then "no one else can enjoy them." On the other hand, readers are warned that books can be consuming, sometimes also "literally," as in *This Book Ate My Dog* or *Wolves*, with the latter suggesting that it can be dangerous to read about certain topics. Finally, there is a suggestion that these dangers could be avoided by sharing the act of reading with others, a significant activity within the examined corpus which will be discussed further on.

READING AS PHYSICAL PERFORMANCE

In the interaction with a picturebook, a reader's body plays a central part in the act of reading, as do the bodies of fictional readers represented in the images in these books. None of them sit up straight; they lean forward, their head bent at an angle. They lie or sit, on the floor, on beanbags, swings, beds, comfy chairs, or even on the books themselves. The look on their faces is usually that of interest and concentration, and the expression of those who are listening or reading along with them is of contentment, wonder, or surprise. The frequent use of the word "love" in relation to book or stories is reflected in the act of holding books close to their bodies with their hands or paws, smelling them, touching them, and especially hugging them.

Because of this close interaction, the reader makes a physical impact on the book. Through the characters of Herb (*Beware of Storybook Wolves* and *Who's Afraid of the Big Bad Book*) or Little Mouse (*Little Mouse's Big Book of Fears* and *Little Mouse's Big Book of Beasts*) and Cedric, the baby dragon (*Again!*), the reader becomes an active agent in the process of what, depending on the point of view, could be considered as either destructive or artistic rewriting. Sometimes, this "de-sacralization" of the book can have unexpected consequences because it results in a new creation which suits the reader better, as in the case of Little Mouse who deals with fears or danger-ous beasts in this way. Thus, pages are torn or scribbled on, images are cut out and glued back in, spines are broken, holes are gnawed or burned through pages, and spines can be broken as readers use hands, claws, or teeth to cre-ate alternative narratives. The traversing of fictional boundaries brings home these transgressive book behaviors even more strongly because of the illusion that it is the very same book that "real" and "fictional" readers have in their hands and can physically interact with.

In the series created by Richard Byrne (*This Book Ate My Dog!*, *We Are in the Wrong Book!* and *This Book Is Out of Control!*—note the exclamation marks) he uses the affordances of the picturebook together with metafic-tion to persuade the reader to carry out this interaction by shaking, blowing, "swiping" and "pressing" buttons in order to help the characters "out" of the book, back into the "correct" book or just to regain control of the stories. The appeal to the reader to interact with the material object they have in their hands implies these readers have the power to "change" the outcome in the storyworld. Although the physical interaction is an illusion, it also calls atten-tion to the potential power that a reader has for creating alternative narratives, which can have social and affective consequences.

THE SPACES FOR THE SOCIAL AND
AFFECTIVE ACT OF READING

The answers to questions about where fictional readers read, and with whom, led to the conclusion that in this corpus these two aspects are closely linked, and they point to reading as a highly social and affective act. Fictional readers in these picturebooks end up making friends (with peers—either humans or animals) and reading with them, usually in communal spaces. The absent or marginal role of adults has already been noted, but it is worth exploring further. In *Books Always Everywhere*, the babies are reading in the company of animals, peers, or perhaps siblings, but there are no adults. Of the five books that show "children" reading with "parents," only two pairs are human (Luna and her father in *Luna Loves Library Day* and Herb and his mother in *Beware of Storybook Wolves*), and it can be assumed they are all reading at bedtime, in their respective "bedrooms." These images conform to more traditional expectations of parents or carers reading before bedtime, although both Cedric (*Again!*) and little chicken (*Interrupting Chicken*) subvert the bedtime story by interrupting or demanding the story be read again and again.

Apart from these parents, the other adult mediators, with one exception, are (female) librarians who suggest titles to shy or reluctant readers, as in the case of *A Library Book for Bear*. These librarians, including "The Little Librarian" who is represented as a child in *The Midnight Library*, are accepting of any would-be reader, whether it is a lion, a bear, or a mouse and invite them to help or join story time. The librarian in *Wild about Books* is used to "conquering resistance" to reading and cunningly starts by reading aloud to encourage the animals to come nearer. Other adult characters tend to be either helpless or naive, such as the bookshop keeper in *The Little Bookshop . . .* or they misunderstand the desire for books and stories that drive the actions of some of the animal characters, such as Ralfy the Rabbit, Library Lion, George the Bear and Franklin the Dragon, among others. These characters are viewed with suspicion by most human adults because they want to read, learn to read, or share stories within the human world. While a couple of understanding adults provide some help, it is either children or other animals who ensure a happy ending by saving the bookshop, finding the lost books or the right books and even encouraging writing.

A teacher appears in only one out of the thirty-six books, *The Detective Dog*, but he is not shown reading to or with a child and he is useless at finding the missing books. This is also one of the only two books in the corpus that contains an image of a classroom. The focus of this classroom is definitely on books and reading as well as on writing and art activities that are tied to the books. The other book that shows a classroom scene is *The Incredible Book-eating Boy,* but no books are included in it. None of the images in any of these picturebooks shows an adult teaching a child to read. Emma's mother supports the idea of George the Bear learning to read, but it is Emma who teaches him (with her mother in the background) in her garden. *The Detective Dog* thus seems to be the exception that proves the rule that school is not about enjoying books or reading for pleasure. Although it could be argued that most intended readers are preschool children and therefore any social or affective positioning of reading occurs in the space of the home or the library, the absence of the school space raises questions about how it is currently perceived in relation to reading and to overall book culture.

Reading is strongly promoted as a social and affective act. In *This Is Not a Picturebook!* the duckling and the bug learn an important lesson together: reading words creates images and makes you feel things (sadness and fear as well as joy). Although there are a few images of readers evidently enjoying books on their own, there is an associated suggestion of loneliness, and the endings strongly imply that reading is more of a pleasure when it is shared, or at least done in a shared space. Ralfy is shown reading on his own at the start of the picturebook, but this solitary reading gets him into trouble which is only sorted when he finds a "book buddy." Dog is surrounded by fictional characters when he reads ("When he read, he forgot that he was alone,"[48]) but he only really looks happy when a girl walks into the shop and reads and plays with him. The crying wolf reader in *The Midnight Library* is consoled when the sad book is shared with The Little Librarian and the owl assistants who (of course) know the book has a happy ending. It may be that this communal aspect of reading is an attempt to mitigate the reality of readers who do not have parents or carers with the economic means to buy these expensive books, the time, or the linguistic or cultural skills to read them. These readers are perhaps assumed to have more "need" of this mediation. So, despite encouraging a strong attachment to books, these books gently push the solitary reader toward a community space where the affection for books, the pleasures of reading and book culture can be (safely and inexpensively) shared.

BOOK CULTURE VS. POPULAR AND DIGITAL CULTURE

Each of these picturebooks acts as a mediator between emerging readers and book culture, stressing bits of knowledge that can help children become more familiar with it. The child who is learning about this culture is placed as more knowing than the animals who want to be part of the reading community but need the "keys" to access it and be accepted. Although being "different" in other respects, Library Lion, George the Bear, and Library Mouse are all "new" to this book culture and their initial efforts are regarded with suspicion. Franklin the Dragon and Dog already love books and stories, but it is only children who recognize and share their passion.

Some books focus on what books can do: provide enjoyment, feed the imagination, offer information and facts. Reading aloud and rereading are represented as extending this enjoyment. Because Library Mouse read so much, "his imagination brimmed over with wonder and fantasy" and he becomes an author himself.[49] Readers are able to "travel" to different places through the fictional version of *The Red Book*. Several picturebooks highlight the links between reading, creative writing, art and music, showing fictional readers painting or writing their own books. Others draw attention not only to the elements that constitute a book (publishing information, title page, blurb, etc.) but also to other texts that surround the practices of reading books (even if some of this is now obsolete): library cards, library stamps, book labeling, ex-libris, book prizes, book ratings, and even book reviews. While the pleasure and value of owning books is less important than access (Ralfy Rabbit and Charlie Cook are the only obsessive book collectors), overall, the texts in the corpus suggest that having books around contributes to learning and literacy and creates links to art and general culture. All of these reminders of what books can "do" encourage implied readers to develop "their understanding of books as a cultural and literary formative arena."[50]

Book culture includes the way books are handled and treated. The librarian in *Wild about Books* gives specific instructions to the animals about looking after their books. The fairy godmother in *Who's Afraid . . .* scolds Herb in no uncertain terms: "What do you expect when you go about scribbling and snippering and generally causing mayhem? This is no way to treat a book, you know!"[51] At least five characters damage books, with the illustrators of these picturebooks ironically setting a "bad" example themselves by "literally" showing and creating the effects of breaking spines, cutting or burning holes, spilling food and taking bites. Finally, book culture also means knowing about libraries and how to behave in them, especially not making loud noises, although libraries are also shown to be hospitable places where other activities can take place (e.g. playing music in the "activity room") and where understanding librarians help find the "perfect" book, share stories or teach how to borrow books.

Although all of these picturebooks seem to be trying to avoid an explicit link between reading and intellectual or cultural snobbery, the inferences are clearly there. The implied reader is culturally positioned as someone who will benefit from accessing this knowledge, becoming "clever" enough to avoid certain behaviors on the one hand and display a familiarity with this culture. However, it remains completely book-centric. Other types of print and/or screen media culture are for the most part ignored: there are very few examples of texts such as magazines, comics, recipes, leaflets, or newspapers. Only one of the characters watches television, but even he is forced to abandon it for a book when a book-loving gorilla knocks the set over.

Digital culture is also ignored. Only one book, *We Are in the Wrong Book!*, refers to an app, but it does not make the reference explicit in words; readers are expected to understand, through the illustrations and app commands, that the characters have ended up in the story app of Little Red Riding Hood. Only two books show a computer: In *Wild about Books*, a librarian also brings a computer to the zoo, presumably to enter borrowing data, but the animals show no interest in it at all. There is also a computer in *Maisy Goes to the Library* which visitors can use. *It's a Book!* is of course about this precise tension between the printed page and screen, with the technologically savvy Jackass discovering what books can do. Yet there is a conspicuous absence of any digital devices in both the background and the foreground. This points to the tension between the codex and digital technology and the anxiety referred to at the beginning of this chapter about children abandoning the latter for the former. It suggests that there is a need to make sure the reading of books is visibly entrenched in a child's mind before they move on to texts afforded by digital technology. Although their perspectives and genres differ, both Pressman and Bhadury suggest that the recent focus on "bookishness" or "self-reflexive narrative" (whether in the case of the adult novel published after 2000 for Pressman or in the case of metafictional children's books for Bhadury) has to do with the codex adopting characteristics of digital technologies, hypertextual texts, and interactive reading practices that "implicitly gesture toward other media."[52] While a discussion of the digital and interactive features in the picturebooks is beyond the scope of this chapter, some of the picturebooks included in this corpus, particularly Richard Byrne's series, are even stronger examples of this trend and it could be argued that they mediate not only between the codex and the screen but also between the knowledge which children acquire early as "digital natives" and knowledge of printed books.

INTERTEXTUAL KNOWLEDGE

Within these picturebooks there is another message about book culture: the pleasure of intertextuality. The inclusion of titles, characters, and other textual or visual references that an intended reader is likely to recognize is one way of cementing a character as a fictional reader. It can also be an invitation to continue reading, with one book introducing another. However, as Peter Hunt has noted, in the past authors could more safely assume that readers would recognize intertextual references.[53] To ensure readers respond to his invitation, which is about reintroducing readers to "classics" of children's literature, Jeffers therefore clearly states the titles of these classics in the endpapers of *A Child of Books*.

Along with real titles, "fake titles" also appear as a humorous device in some of the picturebooks, such as those read by Charlie Cook ("Joust Joking" or "Improving Stories for Wicked Thieves") or by Luna ("Marabella's Book of Magic Mayhem"). These devices, such as the rather belabored titles in

Ralfy's reading lists ("The Rabbit with the Dandelion Tattoo" and "Gone with the Carrots"), are often aimed at the adult readers. In *Books Always Everywhere*, the images also include "joke" book titles that adults will appreciate ("Sitting Pretty" and "100 Best Highchairs"). Most book covers in the illustrations, however, tend to be generic references either to typical children's nonfiction topics (ballet, fish, trucks, bears, dinosaurs, "things to draw and paint") or stories about fictional characters such as mermaids, pirates, knights, and dragons.

Intertextual references involve not only titles and images but also characters, mostly from fairy tales or popular childhood rhymes. Red Reading Hood is of course reading *Little Red Riding Hood*. In *Charlie Cook*, the "Chinese box" structure of one story within another includes Goldilocks and Dr. Foster (who went to Gloucester). Herb has unpleasant encounters with not only Goldilocks but also Hansel and Gretel and other fairy tale characters in *Who's Afraid of the Big Bad Book*. The "Origami Army" that saves "The Little Bookshop" is composed of well-loved book characters such as Alice in Wonderland and the White Rabbit, Elmer the Elephant and characters from *The Wizard of Oz*, and other classics that help stop the destruction of the bookshop with the aid of William Shakespeare and Charles Dickens (Dickens carries a book with his name on it as a shield—presumably to make sure he is recognized at least by some adults). The references therefore become a device to introduce characters that the readers may not recognize.

Presented in these diverse ways, intertextual references support the picturebook in mediating between readers and books. They strengthen the idea of connections between texts and suggest there are many more books to move on to; however, not only do authors/illustrators steer children toward particular texts[54] but the focus also remains book-centric. In addition, this intertextuality implies an ideal reading situation where an adult reader is able to help the child notice and gradually understand the references. The allusions assume an adult reader that possesses "cultural and linguistic competences" and is familiar with "the dominant culture,"[55] including English language children's culture (e.g., nursery rhymes and fairy tales).

FROM PERSONAL PLEASURE TO SOCIAL TRANSFORMATION: THE CONSEQUENCES OF READING

This chapter confirms two of the claims "made on behalf of reading" that Hateley identified in the five picturebooks she discusses: "the reading of specific texts is identified as valuable" and "reading is a social practice constituent of sociocultural agency."[56] Both claims align with the positioning of books and reading as a vehicle for personal and shared pleasure and as a vehicle for transformation as seen in the picturebooks in this study. This positioning emerged from the two questions asked of the picturebook corpus that addressed the consequences of reading: What did the act of reading change? And what did it lead to? The answers are in all cases underpinned by the value accorded to books and reading. In some picturebooks, the message about this value is conveyed more subtly and has personal consequences for the fictional reader; in others, it becomes a rallying cry for society to help preserve book-centric culture.

For the most part, the immediate pleasures of reading are to do with providing a space for the child reader to have imaginary adventures in which books and elements connected to book culture (e.g., fictional readers) play a vital role. The boy in *Look!* who is passively watching TV and ignoring his gorilla friend eventually realizes it is more fun to look at a book together. "Bookishness" is encouraged as a source of pleasure, as is imagining alternative narratives (the wolf in *Little Red Reading Hood* discovers he does not have to be bad). Reading is encouraged not only for the fun and pleasure it can bring but also because it helps the reader become a "better" person, provided we are really able to access and make "proper" sense of what we read.

In addition to implying that the readers in the stories will continue to read into the future, a few of these books show that the characters' experiences with reading will, as Heath concludes, "influence their process of bringing imagination into action" and lead to other creative activities.[57] Heath specifically refers to examples that include activities such as building, drawing, singing, dancing, or acting. Examples from this selection include George the Bear who, along with learning to read, seems to have also taken up art and music. Dog's love of books inspires him to open his own bookshop and some characters such as Library Mouse and little chicken in *Interrupting Chicken* start writing their own stories (little chicken also draws pictures). The wild animals in the zoo also write poetry and literary reviews as well as novels and, in the end, literally construct their own library. Thus, the consequences of reading are shown to be personal and social as well as intellectual and cultural, both in the shorter and longer term.

It is clear that knowledge acquired from books is useful and this is shown through characters who use this knowledge to change their lives. Little Mouse's knowledge about the world garnered from books and other texts allow him to take control over dangerous beasts and his own fears. Otto the bear's map reading and ability to plan and write allow him to find another book in which to "live" when he arrives, exhausted and cold, at a library, described as "a place that looked full of light and hope."[58] Finally, familiarity with an army of fictional characters in childhood can help children to triumph over ideological and commercial attempts to limit access to books and reading spaces, such as the closure of places through which that familiarity is developed (e.g., bookshops and libraries): "They are only made of paper," yells the Mayor who wants to develop the land where the bookshop exists. The Origami army replies: "We are not just made of paper. We are made of IDEAS! . . . And IMAGINATION! . . . We are made of things you can *never* destroy!"[59] Thus, the ways in which the visual images and other affordances of these picturebooks position books and the act of reading in children's thinking are crucial to the society that produces them because, through their interaction with these material artifacts, children learn to embody the social, cultural, educational, economic, and affective narrative of literacy itself and therefore ensure the continuation of this narrative.

NOTES

1. Jessica Pressman, "The Aesthetic of Bookishness in Twenty-First-Century Literature," *The Michigan Quarterly Review* 48, no. 4 (2009): 465–82, 465.

2. Pressman, "The Aesthetic of Bookishness," 465.

3. Claudia Nelson, "Writing the Reader: The Literary Child in and beyond the Book," *Children's Literature Association Quarterly* 31, no. 3 (2006): 222–36, 223.

4. While the act of writing or learning to write also appears in picturebooks, it is less common and is more usually found in books directed at children who are beginning to write or in literature for older readers who are beginning to keep diaries or write literature themselves.

5. Erica Hateley, "Reading: From Turning the Page to Touching the Screen," in *(Re)imagining the World. Children's Literature Response to Changing Times*, eds. Yan Wu, Kerry Mallan and Roderick McGillis (Berlin Heidelberg: Springer-Verlag, 2013), 1–13, 3.

6. Evelyn Arizpe and Vivienne Smith, eds., *Children as Readers in Children's Literature: The Power of Text and the Importance of Reading* (London: Routledge, 2016).

7. Nelson, "Writing the Reader;" Poushali Bhadury, "Metafiction, Narrative Metalepsis, and New Media Forms in the Neverending Story and the Inkworld Trilogy," *The Lion and the Unicorn* 37, no. 3 (2013): 301–26; Joe Sutliff Sanders, "The Critical Reader in Children's Metafiction," *The Lion and the Unicorn* 33, no. 3 (2009): 349–61.

8. Nelson, "Writing the Reader," 226.

9. Frank Serafini, "Images of Reading and the Reader," *The Reading Teacher* 57, no. 7 (2004): 610–17, 616; Rebecca-Anne Do Rozario, "Consuming Books: Synergy of Materiality and Narrative in Picturebooks," *Children's Literature* no. 40 (2012): 151–66, 151; Nina Goga, "Learn to Read. Learn to Live: The Role of Books and Book Collections in Picturebooks," in *Picturebooks. Representation and Narration,* ed. Bettina Kümmerling-Meibauer (London: Routledge, 2014), 201–12, 212; Hateley, "Reading;" Morag Styles and Mary Anne Wolpert, "What Else Can This Book

Do?" in *Children as Readers in Children's Literature: The Power of Text and the Importance of Reading*, eds. Evelyn Arizpe and Vivienne Smith (London: Routledge, 2016), 93–106.

10. This chapter originated from papers presented at the RSE Susan Manning workshop "Mediating Children's Reading," The Institute for Advanced Studies in the Humanities, University of Edinburgh, June 21, 2016, and the UKLA (United Kingdom Literacy Association) Conference in 2016 (with Vivienne Smith). It extends the work Arizpe and Smith carried out for the project "Reading Fictions" (funded by the British Academy), which resulted in the edited book, *Children as Readers in Children's Literature: The Power of Text and the Importance of Reading* (eds. Arizpe and Smith, Routledge, 2016). I am grateful to Vivienne Smith for the contribution to the ideas in this chapter and our continuing conversations on this topic.

11. Arizpe and Smith, *Children as Readers*, xi–xxvi, xiii.

12. Shirley B. Heath, "What No Bedtime Story Means: Narrative Skills at Home and School," *Language and Society* 11, no. 1 (1982): 49–76 and Shirley B. Heath, *Ways with Words* (Cambridge: Cambridge University Press, 1983).

13. Heath, "What No Bedtime Story Means," 49.

14. Patricia Crain, *Reading Children. Literacy, Property and the Dilemmas of Childhood in Nineteenth-Century America* (Philadelphia, PA: University of Pennsylvania Press, 2016).

15. Crain, *Reading Children*, 30.

16. Andrew O'Malley, *The Making of the Modern Child: Children's Literature and Childhood in the Late Eighteenth Century* (London: Routledge, 2003).

17. Matthew O. Grenby, *The Child Reader, 1700–1840* (Cambridge: Cambridge University Press, 2011).

18. Evelyn Arizpe and Morag Styles with Shirley B. Heath, *Reading Lessons from the Eighteenth Century: Mothers, Children and Texts* (Lichfield: Pied Piper Press, 2006).

19. Grenby, *The Child Reader*, 283.

20. Margaret Mackey, "Postmodern Picture Books and the Material Conditions of Reading," in *Postmodern Picturebooks. Play, Parody and Self-Referentiality,* eds. Lawrence R. Sipe and Syliva Pantaleo (London: Routledge, 2008), 103–17, 105.

21. David Lewis, "Pop-Ups and Fingle-Fangles: The History of the Picture Book," in *Talking Pictures: Pictorial Texts and Young Readers*, eds. Victor Watson and Morag Styles (London: Hodder and Stoughton, 1996), 5–22, 13.

22. Hateley, "Reading," 2, 3.

23. Hateley, "Reading," 11.

24. Do Rozario, "Consuming Books," 151.

25. Do Rozario, "Consuming Books," 165.

26. Gunther Kress, *Literacy in the New Media Age* (London: Routledge, 2003), 51.

27. Mackey, "Postmodern Picture Books," 115.

28. Some of the books they discuss, mainly *Who's Afraid of the Big Bad Book* by Lauren Child; *Wolves* by Emily Gravett; *The Incredible Book-eating Boy* by Oliver Jeffers; and *It's a Book!* by Lane Smith, have been the subject of much scholarly

attention, so although they were included the current *corpus*, I have tried to refer less to these and more to less well-known ones.

29. Styles and Wolpert, "What Else Can This Book Do?" 95.

30. Jane Austen, *Northanger Abbey*, ed. Anne Henry Ehrenpreis (London: Penguin, 1972).

Bonny Becker and Kady MacDonald Denton, *A Library Book for Bear* (London: Walker Books, 2015).

Jane Blatt and Sarah Massini, *Books Always Everywhere* (London: Nosy Crow, 2013).

Hrefna Bragadottir, *Baxter's Book* (London: Nosy Crow, 2016).

Anthony Browne, *I Like Books* (London: Walker Books, 2009).

Richard, Byrne, *This Book Just Ate My Dog!* (Oxford: Oxford University Press, 2014).

Richard Byrne, *We Are in the Wrong Book!* (Oxford: Oxford University Press, 2016).

Richard Byrne, *This Book is Out of Control!* (Oxford: Oxford University Press, 2017).

Jen Campbell and Katie Harnett, *Franklin's Flying Bookshop* (London: Thames and Hudson, 2017).

Lauren Child, *Beware of Storybook Wolves* (London: Hodder Children's Books, 2000).

Lauren Child, *Who's Afraid of the Big Bad Book?* (London: Hodder Children's Books, 2002).

Emma Chichester Clark, *Bears Don't Read!* (London: HarperCollins, 2014).

Kate Cleminson, *Otto the Book Bear* (London: Jonathan Cape, 2011).

Joseph Coelho and Fiona Lumbers, *Luna Loves Library Day* (London: Andersen Press, 2017).

Lucy Cousins, *Maisy Goes to the Bookshop* (London: Walker Books, 2007).

Lucy Cousins, *Maisy Goes to the Library* (London: Walker Books, 2017).

Helen Doherty and Thomas Doherty, *The Snatchabook* (London: Alison Green Books, 2013).

Julia Donaldson and Axel Scheffler, *Charlie Cook's Favourite Books* (London: Macmillan Children's Books, 2005).

Julia Donaldson and Sara Ogilvie, *The Detective Dog* (London: Macmillan Children's Books, 2016).

Jonathan Emmett and Poly Bernatene, *Prince Ribbit* (London: Macmillan Children's Books, 2016).

Michael Foreman, *The Little Bookshop and the Origami Army!* (London: Andersen Press, 2015).

Emily Gravett, *Wolves* (London: Macmillan Children's Books, 2006).

Emily Gravett, *Little Mouse's Big Book of Fears* (London: Macmillan, 2007).

Emily Gravett, *Again!* (London: Simon & Schuster, 2011).

Emily Gravett, *Little Mouse's Big Book of Beasts* (London: Macmillan, 2016).

Oliver Jeffers, *The Incredible Book Eating Boy* (London: HarperCollins, 2006).

Oliver Jeffers and Sam Winston, *A Child of Books* (London: Walker Books, 2016).

Kazuno Kohara, *The Midnight Library* (New York: Roaring Book Press, 2014).

Daniel Kirk, *Library Mouse* (New York: Abrams Books for Young Readers, 2007).

Michelle Knudsen and Kevin Hawkes, *Library Lion* (Somerville, MA: Candlewick Press, 2006).

Barbara Lehman, *The Red Book* (Boston, MA: Houghton Mifflin, 2004).

Charlotte Lennox, *The Female Quixote or The Adventures of Arabella*, ed. Margaret Dalziel (Oxford: Oxford University Press, 1989).

Jeff Mack, *Look!* (New York: Philomel Books, 2015).

Emily MacKenzie, *Wanted! Ralfy Rabbit, Book Burglar* (London: Bloomsbury, 2015).

Lucy Rowland and Ben Mantle, *Little Red Reading Hood* (London: Macmillan, 2018).

Sergio Ruzzier, *This Is Not a Picture Book!* (San Francisco, CA: Chronicle Books, 2016).

Judy Sierra and Marc Brown, *Wild about Books* (London: Frances Lincoln, 2004).

Lane Smith, *It's a Book* (London: Macmillan Children's Books, 2010).

David Ezra Stein, *Interrupting Chicken* (Somerville, MA: Candlewick, 2010).

Louise Yates, *Dog Loves Books* (London: Jonathan Cape, 2010).

31. That is not to say that this theme is not found in picturebooks published in other languages.

32. Wilma D. Kuhlman and Mary J. Lickteig, "Literacy as Change Agent: Messages about Reading and Writing. Children's Literature," *Journal of Children's Literature* 24, no. 2 (1998): 84–93; Janelle B. Mathis and Lindsay Patterson, "Literacy to Inform and Transform: Empowering Lessons from Children's Literature," in *53rd Yearbook of the National Reading Conference*, ed. J. Worthy (Oak Creek, WI: National Reading Conference, 2005): 264–80.

33. There are plenty of picturebooks where books or reading appear as incidental to the plot.

34. *Books Always Everywhere* and *Detective Dog Nell* make a point of including diverse looking children and Luna, in *Luna Loves Books* has a white mother and a black father (although it seems they have separated). However, in the latter, the main character is Peter, a white middle-class boy whose dog is well bred enough to be allowed to go to school to be read to.

35. Hateley, "Reading," 3.

36. An iconic image that Crain considers a "scopophilic cultural imperative" and which defined childhood in the nineteenth century (Crain, *Reading Children*, 2).

37. This absence is reflected in picturebooks more generally.

38. Robin Bernstein, "'You Do It!': Going-to-Bed Books and the Scripts of Children's Literature," *PMLA* 135, no. 5 (2020): 877–94, 883.

39. Although there are picturebooks that work without words "there is a significance in this lack which contributes to the overall meaning of the narrative" which means the definition still applies (Evelyn Arizpe, "Meaning-Making from Wordless (or Nearly Wordless) Picturebooks: What Educational Research Expects and What Readers Have to Say," *Cambridge Journal of Education* 43, no. 2 (2013): 163–76, 165).

40. Frank Serafini, "Images of Reading and the Reader," 616.

41. With a few exceptions the text is usually short, with at the most four sentences per page. Five out of the thirty-six books are in verse, suggesting that the intended audience are still young enough to be considered to be receptive to rhyme and rhythm.

42. Judy Sierra and Marc, Brown *Wild about Books* (London: Frances Lincoln, 2004).

43. Gérard Genette, *Narrative Discourse: An Essay in Method*, trans. Jane E. Lewin (Ithaca, NY: Cornell UP, 1980).

44. For example, Catherine Snow and Anat Ninio, "The Contracts of Literacy: What We Learn from Learning to Read Books," in *Emergent Literacy: Writing and Reading*, eds. William Teale and Elizabeth Sulzby (Norwood, NJ: Ablex, 1986), 116–38, or Jackie Marsh and Elaine Hallet, *Desirable Literacies: Approaches to Language and Literacy in the Early Years* (London: Sage, 2008).

45. Jane Blatt and Sarah Massini, *Books Always Everywhere* (London: Nosy Crow, 2013).

46. Goga, "Learn to Read. Learn to Live," 204.

47. Oliver Jeffers, *The Incredible Book Eating Bo* (London: HarperCollins, 2006).

48. Emma Chichester Clark, *Bears Don't Read!* (London: HarperCollins, 2014).

49. Daniel Kirk, *Library Mouse* (New York: Abrams Books for Young Readers, 2007).

50. Goga, "Learn to Read. Learn to Live," 210.

51. Lauren Child, *Who's Afraid of the Big Bad Book?* (London: Hodder Children's Books, 2002).

52. Pressman, "The Aesthetic of Bookishness"; Bhadury, "Metafiction," 302.

53. Peter Hunt, "Taken as Read: Readers in Books and the Importance of Reading, 1744–2003," in *Children as Readers*, eds. Arizpe and Smith, 16–27.

54. Nelson, "Writing the Reader," 228.

55. Pierre Bourdieu, "Cultural Reproduction and Social Reproduction," in *Power and Ideology in Education*, eds. Jerome Karabel and A.H. Halsey (Oxford: Oxford University Press, 1977), 487–511, 494.

56. Hateley, "Reading," 6. However, there is little evidence to support her third claim of "shared or mediated adult-child reading experiences" and especially in relation to "familial relationships."

57. Shirley B. Heath, "'This Is My Show!' Beyond Reading to Envisioning and Enacting," in *Children as Readers*, eds. Arizpe and Smith, 119–31, 124.

58. Kate Cleminson, *Otto the Book Bear* (London: Jonathan Cape, 2011).

59. Michael Foreman, *The Little Bookshop and the Origami Army!* (London: Andersen Press, 2015).

Chapter 8

"My World Has Become Smaller"

Cortically Remapping Postfeminist Confinement in Louise O'Neill's Asking For It

Fiona McCulloch

When eighteen-year-old Emma O'Donovan is gang-raped in Louise O'Neill's young adult (YA) novel *Asking For It* (2015), she narrates, "My world has become smaller [. . .] shrinking to fit the parameters of this house."[1] In this exegesis of O'Neill's text, I argue that postfeminism is a patriarchal assault on feminism which has permeated popular culture via, for instance, media and social media, and has straightjacketed young women and girls into an interpellative femininity whose coded contradictions lead to a simulation of empowerment that is, in effect, tantamount to their own imprisonment. I employ Angela McRobbie's critique of postfeminism's contradictory snares and focus on it further here. Far from reaping the rewards of historical feminist struggle, contemporary gender politics ensure that the "fairer sex" continues to be policed, cajoled, and duped into a role that suits neoliberal politics at the expense of feminist discourses. Neoliberalism is a corporate system of global capitalism that dismantles collective citizen empowerment by privileging free market individualism and perpetuating numerous inequalities, including gender.[2] Rather than becoming collectively empowered, women's wings are clipped and tongues stilled in favor of individualism, choice, corporatization, and image.

While young women are hegemonically seduced and individualized by a head-turning array of consumer products, they are simultaneously punished by neopatriarchal rebuffs to those newfound "freedoms." It is *neo*patriarchal because patriarchy has shapeshifted into a Trojan horse that offers women apparent unconstrained freedoms yet its subterfuge conceals age-old interpellative apparatus to corral any aberrations.[3] Internalized and disseminated

199

by women, neopatriarchy weaponizes postfeminism to constrain women within its hegemonic matrix. According to Beatrix Campbell, "the world is being governed by a neopatriarchal and neoliberal matrix that assails—and provokes" feminism, its "new form of articulation" ranging "from sexual violence to [. . .] equality laws [. . .] time, money and care."[4] Campbell regards neopatriarchy as a deliberate neoliberal tool to subjugate women and roll back any rights gained by feminism and the welfare state, while Carole Jones deploys McRobbie's postfeminist critique in urging feminism "to escape its neopatriarchal containment."[5] Likewise, O'Neill depicts Emma's shrinking "neopatriarchal containment" as a call for cultural and political change— through the pedagogical strategy of YA fiction, *Asking For It* interrogates postfeminism's enablement of the rape culture experienced by its protagonist.

Postfeminism instills narratives of individual responsibility and blame that permeate young women's consciousness in order to suffuse and fragment collective feminist struggle against sociopolitical issues like rape culture. I argue that the proliferation of such narratives detrimentally impinges upon adolescents bodily, cognitively, and cortically to restrict their maturation and impact their development. Against this backdrop O'Neill's narrative strives to overturn the negative impact of postfeminist conditioning (fuelled by corporately driven social media) by cortically remapping and thus empowering those otherwise silenced and inhibited by neopatriarchy's dominant discourses. For O'Neill, "the feminist aspect was what most interested me [. . .] The late 90s and early 2000s were like a feminist wasteland where people were saying that we were living in a post-feminist era and we don't need feminism anymore."[6] In that sense, she provides much-needed textual mediation to help adolescents navigate situations that may well reflect their own current or future lived experiences. YA fiction's maturation themes are crucial insofar as it transcends material deemed suitable for young minds and instead develops a space to ponder the post-innocent framework of children's literary studies by confronting themes that many gatekeepers may find objectionable and wish to censor.[7] Emma Yates-Bradley writes, "O'Neill has been visiting schools" to "discuss [. . .] *Asking For It* [. . .] She has had a mixed response. Even seasoned publishers have been reluctant to put out her novels [. . .] When I went to buy the novel from Waterstones, I was told that the book had been taken out of the YA section after complaints from parents."[8] With regard to its reception, O'Neill predicted, "I think this book is probably going to infuriate a lot of people."[9] Similarly, Laurie Halse Anderson's YA rape novel *Speak* (1999) has faced censorship,[10] while *The Wall Street Journal* commented that "the current generation of young adult fiction is 'too dark' for readers."[11]

As YA fiction, *Asking For It* forms part of an emergent dialogical engagement with postfeminist rape culture and attempts to challenge its intended reader into rethinking the politics of victim blaming and gender relations in a neopatriarchal matrix. For instance, Anderson's *Speak* portrays the way in which rape silences its victim, while Sarahbeth Caplin's *Someone You Already Know* (2012) traces the impact of rape upon two teenage girls—one attacked by her boyfriend and the other by a stranger, while in television, Ryan Murphy and Brad Falchuk's *American Horror Story: Coven* portrays the gang rape of Madison Montgomery during a university fraternity party. As a witch, she wreaks revenge by crashing the frat boys' bus, perhaps empowering those victim-viewers without supernatural abilities, though clearly such fatal justice is problematic. Aaron Hartzler's *What We Saw* (2015) is based on the Steubenville High School rape case of August 2012, while Allison J. Kennedy's *The Choice* (2014) charts the story of her protagonist May who, like O'Neill's Emma and Anderson's Melinda, is raped at a party; May later finds out she is pregnant due to this attack. Most recently, Amber Smith's *The Way I Used to Be* (2016) focuses on the rape of fourteen-year-old Eden by her brother's best friend. Meanwhile, Kirby Dick's documentary film *The Hunting Ground* (2015) explores the prevalence of rape across US university campuses and includes "Till It Happens to You," a song cowritten and performed by Lady Gaga, herself a rape survivor. Similarly, Madonna utilized Billboard's 2016 Woman of the Year platform to reiterate her disclosure of being "raped on a rooftop with a knife digging into my throat,"[12] and articulate postfeminism's neopatriarchal paradoxes which disempower young women, resonating with Emma's experiences in O'Neill's text, including the hostility of other women.

Similar to Hartzler, O'Neill's decision to set *Asking For It* in a small town is influenced by her research into "the Steubenville case and the Maryville case."[13] O'Neill also presented a documentary for Irish Television, entitled *Asking For It?: Reality Bites* (November 2016), which explores rape culture and slut-shaming in Ireland. Director Traolach O Buachalla collaborated with O'Neill for the program, conceding her novel awakened his consciousness to "living within the confines of a rape culture," and insisting "these conversations [. . .] will impact on how the next generation is raised."[14] *Asking For It*'s mediation triggers a debate which resonates in twenty-first-century Ireland and beyond, extending the conversation with a television documentary that examines a nation's role in perpetuating rape culture in the hope its future citizens inherit a more equal society. The documentary gained significant impact and trended on social media, signaling a desire to acknowledge a social blight articulated by YA fiction. Its producers "approached Louise off the back of her book" and regarded her involvement as integral to creating "an extremely informative hour of television that addressed one of the most pertinent issues in Ireland today."[15] Crucially, this YA novel influences a television documentary that reaches across age groups to begin a much-needed social discussion, demonstrating the sociopolitical aspect of a literary text's ability to amplify a dialogue within communities.

To briefly recount *Asking For It*'s plot, Emma is a popular, attractive young woman who parties, studies, is part of a clique of "cool" girls, engages in casual sexual encounters, and consumes recreational alcohol and drugs. It transpires as the narrative unfolds that Emma's behavior is not enjoyed by her but is symptomatic of Althusserian interpellation with peer pressure and a desperate desire to fit in and belong, rather than be bullied or ignored. Meanwhile, her middle-class parents remain blissfully ignorant of her life-style and choose to believe in the image of their perfect nuclear family and dutiful virginal daughter. When that image is shattered, they are subject to the hegemonic discourses that depict Emma as "fucking asking for it."[16] Settled in the small fictional Irish town of Ballinatoom, the parameters of their world are confined to the family and local community, signaling a generational and cultural clash that leaves a chasm between parent/child and local/global. From the outset, the text mentions seemingly in passing the trappings of modern life, including social media and an "iPhone,"[17] all of which steer the narrative toward a crescendo of online trolling against Emma once she has been gang-raped, accusing her of being the whorish instigator. Her parents' lack of familiarity with Facebook accentuates the vulnerable spaces where Emma's attack continues unabated.

All the while, O'Neill interrogates the contradictions of a neopatriarchal culture that endorses rape and slut-shaming, while simultaneously luring young women into projecting a sexualized image, maintained by an array of consumer products (including makeup, haircare, plastic surgery, clothes, alcohol, drugs, porn) that boost a multimillion-pound corporate (including illicit) industry. Young women are expected to play hard but are simultaneously punished by the gender inequalities of neopatriarchal policing. Neopatriarchy proffers women and girls new illusory freedoms, while its covert manipulandum belies its professed liberations, exposed as the same old patriarchal restraints and inequalities. Young women like Emma are demonized rather than supported: "I am Eve. I am the snake in the garden of Eden. I am temptation."[18] She is imprisoned within patriarchy's discursive binary reducing women to Angels/Whores. According to Catharine A MacKinnon, women's voices are erased: "The law of rape divides women into spheres of consent according to indices of relationship to men."[19] The politics of rape responds to gender hierarchies that remove women's agency in favor of discursively interpellated subject positions that silence them from the outset. MacKinnon continues: "The paradigm categories are the virginal daughter and other young girls, with whom all sex is proscribed, and the whorelike wives and prostitutes, with whom no sex is proscribed. Daughters may not consent; wives and prostitutes [. . .] cannot but. Actual consent or nonconsent, far less actual desire, is comparatively irrelevant."[20] Despite marital rape laws apparently shifting toward protecting "wives," the "virginal daughter" is problematized by postfeminism actively encouraging young women to become ever more sexualized. Arguably, we live in acutely sexualized times where daughters are now steeped in sex rather than secluded from it which, in turn, maintains their subjugation.

According to Natasha Walter, "The hypersexual culture is not only rooted in continuing inequality, it also produces more inequality,"[21] since it further disenfranchises young women by serving the demands of neopatriarchy. The paradox is that if you are no longer cast as the virginal daughter in society, then you are the wanton whore and, as such, you are *asking for it*. So, Emma's erstwhile confident embracing of her burgeoning sexuality to respond to the demands of postfeminism contravenes traditional patriarchal Angelic depictions of "good girl" femininity espoused by her parents and promoted by the rural Catholic Irish community around her and signals a cultural, religious, and generational fissure at odds with the tensions and pressures of corporate globalization.[22] Suffering post-traumatic stress disorder from the attack, she is clearly not responding well to therapy, which is instigated to deflect discussion from the family home, enabling her parents to secure silence around a topic their repression has rendered taboo. The perpetuated hush within the home is amplified by Emma's lack of recovery: despite therapy, she confesses in her narrative that she has attempted suicide twice, and indicates that this pattern will continue since her inhospitable home fails to accommodate her needs. For Emma, the menacing silence pervading her home life serves as a constant reminder that she is regarded differently by her family, thus perpetuating her trauma and disrupting her selfhood. Postfeminism's depoliticized individualism ensnares the likes of Emma in an inescapable cycle of victim blaming and isolation, so that her ontological sense of self is diminished and she is psychologically crushed in a manner that cannot fail to have a detrimental neurological impact upon a malleable adolescent cortex.

O'Neill's portrayal of Emma's ontological unraveling due to the trauma of rape and its aftermath resonates with Naomi Wolf's findings regarding rape as a calculated tactic used, for instance, during war, rather than a "personal perversion."[23] This directly challenges postfeminism's propensity to individualize rape victims and perpetrators; instead, it becomes a sociopolitical weapon. In that light, "Rape is a strategy of *actual physical and psychological control of women*, traumatizing via the vagina as a way to imprint the consequences of trauma on the female brain,"[24] although rape can include other orifices too. Wolf continues, "We should understand that one never fully 'recovers' from rape; one is never just the same after as before. Rape, properly understood, is more like an injury to the *brain* than a violent variation on sex. Rape, properly understood, is always aimed not just at the female

Fiona McCulloch

sex organ but at the female brain."[25] Wolf's point resonates with MacKinnon insofar as both regard rape very much as a sexual injury in relation to gender inequalities, but she exceeds this to emphasize that it is not just a bodily and psychological injury but also a neurological issue. In light of developments in the field of neuroscience where the brain, once considered a fixed concrete organ, and since discovered to be plastic in its capacity for change, Wolf's argument *is* persuasive, and corresponds directly to Emma's experience insofar as she is changed utterly as a result of her attack.

As such, the neuroscientific field of cortical remapping is vital in relation to Emma: not only does the rape reduce her ontological confidence, but also the litany of hostile language that she is privy to thereafter. The refrain, "*slut, bitch, skank, whore*"[26] is internalized by Emma which, in turn, *must* alter her neurological pathways so that her entire sense of self is realigned or remapped by a crushing social narrative that recasts her as wanton slattern. Wolf argues:

Is all rape about sexual aggression or male neurosis? Or can the sustained cultural presence of rape also or even instead at times, be about reprogramming women at a core physical level to be less brave, less secure, less robust in other ways, and to go through the rest of their lives, potentially, with a less stable sense of self?[27]

Wolf's view of rape as a "sustained cultural presence" equates with the postfeminist climate of rape in which Emma finds herself trapped, and emphasizes its permeation as a cultural incidence. Emma's gendered cortical "reprogramming" means that she is punitively transformed into a passively static femininity, ensuring she becomes "less brave, less secure" and "with a less stable sense of self" to reiterate Wolf. This self-diminishment, in turn, fuels and accentuates her tendency toward self-annihilation: "I wish I was dead."[28] In addressing rape culture, O'Neill refutes such systematic silencing of victims whose adolescent neuroplasticity is detrimentally and dangerously reshaped. Instead, she offers a vital cortically dialogic counternarrative that challenges neopatriarchal vitriol in favor of feminist self-belief. By offering an alternative to the hegemonic discourse of victim blaming, *Asking For It* pedagogically serves to realign YA readers' grey matter so that they can rethink the politics of rape which, in turn, contributes to the neurological wellbeing of future citizens.

The relationship between Emma (narrator) and reader encourages a dialogic interrogation of discourses that otherwise ensnare and silence rape survivors. Crucially, for Mikhail Bakhtin, fiction's dialogic multifarious heteroglossia ensures "The novel [. . .] is plasticity itself. It is a genre that is ever questing":[29] not only does the novel format speak to the quest-like structure of many children's and YA literary journeys, but its "plasticity" is equally prone to evolutionary malleability akin to the plasticity of a reader's cortical development. With that in mind, O'Neill's reader is ideally positioned to benefit from textual mediation's cortical process of remapping as it strives to resist rape culture's discursive hegemony, utilizing a medium that is always "plasticity itself." Fictional "plasticity" in a YA novel addressing rape culture is paramount to challenge the injurious brain "reprogramming" identified by Wolf and encourage adolescent readers to seek—like Bakhtin's "ever quest-ing" novel—a dialogic counternarrative.

While the power imbalance between author/reader is well documented in children's literature and undoubtedly more acutely evident than in adult literature,[30] nevertheless, as I previously argued,[31] spatial exchange occurs in language's impurity and instability. Similarly, Bakhtin identifies fiction's interrogative heteroglossia and "Hybridization," given its malleability, renewal, and social evolution of "different times, epochs."[32] Likewise, David Rudd deduces, "children's literature can never be pure [. . .] it is always a hybrid, negotiated space."[33] In many ways Bakhtin's hybrid dialogical read-ing experience resonates with Homi K Bhabha's cultural interstitial space as a means of locating a postcolonial hybrid subject who is a fusion of self/other. The relationship between novel and reader formulates a hybrid space where self/other can be renegotiated; rather than such fiction "colonizing" the child, hybridity unleashes the postcolonial agency of readerly interlocution.[34] Children's literature too is an expansive fluid rubric: YA fiction's matura-tion undoubtedly offers more resistant reading than a younger child's textual response may afford, particularly since YA fiction's intended adolescent readers themselves occupy an interstitially hybrid in-between space bridging the stages of child/adult.

Indeed, Roberta Seelinger Trites identifies the rise of YA fiction as symp-tomatic of "questioning and dismantling of Cartesian unified selfhood, so that adolescent development defies Romantic notions of childhood and, instead, problematises subjectivity and its relationship with the capitalist state. It is a notable shift from "individual psychology" to a "questioning of social institutions and how they construct individuals."[35] Ultimately, YA "novels are about power" insofar as they depict individuals struggling to navigate their position within a matrix of social constructions and how their resistant empowerment might offer agency.[36] In turn, adolescent readers can rene-gotiate their felt disempowerment, even if temporarily, during a dialogical relationship with the text through its mediative applicability. By that token, a purely cognitive interiorized approach to mediation is redundant, since YA fiction is borne of a necessity to comprehend one's constructed subjectivity within ideological frameworks and their discursive hegemonies. Rather, as I argue elsewhere,[37] YA fiction negotiates a reader's sociopolitical positioning and encourages an interrogation of a hegemonic status quo. I concur with

Botelho and Rudman's proposal to move "reading and writing away from an exclusively cognitive model which positions literacy as an internal, individual, psychological act, to literacy as a sociocultural, multiple, and political practice."[38] Just as feminist collectivism resists postfeminism's isolationism, it is imperative that textual mediation is regarded sociopolitically rather than as a singular reading practice. Insofar as YA fiction is entwined with power, it is inevitable that its reading must surpass apolitical sole interiority and individual reader-response, and become itself a political and cosmopolitan act that comprehends and inserts other voices in what Bakhtin views as a hybrid sociological enterprise: a novel's dialogic composition "is determined by the very socio-ideological evolution of languages and society."[39] Reading, then, is an evolving sociolinguistic process, its mutability in many ways mirroring adolescent readers' transitions in their developmental progress.

Before further considering how cortical remapping operates within *Asking For It* as a viable neuropolitical counterdiscourse that interrogates and dismantles neoliberal postfeminism and enables adolescent neuroplasticity's reshaping, it is advantageous to further critically outline postfeminist hegemony. According to McRobbie, neoliberal "post-feminism is equated with a 'double movement,' gender retrenchment is secured, paradoxically, through the wide dissemination of discourses of female freedom and (putative) equality. Young women are able to come forward on condition that feminism fades away."[40] For O'Neill's protagonist, the price of actively engaging in these new codes of adolescent femininity is a brutal degradation of the female body, causing her to shrink into the familial home's domestic confines. Once she is discarded as a post-rape product, she is returned to the correctional facility of domesticity's doll house. In O'Neill's depiction of a climate of rape culture, the victim becomes pilloried as a wanton "whore" who was clearly "asking for it."[41] Blamed for internalizing neoliberal consumerism by participating in its hedonistic lifestyle and perfecting her glamorous image, Emma's community focuses, not upon male violence but female lasciviousness. Yet "commercial values now occupy a critical place in the formation of the categories of youthful femininity," ensnaring them in a "commercial culture" that "speaks on their behalf."[42] While professing to liberate women, corporatization silences and replaces their political voice with a discursive consumerism that leaves them disempowered, just as Emma's commercialized interpellated subjectivity serves as the forum for her demonization.

Language used to hold women in check for centuries halts Emma's hitherto "freedom": vilified as a whore, she is imprisoned in the home's (the traditional confine of the Victorian Angel) corrective parameters, thus blaming *her* for the acts of gendered sexual violence against her. Similarly, MacKinnon argues that the politics of rape are imbued with a fundamental inequality that privileges the male perpetrator rather than the female victim's perspective, since it serves a social and legal system that is predicated upon patriarchal values. Thus, "It expresses and reinforces women's inequality to men. Rape with legal impunity makes women second-class citizens."[43] She continues, "the social conception of rape is shaped to interpret particular encounters" and "the legal conception of rape authoritatively shapes that social conception. When perspective is bound up with situation, and situation is unequal, whether or not a contested interaction is authoritatively considered rape comes down to whose meaning wins."[44] Ultimately, "meaning" is inherently skewed in favor of the perpetrator, since the dominant perspective already privileges the male gaze, though whether "legal conception" authorizes "social conception" is disputable as social and cultural discourses are equally likely to influence legality. Thus, "If sexuality is relational, specifically if it is a power relation of gender, consent is a communication under conditions of inequality. It transpires somewhere between what the woman actually wanted, what she was able to express about what she wanted, and what the man comprehended she wanted."[45] From the outset, according to MacKinnon, the dice are loaded with a gender inequality that translates to low levels of convictions but, rather than regarding this as authorized by legal narratives, such entrenched gender disempowerment systematically permeates all social relations, just as Wolf identifies rape's "sustained cultural presence." Similarly, to understand a trial's inherent bias, while making their documentary, O'Buachalla explains he and O'Neill sought legal expertise: "You are being judged by your peers [who] have been raised in a culture, a rape culture, a culture that even *allows* the thought that a victim could possibly have provoked that kind of crime."[46] Emma's fictional experience, then, resonates with legal and cultural permeations within and beyond its pages, mediating a wider readerly interlocution.

A solicitor informs Emma and her parents that rape convictions are so "low in this country" they stand at "only one per cent."[47] O'Neill's fictional narrative precisely mirrors the legal and social injustice accounted for by MacKinnon and emphasizes the manner in which legal/cultural conceptions are framed within narratives that cognitively impair and entrench neural pathways. As such, O' Neill argues, "I couldn't give the book a happy ending" as "it needed to be true to the story and the bigger truth [. . .] the legal system in Ireland seemed set up to protect rapists. There is no legal definition of consent."[48] *Asking For It* is borne of a need to rectify injustice and mediate with its reader to interrogate such legal imbalance. However, apart from the legal imbalance of convictions, Emma's trauma equally stems from extreme hostility within her local community and online forums, emphasizing the cultural conditioning of rape narratives weighted against victims.

MacKinnon more recently notes, "Women are sexually assaulted because they are women: not individually or at random, but on the basis of sex, because of their membership in a group defined by gender."[49] Hierarchical gender binaries situate masculinity in an authoritatively dominant position, argues MacKinnon, so that those who are feminized are automatically compromised; as such, "Females—adults and children—are most of the victims of sexual assault. The perpetrators are, overwhelmingly, men. Men do this to women and to girls, boys, and other men, in that order. Women hardly ever do this to men."[50] In that light, the postfeminist propensity to isolate and individualize rape victims becomes a deliberate attempt to depoliticize and divide feminist solidarity, so diffusing its collective sociopolitical and critical capacity to challenge dominant narratives.

For Sarah Projansky, "representations of rape and discourses of post-feminism" are intertwined "because each is a dominant means through which contemporary popular culture discursively defines feminism," and, in light of this intersection argues, "postfeminist discourses work hegemonically to transform feminism in the service of heterosexual masculinity and a dispersed, depoliticized, and universalized white, middle-class feminine/feminist identity."[51] Like McRobbie, Projansky regards postfeminism as detrimental to collective feminist politics, but further probes its "universalized" whitewashing as well as heteronormativity. Unlike MacKinnon, though, Projansky (following McRobbie) notes the *cultural* manifestation of postfeminism's systemic separation, dismantling, and depoliticization of feminism through an array of discursive positionings, so that "contemporary popular culture['s]" influence permeates individual rape cases which are resultantly diminished and undermined within an already misogynistic legal discourse. Though O'Neill's heroine is problematically white and economically privileged, she nevertheless opens up a dialogic space within YA fiction to consider representations of rape that is much needed and hopefully will encourage other voices to follow in this genre. For Sorcha Gunne and Zoe Brigley Thompson, literary narratives function as "reconfigurations of rape narratives" so that dominant discourses can be interrogated and alternative accounts presented.[52] Arguably, it is even more urgent that such narratives arrive in the form of YA fiction in order to educate and empower tomorrow's citizens. The act of reading allows spatial intervention to offer resistant perspectives, encouraging fledgling citizens to reshape patriarchal society.

The existence of a mediating dialogue between text/reader is evident in the overwhelmingly positive online responses to O'Neill's novel: Goodreads reviews include comments like, "Emma exists. She's everywhere. Where you are, where I am [. . .] There are Emmas all over the world," "*Asking For It* will make you angry, and rightly so. Louise O'Neill doesn't shy away from reality [. . .] with a happily ever after. [. . .] Even after so many years of education—from school to college to university—I have never within education participated in a conversation about rape. This must change. Let's talk";

"Everybody must read this. It should be read in school, uni, book clubs. By parents and by teenagers. By you! [. . .] Rape culture is a thing, an ugly one and it needs to be acknowledged and fought"; "every single little bit of the story could be, has been and will be something that happens. Happened. Will happen again . . . unless we change an awful lot of attitudes [. . .] we see the impact of social media [. . .] we see inside Emma's head and it is compelling, emotionally raw and absolutely authentic."[53] This is a minuscule snapshot of the immense number of reviews from readers clearly affected by and thoroughly engaged with this novel, and it clearly strikes a major chord with its intended adolescent readership from the in-depth responses real readers provide. Goodreads' metrics as of 20 January 2021 show the novel has received 2,601 reviews and 16,881 ratings, predominantly with 4* and 5* and, while online identities are difficult to confirm, reviews appear to be predominantly by young women.[54]

These reviews also reinforce reading's social applicability, with each individual interaction shared in an online community, where readers can, in turn, engage by liking each other's reviews, so that the reading process becomes an endless interlocution of perspectives.[55] The content of many of the reviews also transcend individualism and point to the need for collective reading of O'Neill's novel in schools, universities, and book clubs; all spaces where mediation can allow diverse groups to congregate, share views and experiences of their textual understanding. One of the important responses is that rape needs to be discussed in public forums, rather than regarded individually, so that the novel's influence becomes a resistance to solitary isolated reactions in its dialogic encouragement toward a more political manifestation of communal meetings.

Just as I utilize dialogical textual interaction to mediate against rape culture, Ingrid Johnston and Jyoti Mangat converge Bakhtin's dialogism and Bhabha's interstices "to consider how postcolonial literary texts are able to provide a space of cultural mediation for readers from various ethnocultural backgrounds" insofar as such literature offers multiple reader identities an intersection at the site of textual interlocution.[56] I regard O'Neill's dialogic intervention in postfeminist hegemonic rape narratives a vital act of adolescent mediation, while Johnston and Mangat consider postcolonial literature's similar function as "cultural mediation" for pedagogical development. However, to my mind, YA fiction's mediative capacity impacts not just culturally but cortically, and the latter is a vital tool to remap sociopolitical status quos.

As with Emma's recognition that "my world gets smaller, wrapping itself around me,"[57] feminism's dismantling ensures it is replaced with postfeminist limitation and confinement, imposing an ineffectual individual voice that remains unheard at the expense of an effective political movement. The space of the YA text as a counterdiscourse to a victim's enforced silence uses Emma's narration to emphasize the stifling incarceration and silencing she endures because of the attack: "the silence pouring around us," and "We eat in silence."[58] Silence spectrally "follows me everywhere":[59] the trauma and shame she feels, exacerbated by her parents' and wider society's response, diminishes her voice. Imprisoned in her own head, she can only communicate through her narrative. This oppressive silence signals postfeminism's Philomela-effect; victim blaming stills tongues in favor of neopatriarchal dominance. She envisions atrophying monotony: "I would realize that I was old [. . .] I would lie awake in the same single bed that I had slept in since I was a child,"[60] her childhood bed punishment for being branded a whore by paradoxically entombing her in infantilized stasis (in Ballina*toom*).

O'Neill's text stresses that Emma's experience is not an isolated incident, and instead urges a collective feminist response to a systematic rape culture otherwise negating young women's lives. When Emma's friend, Jamie, was raped the previous Halloween, Emma warns her *"When you say that word, you can't take it back [. . .] pretend it didn't happen [. . .] It's easier."*[61] Erasing the sign emphasizes the link between society's suppression of articulating rape and, in turn, its prolific existence. Even when Emma is gang-raped she cannot bring herself to utter *"that word."* In a culture of victim blaming, the onus of responsibility shifts and, to preserve one's reputation, young girls like Emma internalize the ideological responsibility for colluding with the perpetrator in a cycle of silence. Unsurprisingly, Jamie's trauma disproves Emma's claim that it is *"easier"* to say nothing.

Narratives that function as "reconfigurations of rape narratives" (to reiterate Gunne and Thompson)—including YA fiction, television, cinema, music—create a spatial forum of mediation where rape culture can be discussed rather than silenced by postfeminist hegemony though, as Projansky's earlier observation alerts, there is a danger that such representations of rape are responding to a postfeminist universalism of white heteronormativity which has infiltrated popular culture. In defense of O'Neill, though, her text does raise issues of heteronormativity through Emma's narrative and also addresses racial politics. Emma's father describes her teenage friend, Eli, as an "African lad" who is "as black as the ace of spades" despite her protests that "Eli's lived in Ballinatoom all his life" and "his mam is Irish."[62] After the rape, Emma acknowledges, "It would have been easier for him to understand if it had been Eli";[63] her father's prejudiced view of Eli correlates to dominant cultural views that women are at risk from black male sexual predators. Similarly, Projansky outlines how "U.S. colonists told *narratives* about Native American men raping white women to justify white male armed violence against Native Americans, while simultaneously using *physical* rape of Native American women as a tool of war against Native Americans,"[64] and notes that similar atrocities occurred during slavery. Rape, then, is discursively positioned to deflect blame from white men on to racial minorities to obscure historical and current truths, such as slavery, which O'Neill emphasizes in her novel. Neopatriarchy, then, maintains racial stereotypes about rape while simultaneously victim blaming women if the perpetrators are white.

O'Neill argues in her Afterword to *Asking For It*, "We need to talk about rape" and "consent. We need to talk about victim blaming and slut-shaming and the double standards we place upon our young men and women."[65] As with Gérard Genette's (1997) concept of paratextual thresholds, O'Neill's paratext reiterates the novel's sociopolitical and ethical arguments, forming a bridge between reader and fiction and, in turn, functioning as a public space where her text assumes a direct mediating role between internal fictional events and external narratives shaping reality.[66] Jane Wangari Wakarindi similarly views YA fiction through "repoussoir, an element of paratext" that "mediates between the eye of a book's customer and the internal text."[67] O'Neill's paratext, though, reaches beyond individual readers to encourage community engagement and dialogue, as her aforementioned television documentary also demonstrates. Directly defying the gagging that coincides with rape culture, she advocates endlessly speaking out "until the Emmas of this world feel supported and [. . .] believed."[68] *Asking For It* removes the shameful silencing of (predominantly female) rape victims and challenges the commodification of femininity for male consumption and, by doing so, begins to dismantle the societal impact of postfeminism in favor of female adolescent agency. Similar vocalizations include the #MeToo social media campaign triggered by Hollywood's alleged climate of sexual harassment and rape.

As with Wolf's cerebral discussion of the way in which the brain can be reprogrammed, scientific research found that medical students' cortical remapping was enhanced by studying, so that "It is reasonable to assume that plasticity is a characteristic of the nervous system that evolved for coping with changes in the environment. Understanding changes in brain structure as a result of *learning and adaptation* is pivotal in understanding the characteristic flexibility of our brain to adapt."[69] Since neuroplasticity is shaped by external stimuli and, in Draganski et al.'s study, specifically intellectual stimulation from reading medical texts, this "flexibility" is relevant to the field of literary studies. Arguably, fiction is more cortically interactive than the aforementioned study since, for Bakhtin, reading a novel—described as "plasticity itself"—is a dialogic process where the reader actively intervenes as an interlocutor in the text's heteroglossia. As another voice intervening in a novel's polytonal discourse, the reader engages in a critical and aesthetic exchange whose conversational meaning will alter, depending on who is reading it. Paul B. Armstrong likewise argues that literary texts have a "neuroaesthetic" impact, and the multiplicity of fiction mirrors the brain's complexities: "The brain is a peculiar, at times paradoxical, but eminently functional combination of constancy and flexibility, stability and openness to change, fixed constraints and plasticity, and these contradictory, paradoxical qualities are reflected in the workings of literature and literary interpretation."[70] Each literary engagement, then, sparks neuroplasticity's capacity for mutability insofar as reading offers a "neuroaesthetic" mediation between reader and world, just as the literary text's "plasticity" remains heterogeneously dynamic.

Similarly, YA fiction like O'Neill's plays a crucial role in challenging hegemonic rape culture by offering resistant discourses that allow adolescents to actively engage in a dialogic process. In turn, the act of reading YA fiction will enhance their neuroplasticity, thus equipping readers with the intellectual capacity to reconfigure the way in which they perceive rape culture. As such, it becomes pedagogically incumbent upon YA fiction to provide an activist space that enables rape victims to cortically regroup and assert their voices against hegemonic silencing, by offering an empathetic narrative that offsets the hostility predominantly experienced. This differs, though, from cognitive literary studies; as Armstrong asserts, predominantly, "cognitive critics focus on psychology and its studies of the mind rather than on neuroscience and its analysis of the brain" and, though both have "important overlaps and connections," regrettably this mind/brain schism remains "a problem that cognitive literary studies needs to address."[71] By drawing on both of these schools of thought—each, for Armstrong, serves as a valuable "resource for the other"[72]—I believe that critics of YA fiction could exponentially advance discussions of adolescent agency by examining the cortical as well as cognitive significance of such literature's plasticity. Considering the impact of bibliotherapy, John T. Pardeck and Jean Pardeck concur that readers can vicariously experience other lives as well as identify with experiences that may be familiar but traumatic to them: "By reading about a story character's conflicts, cognition, and emotional reactions, clients gain insight into a problem situation," so that it is instrumental in "stimulating discussion about a problem which may not otherwise be discussed because of fear, guilt, or shame."[73] YA readers of *Asking For It* can similarly either vicariously experience the disorientation felt by Emma as a rape victim or, therapeutically relate to her experience, so aiding the processing of their own trauma and "shame" within a rape culture that silences discussions of rape and renders it taboo, thus perhaps curatively journeying from being a victim to a survivor.

But this bibliotherapeutic practice cannot be confined to a discussion of the mind within psychoanalysis' strictures; rather, its purpose must extend beyond this to consider the impact of reading O'Neill's text as a vehicle of empowerment at the neurobiological level by engaging with Emma's cortical impairment at the hands of her rapists and the negative narratives thereafter which diminish her selfhood. Maria Nikolajeva's work on cognitive criticism in children's literature recognizes its crucial pedagogical and psychological function, since "Novice readers have limited life experience of emotions; therefore, fiction can offer vicarious emotional experience for readers to partake of, long before they may be exposed to it in real life."[74] This is absolutely worthwhile but, to throw my hat in with Armstrong, I believe such cognitive criticism can be enhanced alongside cortical literary criticism. O'Neill's text offers a crucial neuropsychological space for those who hopefully never have to endure Emma's suffering, but simultaneously speaks to others who may well have experienced a similar trauma. For Armstrong, the neuroaesthetics of fiction offers a combination of harmony and dissonance so that issues are equally resolved and deferred, and include the jouissance of different literary genres, since "neuroscience may help to clarify literary experiences that theorists since Aristotle have puzzled over, such as how 'pity' and 'terror' combine in the viewer of a tragedy in order to induce 'catharsis.'"[75] The impact of reading O'Neill's text and its potential cathartic capacity is similarly open to neuroscientific probing in terms of how it affects the adolescent's neuroplasticity, and though "The neurological correlates of this experience may not fully explain its mystery [. . .] neurobiological studies of how the brain simulates body states can clarify how these and other aesthetic emotions occur."[76] To read about and experience the trauma of rape through a young woman's narrative, as such connects a vicarious experience to a neurobiological response. Similarly, Diana I Tamir et al. believe fiction's capacity to create simulated environments can ethically enhance neuroplasticity: "Fiction reading, which engenders simulations of vivid and social content, also recruits the default [neural] network" and, as such, "may impact social ability through its effect on the neural system supporting social simulation."[77] They also ponder to what extent different fictional content might impact upon neural variants, just as I argue, specifically, YA rape novels like O'Neill's are vital for cortical reader development and the advancement of an ethical society.

Thus, while Armstrong is concerned with the field of neuroaesthetics, I extend this to consider how the reader's neuroplasticity with regard to *Asking For It* can have a neuropolitical impact insofar as it pedagogically informs them of rape culture's postfeminist isolation and, in turn, encourages a collectively resistant readership equipped to challenge hegemonic narratives. Consequently, fiction's political aesthetic encourages adolescent neuroplasticity to actively engage with the readerly process by simultaneously appreciating the literary text and applying it to external contexts in order to challenge conventional thinking, in this case regarding rape culture. In terms of vicarious experience gleaned by YA fiction's adolescent woman reader, Seelinger Trites considers Sara K. Day's reader-response and narrative theory work on illusory "narrative intimacy" and concludes, "such novels do not and cannot engage in a feminist ethics of care,"[78] given their unreciprocated gap between first-person narrator and external reader. While such impactful narratives indeed emit feelings of vulnerability from the intimate reader/narrator experience, nevertheless it is not entirely one-directional since reciprocation can occur beyond the real reader/fictional narrator alignment. For instance, readers can and do share books and discuss them with friends and online book reviews, thus satisfying much of the emotional and intellectual literary investment Trites identifies as insurmountable. In that sense, a reader's relationship with Emma does offer a "feminist ethics of care" since it invites a mediative dialogical response outside of the private text/reader sphere within a wider community sphere that echoes Bakhtin's socio-ideological reader relationship. Emma's narrative serves a spatial and discursive need for adolescents, particularly young women, to transcend rape culture's coercive silence and to empower themselves at a sociopolitical and cortical level.

Part of Emma's negative "reprogramming" is undoubtedly exacerbated by the online trolling she experiences. Similarly, a recent study concurs that "rape culture is prominent within online social media comment threads and victim blaming is the prevailing attitude in which it is expressed," and, echoing Emma's experience, "women who consume alcohol prior to being raped had higher rates of victim blaming by both sexes, as compared to women who were assaulted while sober."[79] With social media so prevalent in young people's lives, it is acutely disconcerting that "these attitudes seep into the collective thought of society as these attitudes impact how society views rape and sexual assault. Instead of seeing the issue of sexual assault as an epidemic, this victim blaming and questioning attitude clouds one's judgment to believe rape is merely an individual issue and the survivor's fault."[80] Just as neoliberalism reduces feminist sociopolitical concerns to postfeminist individualization, social media—a corporate entity—condenses a major hierarchical gender issue, described as an "epidemic," into isolated micro incidents, and skews or "clouds" the issue which impacts detrimentally on cortical remapping. It is no accident that the depoliticization of young women away from the stigma of feminism and toward identifying with consumerist individualism coincides with a rape culture "epidemic" and a society that shares a predominant consensus of victim blaming due to its mass cortical reprogramming by monologic dominant discourses. To reiterate Jones's call for a renewed "feminist struggle,"[81] it is imperative that young women become alert to the very real need for collective feminism and to resist the trappings of corporate individualism that, quite literally, brainwash its citizens. In that capacity, YA fiction serves a vital mediatory role to assist the neuro-development of adolescent females and males, enabling them to navigate and critically interrogate discursive hegemony, utilizing fiction's dialogical plasticity.

Similarly, Andrew Bretz identifies an "endemic problem of rape culture being perpetuated on university campuses, a problem that is acute across the country from St Mary's and UBC, where frosh week pro-rape chants were defended as being 'traditional,' to the University of Ottawa" and, he continues, perpetrators "are misguided and they accept a system of gender relations that says what they have done is not only not wrong, it is the expected action of a man."[82] Postfeminism's propensity to sexualize young women and condone male sexual violence is urgently in need of redress by a new feminist politics, since "sexism exists on all sides of the gender divide. Many of the 'likes' on the Overheard at Guelph post [a Facebook gossip news group at University of Guelph] were given by women, and women promote and police rape culture as much as men."[83] As with Bretz's identified online rape culture, in O'Neill's text her protagonist suffers similar judgmental trolling and social media invasion of her privacy. Emma's rapists upload images to Facebook: "After one photo, twenty different boys gave my body marks out of ten."[84] Doubly violated by her attackers and the penetrative masculinist lens of social media, she despairs, "All I am is a thing [. . .] a collection of doll parts to be filled in and plugged up and passed on";[85] she is reduced to an intrusive assemblage of sexualized body parts, a dehumanized "doll" providing voyeuristic pleasure.

Unsurprisingly, she suffers an ontological schism: "My body is not my own any more. They have stamped their names all over it. Easy Emma":[86] after the rape, a dedicated Facebook page—"Easy Emma"—is established to continue her degradation and punishment. The dislocation is clearly symptomatic of post-traumatic stress disorder and the inability to recollect the heinous acts associated with the images: "Dylan on top of that girl (*me, me, that can't be me, that's not me*) [. . .] She has no face. She is just a body, a life-size doll to play with. She is an It. She is a thing (*me, me, me, me, me*). *I don't remember.*"[87] Her erased identity is accentuated with the removal of her face from the pictures, so that her humanity is supplanted with the role of an objectified sex-toy purely to serve male gratification. The epitome of this disconnect/disjuncture is that "I don't want to be in my body,"[88] leading to two suicide attempts in Emma's desperate desire to numb the pain and disappear: "I want all this to end."[89] Her desire for self-destruction emphasizes the aforementioned cortical remapping experienced by rape victims, fuelled by the discursive weight of social media's witch hunt.

Like Zaleski and Bretz, Irina Anderson and Kathy Doherty also identify a link between rape culture, victim blaming, and neoliberal individualism, while noting that "rape is both socially produced and socially legitimated, as a mechanism that ultimately maintains patriarchal gender power relations."[90]

As with the judgmental vilifying experienced by Emma, critical consensus identifies a culture defined by discursive positions that disempower rape victims and maintain Jones's "neopatriarchal containment." However, the act of reading Emma's trauma serves to mediate between narrative and reader as an empathetic awakening by offering an alternative perception of rape as well as empowering adolescents for potential extra-textual risks, all of which enhances neuropolitical maturation. Just as Bretz identifies "endemic" university rape culture, I first discussed this work as a research paper and, from the responses of a largely postgraduate audience, I identified that, as well as the scholarly importance of such critical work, it provides a vital site of interlocution for students. To discuss rape in a public forum felt daunting to me (perhaps indicative of rape's policed linguistic silencing functioning as a cultural taboo, as mentioned earlier), yet the topic's reception assured me that its critical and literary engagement is desperately needed in university environments and beyond as an urgent mediative practice and shying away from it merely perpetuates its erasure.[91] According to Aiyana Altrows, "Despite its increasing frequency as subject matter within the genre, representations of rape in adolescent fiction have not yet attracted sustained critical attention."[92] Critical engagement with such texts is imperative to advance the intellectual debate and to encourage dialogical spaces of mediative debate, and ensure we are not complicit in neopatriarchal silencing.

Emma's frequentation of spaces like parties and social media forums, as well as school, ensure that she is always under public surveillance, and must perform an image of perfect feminine allure for a masculine gaze. Though noting in parenthesis "(Her skin was so soft against mine),"[93] she suppresses the potential liberation of a real rather than simulated lesbian sexual chemistry between herself and Jamie and, instead, refocuses upon heteronormative endeavors, with "Zach's hands on my waist then, replacing hers."[94] Emma and Jamie's pseudo-lesbian encounter betrays feminist solidarity as an act of postfeminist sabotage: "*You're so hot, Jamie*, they kept saying. I didn't like it. I stroked her hair [. . .] my tongue in her mouth, the boys crowing."[95] The sociopolitical gains of lesbian feminism are inverted in a postfeminist culture that seeks to reductively repackage it as a voyeuristic commodity for male sexual gratification, so that "lesbianism is reconfigured as a popular (rather than pornographic) space of activity for phallic girls within circumscribed scenarios for male pleasure."[96] Contained within the masculine gaze's surveillance, Emma and Jamie's simulated sapphic encounter is performative spectacle. Such "masquerade disavows the spectral, powerful and castrating figures of the lesbian and the feminist with whom they might conceivably be linked"[97]—lesbianism's "powerful" political dynamic is commodified by postfeminism. Young "phallic" women like Emma are so afraid of feminism's and lesbianism's negative associations that they endorse and identify with neopatriarchal disempowerment. Any young woman who might actually identify as a lesbian or feminist is vilified and cortically conditioned to be ashamed; after she is ostracized and victim blamed by her school peers, Emma finds "There's only one seat left [. . .] next to Josephine Hurley, who everyone knows is a total lesbian."[98] Whether Josephine identifies as a lesbian or not, she is judged negatively to be so and isolated from the heteronormative mainstream. Now that Emma is the victim in a rape case, she is subject to the same social exclusion, signaling that in a postfeminist era there is no space for those who resist its antifeminist politics.

If young women do remain allured by postfeminist trappings that convey the illusory message of choice and freedom, then neopatriarchal dominance will prevail and their confinement will be absolute. While, on the one hand, corporate neoliberalism promises a world of unrestricted possibilities, the sobering truth is that gender is as polarized as ever in the neopatriarchal turn. Emma concedes, "I never thought that this would be my life, the small, small world of this house, and my parents [. . .] There is no escape."[99] While identifying with the consumer-driven perfection of femininity and "phallic" behavior as a partygoer, Emma is punished for transgressing into the male world and is consequently reined in by the domestic sphere's confinement, "tying me down" in predatory bondage.[100] The shrinkage of Emma's world and the destruction of her potential is a stark reminder for O'Neill's reader that women very much remain the second sex.

To comprehend Emma's "phallic" performativity, McRobbie argues that

the position of phallic girl can be understood as made available by the logic of the consumer culture, which in this case confirms and consolidates patriarchal privilege and masculine hegemony by apportioning some limited features of this privilege to young women, within specified conditions that they withhold critique of their male counterparts and that they are complicit with the norms of the new leisure culture where sexuality is redefined within the tabloid language of masculinist pleasures.[101]

Emma's phallic behavior, then, only exists as a simulacra of "masculine hegemony," in which its consumer trappings conspire in "inviting young women to overturn the old sexual double standard and emulate the assertive and hedonistic styles of sexuality associated with young men, particularly in holiday locations and also within the confines of licensed transgression of, for example, weekend heavy drinking culture."[102] Emma frequents such weekend parties associated with drinking and drug culture (both stimulants impair the brain), and so-called sexual liberation which exists strictly within the confines of "masculinist pleasures."

It is clear, though, from her narrative that she does not enjoy this lifestyle, instead finding herself trapped in its seemingly unstoppable hedonistic surge: though rapacious consumerism tells young women to enjoy the party, Emma perpetually hesitates and questions its legitimacy as a form of genuine female political progress. Her hesitancy is a textual mediator, urging the reader to renegotiate real-world circumstances and avoid emulating the vulnerability of O'Neill's protagonist. Such text/reader/society mediation cortically remaps the YA reader trajectory toward empowered and informed citizenship. For instance, she observes a "couple pressed up against the wall, the boy looking like he's trying to mold her body into the pebble-dashed wall."[103] This moment of sexual intimacy is undercut by the physicality of menacing masculinity: Emma's gaze witnesses the feminized girl being rendered as inanimate as the wall against which she is pressed. She recollects too "(Kevin, throwing me against a wall at the party, his teeth sharp.) [. . .] dragging me into a dimly lit bedroom that smells of Play-Doh. Tripping over a headless Barbie."[104] Dispensing with MacKinnon's "virginal daughter," intercourse and innocence collide to amplify images of postfeminist interpellation's enforced sexual activity: aggression against the female body ensures its "headless" disempowerment in a neopatriarchal hegemony where young women cannot protest. Despite Emma's protestation to "*get back to the party*," Kevin, vampirish predator, was "pushing me down" on the "candy-pink duvet."[105] Despite its apparent loosening of restrictions, such encoded masculine hegemony ensures "This playful female phallicism is also underpinned by a range of possible punishments, which give rise to a spiraling of female anxiety and pain for those who misread the rules."[106] Emma's violent reminder—gang rape and its aftermath—of her feminine otherness forces her retreat to the enclosed confines of domesticity's house arrest.

Similarly, Kim Toffoletti argues that postfeminism's sexualization of young women, bolstered by consumer products, signals a Baudrillardian hyperreality, where such "gestures of female emancipation at the site of the body, and their cultural imagining in the media, can only simulate liberation [. . .] providing us with the illusion of female empowerment through the guise of individual choices, rights, and freedoms."[107] The female body is corseted by the strictures of a corporatized image and its mantra of individual improvement, leaving no room for a politicized collective feminist consciousness or real-world protest. O'Neill's text, then, provides a much-needed literary space to allow her reader to develop a resistant consciousness of cortical remapping through its dialogical plasticity. Further, Toffoletti argues that such media intrusion into women's bodies and lives erases privacy in favor of perpetual public scrutiny, where "Each wrinkle, stretch mark, lump, and bump that the woman despises is amplified and available for public consumption."[108] Emma's violation includes an invasive camera lens—"He spreads her legs" and photographs "pink flesh, and I think of the hundreds of likes, of all the people who have seen this, who have seen her like this. Me"[109]—and the further degradation of those images being posted on social media. Gang rape and voyeuristic public exposure dismantle her hitherto teenage self-confidence: "I feel shame ripping through me, breaking me apart."[110] With the predominance of social media in young people's lives, the boundary between reality and virtual reality is transgressed, just as Emma narrates that "I don't even know what I actually remember, what are real memories, what are *mine*, and what's been implanted inside there by the Easy Emma page."[111] She is drowning in a plethora of discourses that interpret her lost weekend, filled with Facebook, her teacher, the police, her family, traditional media, and her friends, so that she feels dissociated from actual events: "those photos and those comments have become my memories."[112] As with Wolf's argument regarding a rape victim's diminishment and reprogramming, even Emma's recollection of events is reduced and reshaped to an uncertain blur. O'Neill requires her reader to consider the impact of narratives and, by doing so, learn to read between the lines as a critical thinker.

Asking For It offers a vital critique of postfeminism's simulacra much needed by YAs insofar as it breaks the complicit silence inscribed by gender hierarchies that endorse and perpetuate rape culture. MeToo momentum has empowered victims of rape and sexual harassment within a collective movement that appears to be challenging neoliberalism's isolationism, just as *Asking For It* queries the authority of neopatriarchal silencing and mediates a pathway for young readers that encourages them to reshape the status quo of gender politics. YA fiction like O'Neill's is a vital mediator to accentuate the hypocrisies and paradoxes of post-truth contemporary society and to help its readership critically rethink other positions. Otherwise, hegemonic discourses will diminish adolescent maturation and confine a future generation of citizens into accepting narratives that hamper the neural pathways of their cerebral development. This restricted intellectual and critical capacity to challenge hegemony aligns with the view that citizens who succumb to such narratives become "political zombies" who are "politically myopic and intellectually shallow."[113] To be zombified suggests a lobotomized populace who have lost the "intrinsic acumen to question and to think critically outside the liberal, capitalist, ideological box."[114] By accepting hegemonic narratives, Emma's peers fail to exercise their grey matter and enable an overarching verisimilitude to restrictively shape their development and ability to generate alternatives to the angel/whore dichotomy of slut-shaming. In turn, this perpetuates an intellectual confinement that mirrors her shrinking world within the enclosed parameters of her family home, ensuring that she is unable to connect with a viable political feminism to aid and empower her.

Asking For It provides a vital counter-voice to postfeminist slut-shaming and victim blaming in a rape culture epidemic that otherwise leaves young women confined and straightjacketed within neopatriarchal narratives. It interrogates neoliberal postfeminism's illusory freedom that simultaneously entraps young women within a neopatriarchal matrix of consumerist individualism. To

return to Bakhtin's assessment of fiction as "plasticity itself" and "ever quest-
ing," activist YA fiction like O'Neill's enhances and revitalizes adolescent
readers' cortical malleability and journey toward maturation. To reiterate
Wolf's contention that rape injures the brain, O'Neill's text charts how cortical reprogramming diminishes gendered adolescent agency, while remapping
that agency through her counternarrative's dynamic neuroplasticity. The act
of reading, then, dialogically opens up a resistant space of cortical remapping
by accessing other narratives that can equip future citizens with the ability to
critically challenge rather than remain complicit within an otherwise zombified hyperreality. For Draganski et al., reading is an intellectual stimulant that
develops the brain's grey matter, while Armstrong recognizes literature's
neuroaesthetic benefits. If YA fiction's mediation vicariously enhances the
empathetic qualities of a reader's cognitive abilities, it is surely a no-brainer
to complement this with literature's cortical possibilities demonstrated within
the field of neuroplasticity. As such, O'Neill's textual heteroglossia is suffused
with neuropolitical potential in its interrogation of postfeminist rape culture
which pedagogically encourages a dynamic citizenship of resistant readers.

NOTES

1. Louise O'Neill, *Asking for It* (London: Quercus, 2015), 197.
2. For further discussion of globalization and neoliberalism, see, for instance,
Zillah Eisenstein, *Global Obscenities: Patriarchy, Capitalism, and the Lure of
Cyberfantasy* (New York: NYU Press, 1998) and David Harvey, *A Brief History of
Neoliberalism* (Oxford: Oxford University Press, 2005).
3. Neopatriarchy, first coined by Hisham Sharabi (1988) in relation to the Arab
World, alludes to patriarchy's evolvement insofar as it reinvents "itself after a time
period in the space of capitalism and cultural or social settings [. . .] This new form
of patriarchy has an ultimate purpose to suppress and repress the women at household
level." Ume Habiba, Rabia Ali and Asia Ashfaq, "From Patriarchy to Neopatriarchy:
Experiences of Women from Pakistan," *International Journal of Humanities and
Social Science* 6, no. 3 (March 2016): 212–21, 216.
4. Beatrix Campbell, *End of Equality: The Only Way is Women's Liberation*
(London, New York, and Calcutta: Seagull Books, 2013), 91.
5. Carole Jones, "'Femininity in Crisis': The Troubled Trajectory of Feminism
in Laura Hird's *Born Free* and Jenni Fagan's *The Panopticon*," *Contemporary
Women's Writing* 9, no. 3 (2015): 385–400, 399.
6. Louise O'Neill, "Louise O'Neill: 'I Think This Book Will Infuriate a Lot of
People because It's Going to Push Those Buttons,'" interview by Patrick Sproull, *The
Guardian*, September 2, 2015, https://www.theguardian.com/childrens-books-site
/2015/sep/02/louise-oneill-asking-for-it-interview.
7. For further consideration of YA fiction censorship see, for example, Caren
J. Town, *"Unsuitable" Books: Young Adult Fiction and Censorship* (New York:

McFarland, 2014); Alexandria K. Mintah, "Young Adult Literature: Ethics, Evils, and the Ever-Present Question of Censorship," *Exigence* 2, no. 1 (2018): 1–15.

8. Emma Yates-Bradley, "Review: Jeanette Winterson in Conversation with Louise O'Neill," *Northern Soul*, February 24, 2016, https://www.northernsoul.me.uk /louise-o-neill/.

9. Sproull, "Interview."

10. See, for instance, Alison Flood, "Authors and Readers Rally to Defend Rape Novel from School Ban," *The Guardian*, September 29, 2010, https://www.theguardian.com/books/2010/sep/29/defend-novel-school-ban.

11. S.E. Smith, "Silence is the Problem: The Darkness of Young Adult Fiction and Why #YAsaves," *Global Comment*, June 7, 2011, http://globalcomment.com/the -darkness-of-young-adult-fiction-and-why-yasaves/.

12. Joe Lynch, "Madonna Delivers Her Blunt Truth during Fiery, Teary Billboard Women in Music Speech," *Billboard*, December 9, 2016, http://www.billboard.com /articles/events/women-in-music/7616927/madonna-billboard-woman-of-the-year -labrinth.

13. Sproull, "Interview."

14. *Masc*, "Traolach O' Buachalla," interview, January 30, 2017, https://masc .life/home/2017/1/16/traolach-o-buachalla.

15. Laura Brennan, "Asking for It? Louise O'Neill Documentary Receives Huge Response," "News in Brief," *The Irish Film and Television Network*, November 2, 2016, http://iftn.ie/news/?act1=record&only=1&aid=73&rid=4289819&tpl=arch-news&force=1.

16. O'Neill, *Asking*, 154.

17. O'Neill, *Asking*, 14.

18. O'Neill, *Asking*, 318.

19. Catharine A. Mackinnon, "Rape: On Coercion and Consent," in *Writing on the Body: Female Embodiment and Feminist Theory*, eds. K. Conboy, N. Medina and S. Stanbury (New York: Columbia University Press, 1997), 42–58, 46.

20. MacKinnon, "Rape," 46.

21. Natasha Walter, *Living Dolls: The Return of Sexism* (London: Virago, 2010), 120.

22. O'Neill, *Asking*, 232.

23. Naomi Wolf, *Vagina: A New Biography* (London: Virago, 2012), 99.

24. Wolf, *Vagina*.

25. Wolf, *Vagina*, 99–100, my italics.

26. O'Neill, *Asking*, 335.

27. Wolf, *Vagina*, 107.

28. O'Neill, *Asking*, 271.

29. Mikhail Bakhtin, quoted in Pam Morris, "Introduction," in *The Bakhtin Reader: Selected Writings of Bakhtin, Medvedev, Voloshinov*, ed. Pam Morris (London and New York: Edward Arnold, 1994), 1–24, 20.

30. See, for instance, Jacqueline Rose, *The Case of Peter Pan: Or the Impossibility of Children's Fiction* (London: Macmillan Press, 1994 [1984]); Deborah Cogan Thacker and Jean Webb, *Introducing Children's Literature: From Romanticism to Postmodernism* (London and New York: Routledge, 2002).

31. Fiona McCulloch, *The Fictional Role of Childhood in Victorian and Early Twentieth Century Children's Literature* (Lewiston, Queenston and Lampeter: Edwin Mellen Press, 2004).

32. Bakhtin, "The Heteroglot Novel," in *The Bakhtin Reader*, ed. Morris, 112–120, 118, 119.

33. David Rudd, *Reading the Child in Children's Literature: An Heretical Approach* (Palgrave Macmillan, 2013), 186–87.

34. Rose, *The Case of Peter Pan*, 26.

35. Roberta Seelinger Trites, *Disturbing the Universe: Power and Repression in Adolescent Literature* (Iowa City, IA: University of Iowa Press, 2000), 16.

36. Trites, *Disturbing the Universe*, 3.

37. See Fiona McCulloch, *Contemporary British Children's Fiction and Cosmopolitanism* (New York and London: Routledge, 2017).

38. Maria Jose Botelho and Masha Kabakow Rudman, *Critical Multicultural Analysis of Children's Literature* (New York and London: Routledge, 2009), 44.

39. Bakhtin, "The Heteroglot Novel," in *The Bakhtin Reader*, ed. Morris, 119.

40. Angela McRobbie, "Top Girls?" *Cultural Studies* 21, no. 4–5 (2007): 718–37, 720.

41. O'Neill, *Asking*, 335, 192.

42. Angela McRobbie, "Young Women and Consumer Culture," *Cultural Studies* 22, no. 5 (2008): 531–550, 533.

43. MacKinnon, "Rape," 52.

44. MacKinnon, "Rape," 52.

45. MacKinnon, "Rape," 52.

46. *Masc*, "Traolach O' Buachalla."

47. O'Neill, *Asking*, 227, 317.

48. Yates-Bradley, "Review."

49. Catharine A. MacKinnon, *Women's Lives, Men's Laws* (Cambridge and London: The Belknap Press of Harvard University Press, 2007 [2005]), 129.

50. MacKinnon, *Women's Lives*.

51. Sarah Projansky, *Watching Rape: Film and Television in Postfeminist Culture* (New York and London: New York University Press, 2001), 13, 14.

52. Sorcha Gunne and Zoe Brigley Thompson, "Introduction: Feminism without Borders: The Potentials and Pitfalls of Retheorizing Rape," in *Feminism, Literature and Rape Narratives: Violence and Violation,* eds. Gunne and Thompson (New York and London: Routledge, 2010), 1–20, 4.

53. Goodreads, "*Asking for It* by Louise O'Neill," https://www.goodreads.com/book/show/25255576-asking-for-it, accessed January 20, 2021.

54. Goodreads, "*Asking for It* by Louise O'Neill."

55. For information on social reading, see DeNel Rehberg Sedo, "Cultural Capital and Community in Contemporary City-Wide Reading Programs," *Mémoires du Livre: Studies in Book Culture* 2, no. 1 (2010), https://www.erudit.org/en/journals/memoires/2010-v2-n1-memoires3974/045314ar/; José-Antonio Cordón-García, Julio Alonso-Arévalo, Raquel Gómez-Díaz and Daniel Linder, *Social Reading: Platforms, Applications, Clouds and Tags* (Oxford, Cambridge, and New Delhi: Chandos Publishing, 2013); Alyssa Harder, Vivian Howard and DeNel Rehberg Sedo, "Creating Cohesive Community through

Shared Reading: A Case Study of One Book Nova Scotia," *Partnerships: The Canadian Journal of Library and Information Practice and Research* 10, no. 1 (2015): 1–21.

56. Ingrid Johnston and Jyoti Mangat, *Reading Practices, Postcolonial Literature, and Cultural Mediation in the Classroom* (Rotterdam: Sense Publishers, 2012), vii.

57. O'Neill, *Asking,* 223.

58. O'Neill, *Asking,* 282, 311–12.

59. O'Neill, *Asking*, 248.

60. O'Neill, *Asking*, 313.

61. O'Neill, *Asking*, 93–94.

62. O'Neill, *Asking*, 61.

63. O'Neill, *Asking*, 214.

64. Projansky, *Watching Rape*, 5.

65. O'Neill, *Asking*, 344.

66. Gérard Genette, *Paratexts: Thresholds of Interpretation*, Translated by Jane E. Lewin (Cambridge: Cambridge University Press, 1997).

67. Jane Wangari Wakarindi, "Abstract," from "Paratext and the Making of YA Fiction Genre: The Repoussoir," *Eastern African Literary and Cultural Studies* 5, no. 12 (August 2019): 1–15.

68. O'Neill, *Asking*, 344.

69. Bogdan Draganski, Christian Gaser, Gerd Kempermann, H. Georg Kuhn, Jürgen Winkler, Christian Büchel, and Arne May, "Temporal and Spatial Dynamics of Brain Structure Changes during Extensive Learning," *The Journal of Neuroscience* 26, no. 23 (2006): 6314–17, 6317.

70. Paul B. Armstrong, *How Literature Plays with the Brain: The Neuroscience of Reading and Art* (Baltimore, MD: John Hopkins University Press, 2013), 2, 3.

71. Armstrong, *How Literature Plays*, xiii.

72. Armstrong, *How Literature Plays*, xiii.

73. John T. Pardeck and Jean Pardeck, eds., *Bibliotherapy: A Clinical Approach for Helping Children* (Yverdon, Paris, and Reading: Gordon and Breach Science Publishers, 1993), 2.

74. Maria Nikolajeva, *Reading for Learning: Cognitive Approaches to Children's Literature* (Amsterdam: John Benjamins Publishing, 2014), 79.

75. Armstrong, *How Literature Plays*, 11.

76. Armstrong, *How Literature Plays*, 11.

77. Diana I. Tamir, Andrew B. Bricker, David Dodell-Feder, and Jason P. Mitchell, "Reading Fiction and Reading Minds: The Role of Simulation in the Default Network," *Social Cognitive and Affective Neuroscience* 11, no. 2 (2016): 215–24, 216, 217.

78. Seelinger Trites, *Twenty-First-Century Feminisms in Children's and Adolescent Literature* (MS: University Press of Mississippi, 2018), 181.

79. Kristen. L. Zaleski, Kristin K. Gundersen, Jessica Baes, Ely Estupinian, and Alyssa Vergara, "Exploring Rape Culture in Social Media Forums," *Computers in Human Behaviour* 63 (2016): 922–27, 926, 923.

80. Zaleski, et al., "Exploring Rape Culture," 926.

81. Jones, "Femininity," 399.

82. Andrew Bretz, "Making an Impact?: Feminist Pedagogy and Rape Culture on University Campuses," *ESC: English Studies in Canada* 40, no. 4 (2014): 17–20, 19.

83. Bretz, "Making an Impact," 19.

84. O'Neill, *Asking*, 323.

85. O'Neill, *Asking*, 323.

86. O'Neill, *Asking*, 161.

87. O'Neill, *Asking*, 146.

88. O'Neill, *Asking*, 200.

89. O'Neill, *Asking*, 272.

90. Irina Anderson and Kathy Doherty, *Accounting for Rape: Psychology, Feminism and Discourse Analysis in the Study of Sexual Violence* (London and New York: Routledge, 2008), 4.

91. C.J. Bott, "Why We Must Read Young Adult Books that Deal with Sexual Content," *The Alan Review* 33, no. 3 (Summer 2006): 26–29, https://doi.org/10.21061/alan.v33i3.a.4, importantly argues adults should familiarize themselves with YA rape novels because "Recommendations from teachers and librarians are often the only way teens hear about such books" (26). It is objectionable though, that Bott's interpretation of Gigi's date rape in Chris Lynch's *Inexcusable* concludes she "has some responsibility in the event" (28).

92. Aiyana Altrows, "Rape Scripts and Rape Spaces: Constructions of Female Bodies in Adolescent Fiction," *International Research in Children's Literature* 9, no. 1 (2016): 50–64, 51.

93. O'Neill, *Asking*, 93.

94. O'Neill, *Asking*, 93.

95. O'Neill, *Asking*, 93.

96. McRobbie, "Young Women," 732–33.

97. McRobbie, "Young Women," 725.

98. O'Neill, *Asking*, 126.

99. O'Neill, *Asking*, 310.

100. O'Neill, *Asking*, 310.

101. McRobbie, "Young Women," 733.

102. McRobbie, "Young Women," 732.

103. O'Neill, *Asking*, 86.

104. O'Neill, *Asking*, 29.

105. O'Neill, *Asking*, 29.

106. McRobbie, "Young Women," 733.

107. Kim Toffoletti, "Baudrillard, Postfeminism, and the Image Makeover," *Cultural Politics* 10, no. 1 (2014): 105–19, 117.

108. Toffoletti, "Baudrillard," 114.

109. O'Neill, *Asking*, 147.

110. O'Neill, *Asking*, 147.

111. O'Neill, *Asking*, 303.

112. O'Neill, *Asking*, 201.

113. Armando Navarro, *Global Capitalist Crisis and the Second Great Depression: Egalitarian Systematic Models for Change* (Plymouth: Lexington Books, 2012), 389.

114. Navarro, *Global Capitalist Crisis and the Second Great Depression*.

Bibliography

Adams, Gillian. "The Francelia Butler Watershed: Then and Now." *Children's Literature Association Quarterly* 25, no. 4 (2000): 181–90.

Ahlberg, Allan and Paul Howard. *The Bravest Ever Bear.* London: Walker Books, 1999.

Airne, C.W. *The Story of Roman and Pre-Roman Britain.* "Told in Pictures." Manchester: Sankey, Hudson & Co., c. 1930.

Allington, Daniel. "On the Use of Anecdotal Evidence in Reception Study and the History of Reading." In *Reading in History New Methodologies from the Anglo-American Tradition.* The History of the Book, no. 6, edited by Bonnie Gunzenhauser, 11–28. London: Pickering & Chatto, 2010; Abingdon and New York: Routledge, 2016.

Alteri, Suzan A. "From Laboratory to Library: The History of Wayne State University's Education Library." *Education Libraries* 32, no. 1 (2009): 12–16.

Altrows, Aiyana. "Raperule Scripts and Rape Spaces: Constructions of Female Bodies in Adolescent Fiction." *International Research in Children's Literature* 9, no. 1 (2016): 50–64.

Anderson, Ann, Jim Anderson, Jacqueline Lynch, Jon Shapiro and Ji Eun Kim. "Extra-Textual Talk in Shared Book Reading: A Focus on Questioning." *Early Child Development and Care* 182, no. 9 (2012): 1139–54.

Anderson, Irina and Kathy Doherty. *Accounting for Rape: Psychology, Feminism and Discourse Analysis in the Study of Sexual Violence.* London and New York: Routledge, 2008.

Arizpe, Evelyn. "Meaning-Making from Wordless (or Nearly Wordless) Picturebooks: What Educational Research Expects and What Readers Have to Say." *Cambridge Journal of Education* 43, no. 2 (2013): 163–76.

Arizpe, Evelyn and Vivienne Smith, eds. *Children as Readers in Children's Literature: The Power of Text and the Importance of Reading.* London: Routledge, 2016.

Arizpe, Evelyn and Morag Styles. *Children Reading Picturebooks: Interpreting Visual Texts.* Oxford: Routledge, 2016; Hoboken, NJ: Taylor and Francis, 2016.

Arizpe, Evelyn, Morag Styles and Shirley Brice Heath. *Reading Lessons from the Eighteenth Century: Mothers, Children and Texts.* Lichfield: Pied Piper, 2006.

Armstrong, Paul B. *How Literature Plays with the Brain: The Neuroscience of Reading and Art.* Baltimore, MD: John Hopkins University Press, 2013.

Austen, Jane. *Emma.* Oxford and New York: Oxford University Press, 1989.

Austen, Jane. *Mansfield Park.* Oxford and New York: Oxford University Press, 1989.

Austen, Jane. *Northanger Abbey.* London and New York: Penguin, 1994.

Austen, Jane. *Northanger Abbey,* edited by Anne Henry Ehrenpreis. London: Penguin, 1972.

Bailey, Mary, Colin Harrison and Greg Brooks. "The Boots Books for Babies Project: Impact on Library Registrations and Book Loans." *Journal of Early Childhood Literacy* 2, no. 1 (2002): 45–63.

Baines, Phil. *Puffin by Design: 70 Years of Imagination 1940–2010.* London: Penguin Books, 2010.

Bakhtin, Mikhail. "The Heteroglot Novel." In *The Bakhtin Reader: Selected Writings of Bakhtin, Medvedev, Voloshinov*, edited by Pam Morris, 112–20. London and New York: Edward Arnold, 1994.

Baldwin, Ruth M. *Index to the Baldwin Library of Books in English before 1900, Primarily for Children.* Boston, MA: G. K. Hall, 1981.

Baldwin, Ruth M. *Papers.* George A. Smathers Libraries, University of Florida.

Barrie, J.M. "Wrecked on an Island." *National Observer* 11, no. 274 (February 17, 1894): 345.

Basbanes, Nicholas. *A Gentle Madness: Bibliophiles, Bibliomanes, and the Eternal Passion for Books.* New York: H. Holt & Co., 1995.

Basbanes, Nicholas. "Collectors and Libraries: Some Studies in Symbiosis." *Rare Books and Manuscripts Librarianship* 8, no. 1 (1993): 37–48.

Bateman, John, Janina Wildfeuer and Tuomo Hippala. *Multimodality: Foundations, Research and Analysis – A Problem-Oriented Introduction.* Berlin: De Gruyter, 2017.

Baxter, Richard. *A Treatise of Self-Denial.* 2nd ed. London, 1675.

BBC. "More Animal Main Characters than Non-White People in Children's Books." *BBC Newsround*, November 20, 2020. https://www.bbc.co.uk/newsround/54900501.

Bearne, Eve and Gunther Kress. "Editorial." *Reading* 35, no. 3 (2001): 89–93.

Becker, Bonny and Kady MacDonald Denton. *A Library Book for Bear.* London: Walker Books, 2015.

Benjamin, Walter. "Old Forgotten Children's Books." In *Selected Writings*, *Selected Writings: Volume 1 1913–1926*, edited by Marcus Bullock and Michael W. Jennings, 406–13. Cambridge, MA: Belknap Press of Harvard University Press, 2002.

Benjamin, Walter. "Unpacking My Library." In Walter Benjamin, *Illuminations*, edited with an introduction by Hannah Arendt, translated by Harry Zohn, 58–68. New York: Schocken Books, 1969.

Bernstein, Robin. "'You Do It!': Going-to-Bed Books and the Scripts of Children's Literature." *PMLA* 135, no. 5 (2020): 877–94.

Beyer, Susanne and Lothar Gorris. "We Like Lists because We Don't Want to Die." Interview with Umberto Eco. *SPIEGEL International*, November 22, 2009. https://

www.spiegel.de/international/zeitgeist/spiegel-interview-with-umberto-eco-we
-like-lists-because-we-don-t-want-to-die-a-659577-2.html.

Bezemer, Jeff and Gunther Kress. "Visualizing English: A Social Semiotic History of a School Subject." *Visual Communication* 8, no. 3 (2009): 247–62.

Bhadury, Poushali. "Metafiction, Narrative Metalepsis, and New Media Forms in the Neverending Story and the Inkworld Trilogy." *The Lion and the Unicorn* 37, no. 3 (2013): 301–26.

Blake Stevenson. *Bookbug for the Home—Outreach Programme: Year ¾ Evaluation.* Edinburgh: Scottish Book Trust, 2016.

Blatt, Jane and Sarah Massini. *Books Always Everywhere.* London: Nosy Crow, 2013.

Blouin, Francis X., Jr. "Archivists, Mediation, and Constructs of Social Memory." *Archival Issues* 24, no. 2 (1999): 101–12.

Blouin, Francix X., Jr. "History and Memory: The Problem of the Archive." *PMLA* 119, no. 2 (2004): 296–98.

Board of Education. *Handbook of Suggestions for the Consideration of Teachers and Others Involved in the Work of Public Elementary Schools.* London: HMSO, 1937.

Board of Education. *Report of the Consultative Committee on Books in Public Elementary Schools.* London: HMSO, 1928.

Board of Education. *Report of the Consultative Committee on the Primary School.* London: HMSO, 1931.

Bonci, Angela. *A Research Review: The Importance of Families and the Home Environment.* London: National Literacy Trust, 2011.

Botelho, Maria Jose and Masha Kabakow Rudman. *Critical Multicultural Analysis of Children's Literature.* New York and London: Routledge, 2009.

Bott, C.J. "Why We Must Read Young Adult Books that Deal with Sexual Content." *The Alan Review* 33, no. 3 (Summer 2006): 26–29.

Bourdieu, Pierre. "Cultural Reproduction and Social Reproduction." In *Power and Ideology in Education*, edited by Jerome Karabel and A.H. Halsey, 487–511. Oxford: Oxford University Press, 1977.

Bourdieu, Pierre. *Outline of a Theory of Practice.* Cambridge: Cambridge University Press, 1977.

Bow, Leslie. "Racial Abstraction and Species Difference: Anthropomorphic Animals in 'Multicultural' Children's Literature." *American Literature* 91, no. 2 (2019): 323–56.

Bradshaw, Paul, Tom King, Line Knudsen, James Law and Clare Sharp. *Language Development and Enjoyment of Reading: Impacts of Early Parent-Child Activities in Two Growing Up in Scotland Cohorts.* Edinburgh: The Scottish Government: Children and Families Analysis, 2016.

Bragadottir, Hrefna. *Baxter's Book.* London: Nosy Crow, 2016.

Brantlinger, Patrick. *The Reading Lesson: The Threat of Mass Literacy in Nineteenth-Century British Fiction.* Bloomington, IN: Indiana University Press, 1998.

Brennan, Laura. "Asking for It? Louise O'Neill Documentary Receives Huge Response." *News in Brief*, November 2, 2016, *The Irish Film and Television Network.* http://iftn.ie/news/?act1=record&only=1&aid=73&rid=4289819&tpl=archnews&force=1.

Bretz, Andrew. "Making an Impact?: Feminist Pedagogy and Rape Culture on University Campuses." *ESC: English Studies in Canada* 40, no. 4 (2014): 17–20.

British Association for the Advancement of Science. *Report on the Influence of Schoolbooks upon Eyesight.* London: John Murray, 1913.

Brooks, Greg and Peter Hannon. "Research Issues in Family Literacy." In *Sage Handbook of Early Childhood Literacy*, edited by Jackie Larson and Jackie Marsh, 194–206. London: SAGE, 2013.

Brown, Gillian. "The Metamorphic Book: Children's Print Culture in the Eighteenth Century." *Eighteenth-Century Studies* 39, no. 3, New Feminist Work in Epistemology and Aesthetics (Spring 2006): 351–62.

Browne, Anthony. *I Like Books.* London: Walker Books, 2009.

Bruno, Paul. *Kant's Concept of Genius: Its Origin and Function in the Third Critique.* London and New York: Continuum, 2010.

Buckingham, Jennifer, Kevin Wheldall and Robyn Beaman-Wheldall. "Why Poor Children Are More Likely to Become Poor Readers: The School Years." *Australian Journal of Education* 57, no. 3 (2013): 190–213.

Bus, Adriana G., Marinus H. van Ijzendoorn and Anthony D. Pellegrini. "Joint Book Reading Makes for Success in Learning to Read: A Meta-Analysis on Intergenerational Transmission of Literacy." *Review of Educational Research* 65, no. 1 (1995): 1–21.

Byrne, Richard. *This Book Is Out of Control!* Oxford: Oxford University Press, 2017.

Byrne, Richard. *This Book Just Ate My Dog!* Oxford: Oxford University Press, 2014.

Byrne, Richard. *We Are in the Wrong Book!* Oxford: Oxford University Press, 2016.

Cairns, Elizabeth. *Memoirs of the Life of Elizabeth Cairns.* Glasgow: John Greig, 1762.

Campbell, Beatrix. *End of Equality: The Only Way is Women's Liberation.* London, New York, and Calcutta: Seagull Books, 2013.

Campbell, Jen and Katie Harnett. *Franklin's Flying Bookshop.* London: Thames and Hudson, 2017.

Capshaw, Katharine. "Archives and Magic Lanterns." *Children's Literature Association Quarterly* 39, no. 3 (2014): 313–15.

Carnell, Harriett M.T. *Rice Pudding.* "Betty's Geography Lessons." London: George Gill & Sons, c. 1930.

Carrington, Vicky and Allan Luke. "Literacy and Bourdieu's Sociological Theory: A Reframing." *Language and Education* 11, no. 2 (1997): 96–112.

Catalogue of School Books for Primary Schools. Exeter: Wheaton, 1957.

Chartier, Roger. "Laborers and Voyagers: From the Text to the Reader." In *The Book History Reader,* edited by David Finkelstein and Alistair McCleery, 87–98. London: Routledge, 2002.

Chartier, Roger. *The Order of Books: Readers, Authors and Libraries in Europe between the Fourteenth and Eighteenth Centuries,* translated by Lydia Cochrane. Stanford, CA: Stanford University Press, 1994.

Cheadle, Jacob E. "Educational Investment, Family Context, and Children's Math and Reading Growth from Kindergarten through the Third Grade." *Sociology of Education* 81, no. 1 (2008): 1–31.

Child, Lauren. *Beware of Storybook Wolves.* London: Hodder Children's Books, 2000.

Child, Lauren. *Who's Afraid of the Big Bad Book?* London: Hodder Children's Books, 2002.

Chung, Shunah and Daniel J. Walsh. "Unpacking Child-Centredness: A History of Meanings." *Journal of Curriculum Studies* 32, no. 2 (2000): 215–34. http://dx.doi.org/10.1080/002202700182727.

Clark, Emma Chichester. *Bears Don't Read!* London: HarperCollins, 2014.

Claxton, Guy and Margaret Carr. "A Framework for Teaching Learning: The Dynamics of Disposition." *Early Years* 24, no. 1 (2004): 87–97.

Cleminson, Kate. *Otto the Book Bear.* London: Jonathan Cape, 2011.

Coade, George. *Letter to the Right Honourable W.P. Esq; by George Coade, Merchant, of Exeter.* London: for and by J. Scott, 1758.

Coelho, Joseph and Fiona Lumbers. *Luna Loves Library Day.* London: Andersen Press, 2017.

Cohen, Michele. "'Familiar Conversation:' The Role of the 'Familiar Format' in Education in Eighteenth- and Nineteenth-Century England." In *Educating the Child in Enlightenment Britain: Beliefs, Cultures, Practices*, edited by Mary Hilton and Jill Shefrin, 99–116. Farnham: Ashgate, 2009.

Collins, Fiona M. and Cathy Svensson. "If I Had a Magic Wand I'd Magic Her Out of the Book: The Rich Literacy Practices of Competent Early Readers." *Early Years* 28, no. 1 (2008): 81–91.

Cook, Terry. "Archival Science and Postmodernism: New Formulations for Old Concepts." *Archival Science* 1 (2001): 3–24.

Cook, Terry. "Evidence, Memory, Identity, and Community: Four Shifting Archival Paradigms." *Archival Science* 13 (2013): 95–120.

Cook, Terry. "The Archive(s) Is a Foreign Country: Historians, Archivists, and the Changing Archival Landscape." *The American Archivist* 74, no. 2 (Fall/Winter 2011): 600–32.

Cordón-García, José-Antonio, Julio Alonso-Arévalo, Raquel Gómez-Díaz and Daniel Linder. *Social Reading: Platforms, Applications, Clouds and Tags.* Oxford, Cambridge, and New Delhi: Chandos Publishing, 2013.

Cousin, Glynis. "Exploring Threshold Concepts for Linking Teaching and Research." Conference paper, *The International Colloquium: International Policies and Practices for Academic Enquiry*, Winchester, 2007. Accessed January 2021, https://www.ee.ucl.ac.uk/~mflanaga/Glynis_Cousin_Exploring_.pdf.

Cousin, Glynis. "Threshold Concepts: Undergraduate Teaching, Postgraduate Training, Professional Development and School Education: A Short Introduction and a Bibliography f[r]om 2003 to 2018." Accessed January 2021, https://www.ee.ucl.ac.uk/~mflanaga/thresholds.html.

Cousins, Lucy. *Maisy Goes to the Bookshop.* London: Walker Books, 2007.

Cousins, Lucy. *Maisy Goes to the Library.* London: Walker Books, 2017.

Crain, Patricia. *Reading Children. Literacy, Property and the Dilemmas of Childhood in Nineteenth-Century America.* Philadelphia, PA: University of Pennsylvania Press, 2016.

Crone, Rosalind, Katie Halsey and Shafquat Towheed. "Examining the Evidence of Reading: Three Examples from the Reading Experience Database, 1450–1945." In *New Methodologies from the Anglo-American Tradition.* The History of the Book, no. 6, edited by Bonnie Gunzenhauser, 29–46. London: Pickering & Chatto, 2010; Abingdon and New York: Routledge, 2016.

Cusenza, Joan. *The Eloise Ramsey Collection of Literature for Young People: A Catalogue.* Detroit, MI: Wayne State University Libraries, 1967.

Darnton, Robert. "First Steps toward a History of Reading." *Australian Journal of French Studies* 23 (1986): 5–30, reprinted in *The Kiss of Lamourette: Reflections in Cultural History.* London: Faber & Faber, 1990, 154–187.

Davidson, Emma, Christina McMellon, Laura Airey and Helen Berry. *Evaluating the Impact of Bookbug Bags and Sessions in Scotland.* Edinburgh: Scottish Book Trust, 2018.

Davies, Rebecca. *Written Maternal Authority and Eighteenth-Century Education in Britain: Educating by the Book.* London and New York: Routledge, 2014.

Dearden, Lorraine, Luke Sibieta and Kathy Sylva. "The Socio-Economic Gradient in Early Child Outcomes: Evidence from the Millennium Cohort Study." *Longitudinal and Life Course Studies* 2, no. 1 (2011): 19–40.

DeBaryshe, Barbara D. and Janeen Binder. "Development of an Instrument for Measuring Parental Beliefs about Reading Aloud to Young Children." *Perceptual and Motor Skills* 78, no. 3 (1994): 1303–11.

DeBaryshe, Barbara D., Janeen C. Binder and Martha Jane Buell. "Mothers' Implicit Theories of Early Literacy Instruction: Implications for Children's Reading and Writing." *Early Child Development and Care* 160, no. 1 (2000): 119–31.

Delgado, Pablo, Cristina Vargas, Rakefet Ackerman and Ladislao Salmerón. "Don't Throw Away Your Printed Books: A Meta-Analysis on the Effects of Reading Media on Reading Comprehension." *Educational Research Review* 25 (2018): 23–38.

Delin, Judy, John Bateman and Patrick Allen. "A Model of Genre in Document Layout." *Information Design Journal* 11, no. 1 (2002): 54–66.

DeLuzio, Crista. *Female Adolescence in American Scientific Thought, 1830–1930.* Baltimore, MD: Johns Hopkins University Press, 2007.

de Ritter, Richard. "Leisure to Be Wise: Edgeworthian Education and the Possibilities of Domesticity." *Journal for Eighteenth-Century Studies* 33, no. 3 (2010): 313–33.

Derrida, Jacques. *Dissemination*, translated and introduction by Barbara Johnson. New York: Continuum, 2004.

Deverson, H.J. *The Map that Came to Life.* Oxford: Oxford University Press, 1948.

Deverson, H.J. *The Map that Came to Life.* "Ronald Lampitt." The Visual Telling of Stories. Chris Mullen. Accessed November 2020, http://www.fulltable.com/VTS/aoi/l/lampitt/map.htm.

Doherty, Helen and Thomas Doherty. *The Snatchabook.* London: Alison Green Books, 2013.

Donaldson, Julia and Sara Ogilvie. *The Detective Dog.* London: Macmillan Children's Books, 2016.

Donaldson, Julia and Axel Scheffler. *Charlie Cook's Favourite Books.* London: Macmillan Children's Books, 2005.

Do Rozario, Rebecca-Anne. "Consuming Books: Synergy of Materiality and Narrative in Picturebooks." *Children's Literature* 40 (2012): 151–66.

Douglas, Jennifer. "A Call to Rethink Archival Creation: Exploring Types of Creation in Personal Archives." *Archival Science* 18 (2018): 29–49.

Dowdall, Nicholas, Peter J. Cooper, Mark Tomlinson, Sarah Skeen, Frances Gardner and Lynne Murray. "The Benefits of Early Book Sharing for Child Cognitive and Socio-Emotional Development in South Africa: Study Protocol for a Randomised Controlled Trial." *Trials* 18, no. 1 (2017): 1–13.

Draganski, Bogdan, Christian Gaser, Gerd Kempermann, H. Georg Kuhn, Jürgen Winkler, Christian Büchel, and Arne May. "Temporal and Spatial Dynamics of Brain Structure Changes during Extensive Learning." *The Journal of Neuroscience* 26, no. 23 (2006): 6314–17.

Dymond, D., ed. *A List of Illustrations for Use in History Teaching in Schools.* Pamphlet no. 82. London: The Historical Association, 1930.

Eddy, Matthew Daniel. "The Shape of Knowledge: Children and the Visual Culture of Literacy and Numeracy." *Science in Context* 26, no. 2 (2013): 215–45.

Eisenstein, Zillah. *Global Obscenities: Patriarchy, Capitalism, and the Lure of Cyberfantasy.* New York: NYU Press, 1998.

Ellis, Alec. *A History of Children's Reading and Literature.* Oxford: Pergamon Press, 1968.

Elster, Charles A. "Influences of Text and Pictures on Shared and Emergent Readings." *Research in the Teaching of English* 32, no. 1 (1998): 43–78.

Emmett, Jonathan and Poly Bernatene. *Prince Ribbit.* London: Macmillan Children's Books, 2016.

Felski, Rita. "Introduction." *New Literary History* 45, no. 2 (Spring 2014): v–xi.

Felski, Rita. *The Limits of Critique.* Chicago, IL: The University of Chicago Press, 2015.

Ferguson, Moira. "The Discovery of Mary Wollstonecraft's 'The Female Reader.'" *Signs* 3, no. 4 (1978): 945–57.

Finkelstein, David and Alistair McCleery, eds. *An Introduction to Book History.* 3rd ed. Abingdon: Routledge, 2013.

Fisher, Margery. *Matters of Fact: Aspects of Non-Fiction for Children.* Leicester: Brockhampton Press, 1972.

Fithian, Philip. *Journal & Letters of Philip Vickers Fithian, 1773–1774: A Plantation Tutor of the Old Dominion*, edited by Hunter Dickinson Farish. Williamsburg, VA: Colonial Williamsburg, Incorporated, 1945.

Fletcher of Saltoun. Account of Books Bought by Francis Fletcher, Younger Son of Andrew Fletcher, Lord Milton. *Papers of the Family of Fletcher of Saltoun.* National Library of Scotland. MS 17065.

Fletcher of Saltoun. Library Catalogue for the Family of Fletcher of Saltoun. *Papers of the Family of Fletcher of Saltoun.* National Library of Scotland. MS 17866.

Fletcher of Saltoun. *Papers of the Family of Fletcher of Saltoun.* National Library of Scotland. MS 17890.

Fletcher, Lord Milton. *Saltoun Family Letters.* National Library of Scotland, MS 16688; MS 16746; MS 16693; MS 16503.

Flint, Kate. *The Woman Reader, 1837–1914.* Oxford: Oxford University Press, 1995.

Flood, Alison. "Authors and Readers Rally to Defend Rape Novel from School Ban." *The Guardian*, September 29, 2010. https://www.theguardian.com/books/2010/sep/29/defend-novel-school-ban.

Flood, Alison. "Children's Books Eight Times as Likely to Feature Animal Main Characters than BAME People." *The Guardian*, November 20, 2020. https://www.theguardian.com/books/2020/nov/11/childrens-books-eight-times-as-likely-to-feature-animal-main-characters-than-bame-people.

Foreman, Michael. *The Little Bookshop and the Origami Army!* London: Andersen Press, 2015.

Fowler, Bridget. *Reading Bourdieu on Society and Culture.* Keele: Blackwell Publishing/The Sociological Review, 2000.

Freebody, Peter and Allan Luke. "Literacies Programs: Debates and Demands in Cultural Context." *Prospect: An Australian Journal of TESOL* 5, no. 3 (1990): 7–16.

Fuller, Danielle and DeNel Rehberg-Sedo. *Reading beyond the Book*: *The Social Practices of Contemporary Literary Culture.* London: Routledge, 2015.

Gardner, Emelyn E. and Eloise Ramsey. *A Handbook of Children's Literature: Methods and Materials.* Chicago, IL: Scott, Foresman and Company, 1927.

Gee, James P. "The New Literacy Studies and the 'Social Turn.'" Opinion paper. Washington, DC: Institute of Education Sciences (ERIC), 1998. Accessed May 13, 2019, http://jamespaulgee.com/pdfs/The%20New%20Literacy%20Studies%20and%20the%20Social%20Turn.pdf.

Genette, Gérard. *Narrative Discourse: An Essay in Method*, translated by Jane E. Lewin. Ithaca, NY: Cornell UP, 1980.

Genette, Gérard. *Paratexts: Thresholds of Interpretation*, translated by Jane E. Lewin. Cambridge: Cambridge University Press, 1997.

Gerard, Alexander. *An Essay on Genius.* London: W. Strahan, T. Cadell and W. Creech, 1774.

Gest, Scott D., Nicole R. Freeman, Celene E. Domitrovich and Janet A. Welsh. "Shared Book Reading and Children's Language Comprehension Skills: The Moderating Role of Parental Discipline Practices." *Early Childhood Research Quarterly* 19, no. 2 (2004): 319–36.

Glover, Katharine. "The Female Mind: Scottish Enlightenment Femininity and the World of Letters. A Case Study of the Fletcher of Saltoun Family in the Mid-Eighteenth Century." *Journal of Scottish Historical Studies* 25, no. 1 (2005): 1–20.

Goga, Nina. "Learn to Read. Learn to Live: The Role of Books and Book Collections in Picturebooks." In *Picturebooks. Representation and Narration,* edited by Bettina Kümmerling-Meibauer, 201–12. London: Routledge, 2014.

Goldsmith, Evelyn. "Learning from Illustrations: Factors in the Design of Illustrated Educational Books for Middle School Children." *Word and Image* 2, no. 2 (1986): 111–21.

Goldstone, Bette. "The Postmodern Picture Book: A New Subgenre." *Language Arts* 81, no. 3 (2004): 196–204.

Gonzalez, Norma, Luis Moll and Cathy Amanti, eds. *Funds of Knowledge: Theorizing Practices in Households, Communities and Classrooms.* Mahwah, NJ: Lawrence Erlbaum, 2005.

Goodreads. "*Asking for It* by Louise O'Neill." *Goodreads.* Accessed January 20, 2021, https://www.goodreads.com/book/show/25255576-asking-for-it.

Graff, Harvey. "The Literacy Myth: Literacy, Education and Demography." *Vienna Yearbook of Population Research* 8 (2010): 17–23.

Gravett, Emily. *Again!* London: Simon & Schuster, 2011.

Gravett, Emily. *Little Mouse's Big Book of Beasts.* London: Macmillan, 2016.

Gravett, Emily. *Little Mouse's Big Book of Fears.* London: Macmillan, 2007.

Gravett, Emily. *Wolves.* London: Macmillan Children's Books, 2006.

Gray, Mia and Anna Barford. "The Depth of the Cuts: The Uneven Geography of Local Government Austerity." *Cambridge Journal of Regions, Economy and Society* 11 (2018): 541–63.

Greetham, David. "Who's In, Who's Out: The Cultural Poetics of Archival Exclusion." *Studies in the Literary Imagination* 32, no. 1 (1999): 1–28.

Grenby, Matthew O. *The Child Reader, 1700–1840.* Cambridge: Cambridge University Press, 2011.

Grenby, Matthew O. and Kimberley Reynolds. *Children's Literature Studies: A Research Handbook.* Hampshire: Palgrave Macmillan, 2011.

Grenfell, Michael. *Pierre Bourdieu: Education and Training.* London: Continuum Books, 2007.

Grieve, Ann. "Metafictional Play in Children's Fiction." *Papers* 8, no. 3 (1998): 5–15.

Griffing, Harold and Shepherd Franz. "On the Conditions of Fatigue in Reading." *The Psychological Review* 3, no. 5 (1896): 513–30.

Griswold, Wendy. *Regionalism and the Reading Class.* Chicago, IL and London: University of Chicago Press, 2008.

Guillory, John. "Enlightening Mediation." In *This Is Enlightenment*, edited by Clifford Siskin and William Warner, 37–63. Chicago, IL and London: University of Chicago Press, 2010.

Guillory, John. "Literary Capital: Gray's 'Elegy,' Anna Laetitia Barbauld, and the Vernacular Canon." In *Early Modern Conceptions of Property*, edited by John Brewer and Susan Staves, 389–412. London and New York: Routledge, 1996.

Gunne, Sorcha and Zoe Brigley Thompson. "Introduction: Feminism without Borders: The Potentials and Pitfalls of Retheorizing Rape." In *Feminism, Literature and Rape Narratives: Violence and Violation*, edited by Sorcha Gunne and Zoe Brigley Thompson, 1–20. New York and London: Routledge, 2010.

Gunzenhauser, Bonnie. "Introduction." In *Reading in History: New Methodologies from the Anglo-American Tradition*. The History of the Book, no. 6, edited by

Bonnie Gunzenhauser, 2–9. London: Pickering & Chatto, 2010; Abingdon and New York: Routledge, 2016.

Habiba, Ume, Rabia Ali and Asia Ashfaq. "From Patriarchy to Neopatriarchy: Experiences of Women from Pakistan." *International Journal of Humanities and Social Science* 6, no. 3 (2016): 212–21.

Hagglund, Betty. "The Depiction of Literacy, Schooling and Education in the Autobiographical Writings of Eighteenth-Century Scottish Women." In *Women in Eighteenth-Century Scotland: Intimate, Intellectual and Public Lives*, edited by Katie Barclay and Deborah Simonton, 115–32. Farnham: Ashgate, 2013.

Hamilton, Elizabeth. *Letters on Education.* Dublin: for H. Colbert, 1801.

Hamilton, Elizabeth. *Memoirs of the Late Mrs Elizabeth Hamilton.* Vol. 1. London: Longman, Hurst, Rees, Orme and Brown, 1819.

Hamilton, Janet. *Poems, Essays and Sketches.* Glasgow: James Maclehose, 1870.

Hanawalt, L.L. *A Place of Light: The History of Wayne State University.* Detroit, MI: Wayne State University Press, 1968.

Harder, Alyssa, Vivian Howard and DeNel Rehberg Sedo. "Creating Cohesive Community through Shared Reading: A Case Study of One Book Nova Scotia." *Partnerships: The Canadian Journal of Library and Information Practice and Research* 10, no. 1 (2015): 1–21.

Hart, Betty and Todd R. Risley. "The Early Catastrophe." *American Educator* 27, no. 4 (2003): 6–9.

Hartas, Dimitra. "Families' Social Backgrounds Matter: Socio-Economic Factors, Home Learning and Young Children's Language, Literacy and Social Outcomes." *British Educational Research Journal* 37, no. 6 (2011): 893–914.

Hartley, James and Mark Trueman. "A Research Strategy for Designers: The Role of Headings." *Instructional Science* 14, no. 2 (1985): 99–155.

Harvey, David. *A Brief History of Neoliberalism.* Oxford: Oxford University Press, 2005.

Hateley, Erica. "Reading: From Turning the Page to Touching the Screen." In *(Re) imagining the World. Children's Literature Response to Changing Times*, edited by Yan Wu, Kerry Mallan and Roderick McGillis, 1–13. Berlin Heidelberg: Springer-Verlag, 2013.

Hawes, Joseph M. and N. Ray Hiner. "Hidden in Plain View: The History of Children (and Childhood) in the Twenty-First Century." *Journal of the History of Childhood and Youth* 1, no. 1 (2008): 43–49.

Heath, Shirley Brice. "'This Is My Show!' Beyond Reading to Envisioning and Enacting." In *Children as Readers in Children's Literature: The Power of Text and the Importance of Reading*, edited by Evelyn Arizpe and Vivienne Smith, 119–31. London: Routledge, 2016.

Heath, Shirley Brice. *Ways with Words.* Cambridge: Cambridge University Press, 1983.

Heath, Shirley Brice. "What No Bedtime Story Means: Narrative Skills at Home and School." *Language and Society* 11, no. 1 (1982): 49–76.

Heller, Jennifer. *The Mother's Legacy in Early Modern England.* Farnham: Ashgate, 2011.

Hemmerechts, Kenneth, Orhan Agirdag and Dimokritos Kavadias. "The Relationship between Parental Literacy Involvement, Socio-economic Status and Reading Literacy." *Educational Review* 69, no. 1 (2017): 85–101.

Hershinow, Stephanie Insley. *Born Yesterday: Inexperience and the Early Realist Novel*. Baltimore, MD and London: John Hopkins University Press, 2019.

Hewins, Caroline M. *Books for Boys and Girls: A Selected List*. Chicago, IL: American Library Association Publishing Board, 1915.

Hilton, Mary. *Women and the Shaping of the Nation's Young: Education and Public Doctrine in Britain 1750–1850*. London and New York: Routledge, 2007.

Hilton, Mary and Jill Shefrin, eds. *Educating the Child in Enlightenment Britain: Beliefs, Cultures, Practices*. Farnham: Ashgate, 2009.

Hindman, Annemarie H., Carol M. Connor, Abigail M. Jewkes and Frederick J. Morrison. "Untangling the Effects of Shared Book Reading: Multiple Factors and Their Associations with Preschool Literacy Outcomes." *Early Childhood Research Quarterly* 23, no. 3 (2008): 330–50.

Hines, Margaret and Greg Brooks. *Sheffield Babies Love Books: An Evaluation of the Sheffield Bookstart Project*. Sheffield: City of Sheffield, 2005.

Hochuli, Jost and Robin Kinross. *Designing Books: Practice and Theory*. London: Hyphen Press, 1996.

Hogg, James. *Altrive Tales: Featuring a Memoir of the Author*, edited by Gillian Hughes. Edinburgh: Edinburgh University Press, 2003.

Hogg, James. *Memoir of the Author's Life* in *The Poetical Works of the Ettrick Shepherd*. Vol. 5. Glasgow: Blackie and Son, 1840.

Hood, Michelle, Elizabeth Conlon and Glenda Andrews. "Preschool Home Literacy Practices and Children's Literacy Development: A Longitudinal Analysis." *Journal of Educational Psychology* 100, no. 2 (2008): 252–71.

Hounsell, H.E. and James Hilton. "Pictorial History" *A First Course in History Book 1*. Huddersfield: Schofield & Sims, 1937.

Hunt, Peter. "Taken as Read: Readers in Books and the Importance of Reading, 1744–2003." In *Children as Readers in Children's Literature: The Power of Text and the Importance of Reading*, edited by Evelyn Arizpe and Vivienne Smith, 16–27. London: Routledge, 2016.

Husserl, Edmund. *Ideas Pertaining to a Pure Phenomenology and to a Phenomenological Philosophy. First Book: General Introduction to a Pure Phenomenology*. The Hague: Springer Netherlands, 1982.

"Isotype Revisited." www.isotyperevisited.org. Accessed November 2020.

Jajdelska, Elspeth. *Silent Reading and the Birth of the Narrator*. Toronto, ON: University of Toronto Press, 2007.

Jajdelska, Elspeth. "'Singing of Psalms of Which I Could Never Get Enough': Labouring Class Religion and Poetry in the Cambuslang Revival of 1741." *Studies in Scottish Literature* 41, no. 1 (2016): 88–107.

Jajdelska, Elspeth. *Speech, Print and Decorum in Britain, 1600–1750: Studies in Social Rank and Communication*. Abingdon: Routledge, 2016.

Jajdelska, Elspeth. "'The Very Defective and Erroneous Method': Reading Instruction and Social Identity in Elite Eighteenth-Century Learners." *Oxford Review of Education* 36, no. 2 (2010): 141–56.

Jeffers, Oliver. *The Incredible Book Eating Boy.* London: HarperCollins, 2006.

Jeffers, Oliver and Sam Winston. *A Child of Books.* London: Walker Books, 2016.

Johnson, Lorraine and Brian Alderson. *The Ladybird Story: Children's Books for Everyone.* London: The British Library, 2014.

Johnston, Ingrid and Jyoti Mangat. *Reading Practices, Postcolonial Literature, and Cultural Mediation in the Classroom.* Rotterdam: Sense Publishers, 2012.

Jones, Carole. "'Femininity in Crisis': The Troubled Trajectory of Feminism in Laura Hird's *Born Free* and Jenni Fagan's *The Panopticon.*" *Contemporary Women's Writing* 9, no. 3 (2015): 385–400.

Kant, Immanuel. *An Answer to the Question: What is Enlightenment?*, translated by H.B. Nisbet. London and New York: Penguin, 2009.

Karremann, Isabel. "Mediating Identities in Eighteenth-Century England." In *Mediating Identities in Eighteenth-Century England: Public Negotiations, Literary Discourses, Topography*, edited by Isabel Karremann and Anja Müller, 1–16. London: Routledge, 2011.

Kerr, James. *The Fundamentals of School Health.* London: Allen and Unwin, 1926.

Key, Ellen. *The Century of the Child.* New York and London: George Putnam and Sons, 1909.

Kidd, Kenneth B. "The Child, the Scholar, and the Children's Literature Archive." *The Lion and the Unicorn* 35, no. 1 (2011): 1–23.

Kirk, Daniel. *Library Mouse.* New York: Abrams Books for Young Readers, 2007.

Knott, Sarah and Barbara Taylor, eds. *Women, Gender and Enlightenment.* Hampshire: Palgrave MacMillan, 2005.

Knudsen, Michelle and Kevin Hawkes. *Library Lion.* Sommerville, MA: Candlewick Press, 2006.

Kohara, Kazuno. *The Midnight Library.* New York: Roaring Book Press, 2014.

Kress, Gunther. *Literacy in the New Media Age.* London: Routledge, 2003.

Kress, Gunther. "Perspectives on Making Meaning: The Differential Principles and Means of Adults and Children." In *Handbook of Early Childhood Literacy*, edited by Nigel Hall, Jackie Larson and Jackie Marsh, 154–66. London: SAGE, 2003.

Kuhl, Patricia K. "Early Language Learning and Literacy: Neuroscience Implications for Education." *Mind, Brain and Education: The Official Journal of the International Mind, Brain, and Education Society* 5, no. 3 (2011): 128–42.

Kuhlma, Wilma D. and Mary J. Lickteig. "Literacy as Change Agent: Messages about Reading and Writing Children's Literature." *Journal of Children's Literature* 24, no. 2 (1998): 84–93.

Lang, Anouk. "Explicating Explications: Researching Contemporary Reading." In *Reading in History: New Methodologies from the Anglo-American Tradition*, edited by Bonnie Gunzenhauser, 119–34. London: Pickering & Chatto, 2010; Abingdon and New York: Routledge, 2016.

Lang, Anouk. "Introduction: Transforming Reading." In *From Codex to Hypertext. Studies in Print Culture and the History of the Book*, edited by Anouk Lang, 1–24. Amherst, MA: University of Massachusetts Press, 2012.

Lawler, Steph. "Rules of Engagement: Habitus, Power and Resistance." *Sociological Review* 52, no. 2 (2004): 110–28.

Lehman, Barbara. *The Red Book*. Boston, MA: Houghton Mifflin, 2004.

Lennox, Charlotte. *The Female Quixote or the Adventures of Arabella*, edited by Margaret Dalziel. Oxford: Oxford University Press, 1989.

Lewis, David. "Pop-Ups and Fingle-Fangles: The History of the Picture Book." In *Talking Pictures: Pictorial Texts and Young Readers*, edited by Victor Watson and Morag Styles, 5–22. London: Hodder and Stoughton, 1996.

Lewis, David. *Reading Contemporary Picturebooks*. London: Routledge Farmer, 2001.

Lewis, David. "The Constructedness of Texts: Picture Books and the Metafictive." *Signal* 62 (1990): 131–46.

Library of Congress. "Collecting Levels." *Library of Congress*. Accessed June 24, 2019, https://www.loc.gov/acq/devpol/cpc.html.

Lida. *Scaf the Seal*, translated by Rose Fyleman. London: George Allen and Unwin, c. 1938.

Lines, Katherine. *Four to Fourteen. A Library of Books for Children*. Cambridge: National Book League, 1956.

Littau, Karin. *Theories of Reading: Books, Bodies and Bibliomania*. Cambridge: Polity, 2006.

Locke, John. *An Essay Concerning Human Understanding*. Oxford and New York: Oxford University Press, 2008.

Long, Elizabeth. "Textual Interpretation as Collective Action." In *The Ethnographies of Reading*, edited by Jonathan Boyarin, 180–211. Berkeley, CA: University of California Press, 1993.

Lowe, Bronwyn. *"The Right Thing to Read": A History of Australian Girl-Readers, 1910–1960*. New York and Abingdon: Routledge, 2018.

Luke, Allan. *Reading and Critical Literacy: Redefining the Great Debate*. Conference paper, presented at the 18th New Zealand Conference on Reading, Wellington, NZ, 1992.

Lundin, Anne. "A 'Dukedom Large Enough': The de Grummond Archive." *The Lion and the Unicorn* 35, no. 1 (2001): 303–10.

Lundin, Anne. "Introduction." In *Defining Print Culture for Youth*, edited by Anne Lundin and Wayne A. Wiegand, xi–xxii. New York: Libraries Unlimited, 2003.

Lupton, Christina. *Knowing Books: The Consciousness of Mediation in Eighteenth Century Britain*. Philadelphia, PA: University of Pennsylvania Press, 2012.

Lupton, Christina. *Reading and the Making of Time in the Eighteenth Century*. Baltimore, MD: Johns Hopkins University Press, 2018.

Lwin, Soe Marlar. "Capturing the Dynamics of Narrative Development in an Oral Storytelling Performance: A Multimodal Perspective." *Language and Literature* 19, no. 4 (2010): 357–77.

Lynch, Joe. "Madonna Delivers Her Blunt Truth during Fiery, Teary Billboard Women in Music Speech." *Billboard*, December 9, 2016. http://www.billboard.com/articles/events/women-in-music/7616927/madonna-billboard-woman-of-the-year-labrinth.

Macaulay, David. *Black and White*. Boston, MA: Houghton Mifflin Harcourt, 1991.

Mack, Jeff. *Look!* New York: Philomel Books, 2015.

MacKenzie, Emily. *Wanted! Ralfy Rabbit, Book Burglar.* London: Bloomsbury, 2015.

Mackey, Margaret. "Metafiction for Beginners: Allan Ahlberg's *Ten in a Bed.*" *Children's Literature in Education* 21, no. 3 (1990): 179–87.

Mackey, Margaret. "Postmodern Picture Books and the Material Conditions of Reading." In *Postmodern Picturebooks. Play, Parody and Self-Referentiality*, edited by Lawrence R. Sipe and Sylvia Pantaleo, 103–17. London: Routledge, 2008.

MacKinnon, Catharine A. "Rape: On Coercion and Consent." In *Writing on the Body: Female Embodiment and Feminist Theory*, edited by K. Conboy, N. Medina and S. Stanbury, 42–58. New York: Columbia University Press, 1997.

MacKinnon, Catharine A. *Women's Lives, Men's Laws.* 2005. Cambridge and London: The Belknap Press of Harvard University Press, 2007.

Madeley, H.M. *Time Charts.* Pamphlet no. 50. 2nd ed. London: The Historical Association, 1921.

Makin, Laurie. "Literacy 8–12 Months: What Are Babies Learning?" *Early Years* 26, no. 3 (2007): 269–77.

Mallett, Margaret. *Making Facts Matter: Reading Non-Fiction 5–11.* London: Paul Chapman, 1992.

Marie Neurath. *Picturing Science.* https://www.marieneurath.org/.

Marland, Hilary. *Health and Girlhood in Britain, 1874–1920.* Basingstoke: Ashgate, 2013.

Marmot, Michael. *Fair Society, Healthy Lives: The Marmot Review.* London: University College London, 2010.

Marsh, Jackie and Elaine Hallet. *Desirable Literacies: Approaches to Language and Literacy in the Early Years.* London: SAGE, 2008.

Martinez, Miriam and Janis M. Harmon. "Picture/Text Relationships: An Investigation of Literary Elements in Picture Books." *Literacy Research and Instruction* 51, no. 4 (2012): 323–43.

Masc. "Traolach O' Buachalla." Interview. *Masc*, January 30, 2017. https://masc.life/home/2017/1/16/traolach-o-buachalla.

Mathis, Janelle B. and Lindsay Patterson. "Literacy to Inform and Transform: Empowering Lessons from Children's Literature." In *53rd Yearbook of the National Reading Conference*, edited by J. Worthy, 264–80. Oak Creek, WI: National Reading Conference, 2004.

Matthew, Patricia A. "Biography and Mary Wollstonecraft in *Adeline Mowbray* and *Valperga.*" *Women's Writing* 14, no. 3 (2007): 382–98.

Mayne, John. "Contribution Analysis: An Approach to Exploring Cause and Effect." *The Institutional Learning and Change (ILAC) Briefing* 16 (2008). http://bettere-valuation.org/sites/default/files/ILAC_Brief16_Contribution_Analysis.pdf.

McClay, Jill. "'Wait a Second . . .': Negotiating Complex Narratives in Black and White." *Children's Literature in Education* 31, no. 2 (2000): 91–106.

McCulloch, Fiona. *Contemporary British Children's Fiction and Cosmopolitanism.* New York and London: Routledge, 2017.

McCulloch, Fiona. *The Fictional Role of Childhood in Victorian and Early Twentieth Century Children's Literature.* Lewiston, Queenston, and Lampeter: Edwin Mellen Press, 2004.

McDowell, Paula. *The Invention of the Oral: Print Commerce and Fugitive Voices in Eighteenth-Century Britain*. Chicago, IL and London: University of Chicago Press, 2017.

McIntosh, Carey. *The Evolution of English Prose 1700–1800: Style, Politeness, and Print Culture*. Cambridge: Cambridge University Press, 1998.

McKinley, Meg and Leila Rudge. *No Bears*. London: Walker Books, 2013.

McLaughlin, Thomas. *Reading and the Body: The Physical Practice of Reading*. New York: Palgrave Macmillan, 2015.

McRobbie, Angela. "Top Girls?" *Cultural Studies* 21, no. 4–5 (2007): 718–37.

McRobbie, Angela. "Young Women and Consumer Culture." *Cultural Studies* 22, no. 5 (2008): 531–51.

Meek, Margaret. *How Texts Teach What Readers Learn*. Stroud: Thimble Press, 1988.

Meek, Margaret. "The Critical Challenge of the World in Books for Children." *Children's Literature in Education* 26, no. 1 (1995): 5–23.

Melhuish, Edward. "Why Children, Parents and Home Learning Are Important." In *Early Childhood Matters: Evidence from the Effective Pre-School and Primary Education Project*, edited by Kathy Sylva, Edward Melhuish, Pam Sammons, Iram Siraj-Blatchford and Brenda Taggart, 44–69. Abingdon: Routledge, 2010.

Michaels, Carolyn Clugston. *Children's Book Collecting*. Hamden, CT: Library Professional Publications, 1993.

Middleton, Jacob. "The Overpressure Epidemic of 1884 and the Culture of Nineteenth-Century Schooling." *History of Education* 33, no. 4 (2004): 419–35.

Midgley, C. *The Magic Map: An Introduction to the Fascination of Maps*. Exeter: Wheaton, 1935.

Millard, Elaine and Jackie Marsh. "Sending Minnie the Minx Home: Comics and Reading Choices." *Cambridge Journal of Education* 31, no. 1 (2001): 25–38.

Mintah, Alexandria K. "Young Adult Literature: Ethics, Evils, and the Ever-Present Question of Censorship." *Exigence* 2, no. 1 (2018): 1–15.

Mol, Suzanne E. and Adriana G. Bus. "To Read or Not to Read: A Meta-Analysis of Print Exposure from Infancy to Early Adulthood." *Psychological Bulletin* 137, no. 2 (2011): 267–96.

Moles, Kate. "A Walk in Thirdspace: Place, Methods and Walking." *Sociological Research Online* 13, no. 4 (2008). http://www.socresonline.org.uk/13/4/2.html.

Monro, Alexander (Primus). *The Professor's Daughter: An Essay on Female Conduct Contained in Letters from a Father to a Daughter*. Cambridge: Library edition, 1995.

Morris, Pam. "Introduction." In *The Bakhtin Reader: Selected Writings of Bakhtin, Medvedev, Voloshinov*, edited by Pam Morris, 1–24. London and New York: Edward Arnold, 1994.

Morss, Robert D. "The Neglected Schoolbook." *Monotype Recorder* 34, no. 2 (1935): 3–13.

Mozley, Anne. "On Fiction as an Educator." In *A Serious Occupation: Literary Criticism by Victorian Women Writers*, edited by Solveig C. Robinson, 187–207. Peterborough, ON: Broadview Press, 2013.

Murdoch, Alexander. "Literacy." In *The Edinburgh History of the Book in Scotland. Vol. 2, Enlightenment and Expansion, 1707–1800*, edited by Stephen W. Brown and Warren McDougall, 287–96. Edinburgh: Edinburgh University Press, 2012.

Murphy, Emily. "Unpacking the Archive: Value, Pricing, and the Letter-Writing Campaign of Dr. Lena Y. de Grummond." *Children's Literature Association Quarterly* 39, no. 4 (2014): 551–68.

Murray, Padmini Ray and Claire Squires. "The Digital Communications Circuit." *Book 2.0* 3, no. 1 (2013): 3–24.

National Audit Office. *Financial Sustainability of Local Authorities*. London: NAO, 2018.

National Book League. *Textbook Design Exhibition. Catalogue of an Exhibition of Books Published between May 1962 and May 1965 and Chosen for the National Book League by G. Fielden Hughes, Ruari McLean and Kenneth Pinnock*. London: National Book League, 1966.

Navarro, Armando. *Global Capitalist Crisis and the Second Great Depression: Egalitarian Systemic Models for Change*. Plymouth: Lexington Books, 2012.

Nelson, Claudia. "Writing the Reader: The Literary Child in and beyond the Book." *Children's Literature Association Quarterly* 31, no. 3 (2006): 222–36.

Nelson, James. *An Essay on the Government of Children*. London: for R. and J. Dodlsey, 1753.

Neurath, Marie. "Report on the Last Years of Isotype Work." *Synthese* 8, no ½ (1950–51): 22–27.

Neurath, Otto. *International Picture Language*. London: Kegan Paul, Trench, Trubner & Co., Ltd, 1936.

New London Group. "A Pedagogy of Multiliteracies: Designing Social Futures." *Harvard Educational Review* 66, no. 1 (1996): 60–92.

Nikolajeva, Maria. "Picturebooks and Emotional Literacy." *The Reading Teacher* 67, no. 4 (2013): 249–54.

Nikolajeva, Maria. *Reading for Learning: Cognitive Approaches to Children's Literature*. Children's Literature, Culture, and Cognition, edited by Nina Christensen, Elina Druker and Bettina Kümmerling-Meibauer, vol. 3. Amsterdam: John Benjamins, 2014.

Nikolajeva, Maria. "Reading Other People's Minds through Word and Image." *Children's Literature in Education* 43 (2012): 273–29.

Nikolajeva, Maria. "Verbal and Visual Literacy: The Role of Picturebooks in the Reading Experience of Young Children." In *Handbook of Early Childhood Literacy*, edited by Nigel Hall, Jackie Larson and Jackie Marsh, 235–48. London: SAGE, 2003.

Nikolajeva, Maria and Carole Scott. *How Picture Books Work*. London: Psychology Press, 2001.

Nikolajeva, Maria and Carole Scott. "The Dynamics of Picturebook Communication." *Children's Literature in Education* 31, no. 4 (2000): 225–39.

Noble, Kimberly G., Martha J. Farah and Bruce D. McCandliss. "Socioeconomic Background Modulates Cognition-Achievement Relationships in Reading." *Cognitive Development* 21, no. 3 (2006): 349–68.

Nodelman, Perry. *The Hidden Adult: Defining Children's Literature*. Baltimore, MD: Johns Hopkins University Press, 2008.

Office of National Statistics. "Child Poverty and Education Outcomes by Ethnicity." 2007. https://www.ons.gov.uk/economy/nationalaccounts/uksectoraccounts/

compendium/economicreview/february2020/childpovertyandeducationoutcome
sbyethnicity.

O'Malley, Andrew. *The Making of the Modern Child: Children's Literature and Childhood in the Late Eighteenth Century.* London: Routledge, 2003.

O'Neill, Louise. *Asking for It.* London: Quercus, 2015.

O'Neill, Louise. "Louise O'Neill: 'I Think this Book Will Infuriate a Lot of People because It's Going to Push those Buttons'." Interview by Patrick Sproull. *The Guardian*, September 2, 2015. https://www.theguardian.com/childrens-books-site /2015/sep/02/louise-oneill-asking-for-it-interview.

Open Education Database. "Your Brain on Books: 10 Things that Happen to Our Minds When We Read." n.d. https://oedb.org/ilibrarian/your-brain-on-books-10 -things-that-happen-to-our-minds-when-we-read/.

Opie, Amelia. *Adeline Mowbray.* Oxford and New York: Oxford University Press, 1999.

Osborne, Thomas. "The Ordinariness of the Archive." *History of the Human Sciences* 12, no. 2 (1999): 51–64.

Pahl, Kate. "Habitus in the Home: Texts and Practices in Families." *Ways of Knowing Journal* 2, no. 1 (2002): 45–53.

Pantaleo, Sylvia. "Young Children Interpret the Metafictive in Anthony Browne's *Voices in the Park.*" *Journal of Early Childhood Literacy* 4, no. 2 (2004): 211–233.

Pardeck, John T. and Jean Pardeck, eds. *Bibliotherapy: A Clinical Approach for Helping Children.* Yverdon, Paris, and Reading: Gordon and Breach Science Publishers, 1993.

Park, Hyunjoon. "Home Literacy Environments and Children's Reading Performance: A Comparative Study of 25 Countries." *Educational Research and Evaluation* 14, no. 6 (2008): 489–505.

Patchett, T.S. "A Visual Geography of the World" *Book 1 Africa and Australasia.* London: Educational Publishing Company, 1950.

Pawley, Christine. "Beyond Market Models and Resistance: Organizations as a Middle Layer in the History of Reading." *The Library Quarterly* 79, no. 1 (2009): 79–93.

Peeck, Joan. "Increasing Picture Effects in Learning from Illustrated Text." *Learning and Instruction* 3, no. 3 (1993): 227–38.

Phipps, Alison. "Intercultural Ethics: Questions of Methods and Intercultural Communication." *Language and Intercultural Communication* 13, no. 1 (2013): 10–26.

Phoenix, Anne and Fatima Husain. *Parenting and Ethnicity.* York: Joseph Rowntree Foundation, 2007.

Potkay, Adam. *The Fate of Eloquence in the Age of Hume.* Ithaca, NY: Cornell University Press, 1994.

Power, S., M. Rhys, C. Taylor and S. Waldron. "How Child Centred Education Favours Some Learners More than Others." *Review of Education* 7, no. 3 (2019): 570–92.

Pressman, Jessica. "The Aesthetic of Bookishness in Twenty-First-Century Literature." *The Michigan Quarterly Review* 48, no. 4 (2009): 465–82.

Pressman, Jessica. "'There's Nothing Quite Like a Real Book:' Stop-Motion Bookishness." In *The Printed Book in Contemporary American Culture: Medium,*

Object, Metaphor, edited by Heike Schaefer and Alexander Starre, 155–76. London: Palgrave Macmillan, 2019.

Price, Leah. *How to Do Things with Books in Victorian Britain*. Princeton, NJ, and Oxford: Princeton University Press, 2012.

Price, Leah. "Reading: The State of the Discipline." *Book History* 7 (2004): 303–20.

Projansky, Sarah. *Watching Rape: Film and Television in Postfeminist Culture*. New York and London: New York University Press, 2001.

Proulx, François. *Victims of the Book: Reading and Masculinity in Fin-de-Siècle France*. Toronto, ON: University of Toronto Press, 2019.

Radway, Janice. "*Beyond Mary Bailey* and Old Maid Librarians: Reimagining Readers and Rethinking Reading." *Journal of Education for Library and Information Science* 35, no. 4 (1994): 275–96.

Ramsey, Eloise. *Papers*. Walter P. Reuther Library, Wayne State University.

Ray, Gordon N. *Books as a Way of Life: Essays*, edited by G. Thomas Tanselle. New York: Grolier Club, Pierpont Morgan Library, 1988.

Reay, Diane. "'It's All Becoming a Habitus': Beyond the Habitual Use of Habitus in Educational Research." *British Journal of Sociology in Education* 25, no. 4 (2004): 431–44.

Redmayne, John. *The Changing Shape of Things*. London: John Murray, 1947.

Redmayne, John. *Transport by Land*. London: John Murray, 1948.

Research Centre for Children, Families and Communities. *The Role of the Bookstart Baby Gifting Process in Supporting Shared Reading*. Canterbury: Canterbury Christ Church University, 2016.

Reynolds, Kimberley. *Left Out: The Forgotten Tradition of Radical Publishing for Children in Britain 1910–1949*. Oxford: Oxford University Press, 2016.

Ricoeur, Paul. *Time and Narrative*. Vol. 1. Chicago, IL: University of Chicago Press, 1990.

Riley, Barbara, Alison Kernoghan, Lisa Stockton, Steve Montague, Jennifer Yessis and Cameron D. Willis. "Using Contribution Analysis to Evaluate the Impacts of Research on Policy: Getting to 'Good Enough.'" *Research Evaluation* 27, no. 1 (2017): 16–27.

Rimm-Kaufman, Sara E. and Robert C. Pianta. "An Ecological Perspective on the Transition to Kindergarten: A Theoretical Framework to Guide Empirical Research." *Journal of Applied Developmental Psychology* 21, no. 5 (2000): 491–511.

Robson, Nicola. "Information Books for Children: Their Visual Anatomy and Evolution (1960 to 2005)." Unpublished PhD thesis. Department of Typography & Graphic Communication, University of Reading, 2007.

Rodriguez-Brown, Flora. "Family Literacy: A Current View of Research on Parents and Children Learning Together." In *Handbook of Reading Research Volume IV*, edited by Michael Kamil, David Pearson, Elizabeth Moje Birr and Peter Afflerback, 726–53. London: Routledge, 2011.

Rogerson, Ian. *Noel Carrington and His Puffin Picture Books*. Exhibition Catalogue. Manchester: Manchester Polytechnic Library, 1992.

Rose, Jacqueline. *The Case of Peter Pan of the Impossibility of Children's Fiction.* 1984. Philadelphia, PA: Pennsylvania University Press, 1992; London: Macmillan Press, 1994.

Rose, Jonathan. *The Intellectual Life of the British Working Classes.* New Haven, CT: Yale University Press, 2001.

Rosenblatt, Louise M. "The Aesthetic Transaction." *Journal of Aesthetic Education* 20, no. 4 (1986): 122–28.

Rothstein, Eric. *Systems of Order and Inquiry in Later Eighteenth-Century Fiction.* Berkley, Los Angeles, CA, and London: University of California Press, 1975.

Rous, Francis. *The Psalms of David in Meeter,* modified by the General Assembly of the Church of Scotland, translators. Edinburgh: printed by Evan Tyler, 1650.

Rowland, Lucy and Ben Mantle. *Little Red Reading Hood.* London: Macmillan, 2018.

Rowland, T.J.S. *Living Things for Lively Youngsters.* London: Cassell, 1933.

Rubin, Joan Shelley. "What Is the History of the History of Books?" *The Journal of American History* 90, no. 2 (2003): 555–75.

Rudd, David. *Reading the Child in Children's Literature: An Heretical Approach.* London: Palgrave Macmillan, 2013.

Rule, Andrew. *Diary.* National Library of Scotland. Advocates MS 34.7.12.

Ruzzier, Sergio. *This Is Not a Picture Book!* San Francisco, CA: Chronicle Books, 2016.

Ryan, Mary and Michele Anstey. "Identity and Text: Developing Self-Conscious Readers." *Australian Journal of Language and Literacy* 26, no. 1 (2003): 9–22.

Sanchez-Eppler, Karen. "In the Archives of Childhood." In *Children's Table: Childhood Studies and the Humanities,* edited by Anna Mae Duane, 213–37. Atlanta, GA: University of Georgia Press, 2013.

Sanders, Joe Sutliff. "The Critical Reader in Children's Metafiction." *The Lion and the Unicorn* 33, no. 3 (2009): 349–61.

Sawyer, Charles J. and F.J. Harvey Darton. *English Books 1475–1900: A Signpost for Collectors.* London: Chas. J. Sawyer, Ltd, 1927.

Schwartz, Joan M. and Terry Cook. "Archives, Records, and Power: The Making of Modern Memory." *Archival Science* 2 (2002): 1–19.

Schwebel, Sara. "Taking Children's Literature Scholarship to the Public." *Children's Literature Association Quarterly* 38, no. 4 (2013): 470–75.

Scottish Book Trust. "About Us." Accessed January 28, 2022. https://www.scottish-booktrust.com/.

Sedo, DeNel Rehberg. "Cultural Capital and Community in Contemporary City-Wide Reading Programs." *Mémoires du Livre: Studies in Book Culture* 2, no. 1 (2010). https://www.erudit.org/en/journals/memoires/2010-v2-n1-memoires3974/045314ar/.

Sénéchal, Monique and Jo-Anne LeFevre. "Continuity and Change in the Home Literacy Environment as Predictors of Growth in Vocabulary and Reading." *Child Development* 85, no. 4 (2014): 1552–68.

Sénéchal, Monique and Laura Young. "The Effect of Family Literacy Interventions on Children's Acquisition of Reading from Kindergarten to Grade 3: A Meta-Analytic Review." *Review of Educational Research* 78, no. 4 (2008): 880–907.

Serafini, Frank. "Expanding the Four Resources Model: Reading Visual and Multi-Modal Texts." *Pedagogies: An International Journal* 7, no. 2 (2012): 150–64.

Serafini, Frank. "Images of Reading and the Reader." *The Reading Teacher* 57, no. 7 (2004): 610–17.

Serafini, Frank. "Paths to Interpretation: Developing Students' Interpretive Repertoires." *Language and Literacy* 17, no. 3 (2015): 118–33.

Shapiro, John, Jim Anderson and Ann Anderson. "Diversity in Parental Storybook Reading." *Early Child Development and Care* 127–128 (1997): 47–59.

Sharpe, William. *A Dissertation upon Genius, Or, an Attempt to Shew that the Several Instances of Distinction, and Degrees of Superiority in the Human Genius are Not, Fundamentally, the Result of Nature, But the Effect of Acquisition.* London: Bathurst, 1755.

Shaw, Marion. *Elijah's Mantle, or, the Memoirs and Spiritual Exercises of Marion Shaw.* Glasgow: printed by John Bryce, 1765.

Sheffield Hallam. *The Contribution of Early Years Bookgifting Programmes to Literacy Attainment: A Literature Review.* Sheffield: Sheffield Hallam University, 2014. https://www.booktrust.org.uk/globalassets/resources/research/final-book-gifting-lit-review.pdf.

Shirley, Betsy Beinecke. *Read Me a Story, Show Me a Book: American Children's Literature, 1690–1988 from the Collection of Betsy Beinecke Shirley.* New Haven, CT: Beinecke Library, Yale University, 1991.

Short, Kathy. "Researching Intertextuality within Collaborative Classroom Learning Environments." *Linguistics and Education* 4, no. 3–4 (1992): 313–33.

Shuttleworth, Sally. *The Mind of the Child: Child Development in Literature, Science and Medicine.* Oxford: Oxford University Press, 2010.

Sierra, Judy and Marc Brown. *Wild about Books.* London: Frances Lincoln, 2004.

Simms, Eva-Maria. "Questioning the Value of Literacy: A Phenomenology of Speaking and Reading in Children." In *Handbook of Research on Children's and Young Adult Literature*, edited by Wolf, Coats, Enciso and Jenkins, 20–31. New York and London: Routledge, 2011.

Simpson, James. *Burning to Read: English Fundamentalism and Its Reformation Opponents.* Cambridge, MA: Harvard University Press, 2007.

Sipe, Lawrence. "How Picture Books Work: A Semiotically Framed Theory of Text-Picture Relationships." *Children's Literature in Education* 29, no. 2 (1998): 97–108.

Sipe, Lawrence and Caroline McGuire. "The Stinky Cheese Man and Other Fairly Postmodern Picture Books for Children." In *Shattering the Looking Glass: Challenge, Risk and Controversy in Children's Literature*, edited by Susan Lehr, 273–88. Norwood, MA: Christopher-Gordon Publishers, 2008.

Siskin, Clifford and William Warner, eds. *This Is Enlightenment.* Chicago, IL and London: University of Chicago Press, 2010.

Siskin, Clifford and William Warner. "If this Is Enlightenment Then What Is Romanticism?" *European Romantic Review* 22, no. 3 (2011): 281–91.

Slater, J. Herbert. *Round and about the Book-Stalls: A Guide for the Book-Hunter.* London: L. U. Gill, 1891.

Smith, Adam. *Lectures on Rhetoric and Belles Lettres*, edited by J.C. Bryce. Oxford: Clarendon Press, 1983.

Smith, Lane. *It's a Book*. London: Macmillan Children's Books, 2010.

Smith, S.E. "Silence is the Problem: The Darkness of Young Adult Fiction and Why #YAsaves." *Global Comment*, June 7, 2011. http://globalcomment.com/the-darkness-of-young-adult-fiction-and-why-yasaves/.

Smith, Vivienne. *Making Reading Mean*. Royston, Herts: UKLA, 2005.

Smout, T.C. "Born again at Cambuslang: New Evidence on Popular Religion and Literacy in Eighteenth-Century Scotland." *Past and Present* 97 (1982): 114–27.

Snow, Catherine and Anat Ninio. "The Contracts of Literacy: What We Learn from Learning to Read Books." In *Emergent Literacy: Writing and Reading*, edited by William Teale and Elizabeth Sulzby, 116–138. Norwood, NJ: Ablex, 1986.

Son, Seung-Hee and Frederick J. Morrison. "The Nature and Impact of Changes in Home Learning Environment on Development of Language and Academic Skills in Preschool Children." *Developmental Psychology* 46, no. 5 (2010): 1103–18.

Souto-Manning, Mariana. "Negotiating Culturally Responsive Pedagogy through Multicultural Children's Literature: Towards Critical Democratic Literacy Practices in a First Grade Classroom." *Journal of Early Childhood Literacy* 9, no. 1 (2009): 50–74.

Spratt, Jenny and Kate Philip. *An Appraisal of Bookstart in Sighthill*. Edinburgh: Bookstart, 2007.

St Clair, William. *The Reading Nation in the Romantic Period*. Cambridge: Cambridge University Press, 2004.

Stephenson, E.M. "Nature at Work." *Primary Series, Book 1*. London: A&C Black, c. 1940.

Steuart, Amelia. *Diary of Amelia Steuart of Dalguise. Journals of Mrs Steuart of Dalguise*. National Library of Scotland MS 983.

Stiff, Paul, ed. *Modern Typography in Britain: Graphic Design, Politics and Society, Typography Papers 8*. London: Hyphen Press, 2009.

Stiff, Paul. "Showing a New World in 1942: The Gentle Modernity of Puffin Picture Books." *Design Issues* 23, no. 4 (Autumn 2007): 22–38.

Storrs, Carina. "This Is Your Child's Brain on Reading." *CNN*, February 3, 2016. https://edition.cnn.com/2015/08/05/health/parents-reading-to-kids-study/index.html.

Street, Brian. *Literacy in Theory and Practice*. Cambridge: Cambridge University Press, 1984.

Styles, Morag and Mary Anne Wolpert. "What Else Can this Book Do?" In *Children as Readers in Children's Literature: The Power of Text and the Importance of Reading*, edited by Evelyn Arizpe and Vivienne Smith, 93–106. London: Routledge, 2016.

Sylva, Kathy, Edward Melhuish, Pam Sammons, Iram Siraj-Blatchford and Brenda Taggart. *The Effective Provision of Pre-school Education Project: Final Report: A Longitudinal Study Funded by the Dfes 1997–2004*. London: Institute of Education, University of London/Department for Education and Skills/Sure Start, 2004.

Talley, Lee A. "Young Adult." In *Keywords for Children's Literature*, edited by Philip Nel and Lissa Paul, 228–32. New York and London: New York University Press, 2011.

Tamir, Diana I., Andrew B. Bricker, David Dodell-Feder and Jason P. Mitchell. "Reading Fiction and Reading Minds: The Role of Simulation in the Default Network." *Social Cognitive and Affective Neuroscience* 11, no. 2 (2016): 215–24.

Targ, William, ed. *Bibliophile in the Nursery: A Bookman's Treasury of Collectors' Lore on Old and Rare Children's Books.* Cleveland, OH: World Pub. Co., 1957.

Taylor, Joan Bessman. "Producing Meaning through Interaction: Book Groups and the Social Context of Reading." In *From Codex to Hypertext*, edited by Anouk Lang, 142–158. Amherst, MA: University of Massachusetts Press, 2012.

Tett, Lyn and Jim Crowther. "Families at a Disadvantage: Class, Culture and Literacies." *British Educational Research Journal* 24, no. 4 (1998): 449–60.

Thacker, Deborah Cogan and Jean Webb. *Introducing Children's Literature: From Romanticism to Postmodernism.* London and New York: Routledge, 2002.

The Children's Reading Company. March 18, 2019. https://childrensreadingcompany .com/.

The Children's Reading Connection. March 18, 2019. https://www.childrensreadin gconnection.org/.

The Children's Reading Foundation of the Mid-Colombia. March 18, 2019. read-20minutes.com.

Tizard, Barbara and Martin Hughes. *Young Children Learning: Talking and Thinking at Home and at School.* London: Fontana Press, 1986.

Toffoletti, Kim. "Baudrillard, Postfeminism, and the Image Makeover." *Cultural Politics* 10, no. 1 (2014): 105–19.

Torr, Jane. "The Pleasure of Recognition: Intertextuality in the Talk of Preschoolers during Shared Reading with Mothers and Teachers." *Early Years* 27, no. 1 (2007): 77–91.

Towheed, Shafquat. "Introduction." In *The History of Reading Vol. 3. Methods, Strategies, Tactics*, edited by Rosalind Crane and Shafquat Towheed, 1–12. Basingstoke: Palgrave Macmillan, 2011.

Town, Caren J. *"Unsuitable" Books: Young Adult Fiction and Censorship.* New York: McFarland, 2014.

Towsey, Mark. "Women as Readers and Writers." In *The Cambridge Companion to Women's Writing in Britain, 1660–1789*, edited by Catherine Ingrassia, 21–36. Cambridge: Cambridge University Press, 2015.

Trites, Roberta Seelinger. *Disturbing the Universe: Power and Repression in Adolescent Literature.* Iowa City, IA: University of Iowa Press, 2000.

Trites, Roberta Seelinger. *Twenty-First-Century Feminisms in Children's and Adolescent Literature.* MS: University Press of Mississippi, 2018.

Tunnicliffe, Charles. *What to Look for in Winter.* Loughborough: Wills & Hepworth, 1959.

Twyman, Michael. *A History of Chromolithography: Printed Colour for All.* London: British Library, 2013.

Twyman, Michael. "The Bold Idea: The Use of Bold-Looking Types in the Nineteenth Century." *Journal of the Printing Historical Society* 22 (1993): 107–43.

Twyman, Michael. "The Emergence of the Graphic Book in the 19th Century." In *A Millennium of the Book: Production, Design and Illustration in Manuscript and Print,* edited by Robin Myers and Michael Harris, 135–80. Winchester: St Paul's Bibliographies, 1994.

Twyman, Michael. "Typography without Words." *Visible Language* 15, no. 1 (181): 5–12.

Van Kleeck, Anne. "Research on Book Sharing: Another Critical Look." In *On Reading Books to Children: Parents and Teachers,* edited by Anne van Kleeck, Steven A. Stahl and Eurydice B. Bauer, 271–320. New York: Routledge, 2003.

Vernon, Magdalen D. "The Instruction of Children by Pictorial Illustration." *The Journal of Educational Psychology* 24 (1953): 171–79.

Vernon, Magdalen D. "The Value of Pictorial Illustration." *The Journal of Educational Psychology* 23, no. 1 (1953): 180–87.

Vincent, David. *Bread, Knowledge and Freedom: A Study of Nineteenth-Century Working Class Autobiography.* London: Europa, 1981.

Wakarindi, Jane Wangari. "Abstract," from "Paratext and the Making of YA Fiction Genre: The Repoussoir." *Eastern African Literary and Cultural Studies* 5, no. 12 (August 2019): 1–15.

Walker, Sue. *Book Design for Children's Reading: Typography, Pictures, Print.* London: St Bride Library, 2013.

Walker, Sue. "Explaining History to Children: Otto and Marie Neurath's Work on the 'Visual History of Mankind.'" *Journal of Design History* 24, no. 4 (2012): 345–62.

Walker, Sue. "Graphic Explanation for Children, 1944–1971." In *Isotype. Design and Contexts 1925–1971,* edited by Christopher Burke, Eric Kindel and Sue Walker, 390–437. London: Hyphen Press, 2013.

Walker, Sue, Alison Black, Ann Bessemans, Kevin Bormans, Maarten Renckens and Mark Barratt. "Designing Digital Texts for Beginner Readers; Performance, Practice and Process." In *Learning to Read in a Digital World,* edited by Mirit Barzillai, Jenny Thomson, Sascha Schroeder and Paul van den Broek, 31–56. Amsterdam: John Benjamins Publishing Company, 2018.

Walter, Natasha. *Living Dolls: The Return of Sexism.* London: Virago, 2010.

Warde, Beatrice. "Improving the Compulsory Book." *The Penrose Annual* 44 (1950): 37–40.

Watts, Isaac. *The Improvement of the Mind: Or a Supplement to the Art of Logick.* London: for J. Brackstone and T. Longman, 1749.

Watts, Lynne and John Nisbet. *Legibility in Children's Books: A Review of Research.* Slough: NFER Publishing Company, 1974.

Webb, Harold. "Kingsway Pictorial Science" *Book 3.* London: Evans Brothers Limited, 1950.

Westell, Percival. "Naturecraft Readers." *Book II, In City, Field and Farm.* Edinburgh: McDougall's Educational Co., c. 1940.

What Works Clearinghouse. *Fast Forward Language: English Language Learners.* US Department of Education, Institute of Education Sciences, 2006. https://files .eric.ed.gov/fulltext/ED540656.pdf.

Wheaton. *Catalogue of School Books for Primary Schools.* Exeter: Wheaton, 1957.

Whitehurst, Graver J. and Christopher J. Lonigan. "Child Development and Emergent Literacy." *Child Development* 69, no. 3 (1998): 848–72.

Whyman, Susan. *The Pen and the People: English Letter Writers 1660–1800.* Oxford: Oxford University Press, 2009.

Wiesner, David. *The Three Pigs.* Boston, MA: Houghton Mifflin Harcourt, 2001.

Williams, Abigail. *The Social Life of Books: Reading Together in the Eighteenth-Century Home.* New Haven, CT: Yale University Press, 2017.

Williams-Ellis, Amabel. *How You Began: A Child's Introduction to Biology.* London: Gerald Howe Ltd, 1928.

Witherspoon, John. *The Selected Writings of John Witherspoon*, edited by Thomas P. Miller. Southern Illinois University Press, 1990.

Withrington, D.J. "The S.P.C.K. and Highland Schools in Mid-Eighteenth Century." *Scottish Historical Review* XLI 132 (1962): 89–99.

Wolf, Maryanne. "Skim Reading Is the New Normal. The Effect on Society Is Profound." *The Guardian*, August 25, 2018. https://www.theguardian.com/commentisfree/2018/aug/25/skim-reading-new-normal-maryanne-wolf.

Wolf, Naomi. *Vagina: A New Biography.* London: Virago, 2012.

Wolf, Shelby A., Karen Coats, Patricia Enciso and Christine A. Jenkins, eds. *The Routledge Handbook of Research on Children's and Young Adult Literature.* New York and London: Routledge, 2011.

Wollstonecraft, Mary. *A Short Residence in Sweden.* London and New York: Penguin Classics, 1987.

Wollstonecraft, Mary. *A Vindication of the Rights of Woman with Strictures on Political and Moral Subjects.* London: J. Johnson, 1796.

Wright, Louis B. *Middle-Class Culture in Elizabethan England.* Chapel Hill, NC: University of Carolina Press, 1935.

Yates, Louise. *Dog Loves Books.* London: Jonathan Cape, 2010.

Yates-Bradley, Emma. "Review: Jeanette Winterson in Conversation with Louise O'Neill." *Northern Soul*, February 24, 2016. https://www.northernsoul.me.uk/louise-o-neill.

Ylla and Paulette Falconnet. *Two Little Bears.* London: Hamish Hamilton, 1954.

Yonge, Charlotte Mary. *What Books to Lend and What to Give.* London: National Society's Depository, 1887.

Zaleski, Kristen L., Kristin K. Gundersen, Jessica Baes, Ely Estupinian, and Alyssa Vergara. "Exploring Rape Culture in Social Media Forums." *Computers in Human Behaviour* 63 (2016): 922–27.

Zubatsky, David. "The History of American Colleges and Their Libraries in the Seventeenth and Eighteenth Centuries: A Bibliographical Essay." *Occasional Papers* 140. Champaign, IL: University of Illinois Graduate School of Library Science, October 1979.

Index

About the Authors

Suzan Alteri is the curator of the Arne Nixon Center of Children's Literature at California State University Fresno. Previous positions have been at the University of Florida and Wayne State University. Recent publications include the digital bibliography project "Guiding Science: Publications from the Romantic and Victorian Ages," and others have appeared in *Digital Humanities Quarterly*, the *Journal of Interactive Teaching and Pedagogy*. Her research interests are varied but focus on text and bibliographic analysis of women-authored science books for children, women book collectors, archival pedagogy, and diversity and racism in children's books.

Evelyn Arizpe holds the chair of Children's Literature at the School of Education, University of Glasgow, and is leader of the Erasmus Mundus Joint Master's Degree program "Children's Literature, Media and Culture." She has taught and published widely both nationally and internationally and has coauthored *Children Reading Picturebooks: Interpreting Visual Texts* (2003/2016) and *Visual Journeys through Wordless Narratives* (2014). She has also coedited *Children as Readers in Children's Literature: The Power of Text and the Importance of Reading* (2016) and *Young People Reading: Empirical Research across International Contexts* (2018). Her current research involves children's literature and the arts in projects on migration, conflict, and peacebuilding funded by the British Academy and the Arts and Humanities Research Council in the UK.

Tracy Cooper joined Scottish Book Trust's Early Years (Bookbug) Team in 2010 after working with a family literacy program in Nova Scotia, Canada. Tracy has an MSc in Developmental Linguistics and a passion for stories, songs, and rhymes. Tracy established Bookbug's flagship training program and has traveled the length and breadth of Scotland to deliver Bookbug Training to inspire and encourage practitioners to creatively and enthusiastically share stories, songs, and rhymes with children and families.

Emma Davidson is a Leverhulme Early Career Senior Research Fellow based at the University of Edinburgh. Emma's broad research interests include public libraries and third spaces, community studies and understanding social infrastructure. Funded by the Leverhulme Trust, she is currently researching the everyday social worlds of the public libraries and the challenges they face under austerity.

Rebecca Davies is associate professor of English Literature at Inland University of Applied Sciences in Norway. She specializes in discussions of motherhood and childhood education, cognition, and intellectual history in the long eighteenth century. Her monograph *Written Maternal Authority and Eighteenth–Century Education in Britain* was published in 2014, and she is currently working on a project examining the relationship between genius and education.

Jennifer Farrar is a lecturer at the University of Glasgow, Scotland, in children's literature and literacies. Her research interests include student teachers' knowledge and use of children's literature and its potential as a vehicle for critical literacies. Her current research explores the intersection of political and critical literacies within initial teacher education. Recently published articles have explored the status of critical literacies in Scottish educational policy (2019) and critical literacy's role in Scotland's new LGBTI-inclusive curriculum (2020).

Anne Marie Hagen is associate professor in English at the Norwegian Defence University College, Oslo, Norway. She specializes in the history of reading and publishing from the nineteenth century to the present, with emphasis on books for children and military life-writing. Her recent research has focused on life-writing in higher education (*Scandinavian Journal of Military Studies* 2019), and the intersection of life-writing genres, gender and heroism in Victorian and Edwardian books for children (chapter forthcoming). She is currently working on fiction and social reading in professional military education, and the interplay between Afghanistan memoirs and public discourses on war.

Elspeth Jajdelska is a senior lecturer in English at the University of Strathclyde. She has published two monographs on the history of reading in the seventeenth and eighteenth centuries, *Silent Reading and the Birth of* *the Narrator* (2007) and *Speech, Print and Decorum in Britain, 1600–1750* (2016). She has also published on laboring class Scottish reading and writing in the eighteenth century, and on the role of paratexts in eighteenth-century readers' experiences of medical books. She is currently working on cognitive accounts of readers' experience of fiction.

Fiona McCulloch is currently an independent scholar. She was Lynn Wood Neag Distinguished Visiting Professor of British Literature at the University of Connecticut in 2015. As well as publishing several peer-reviewed articles, her books include *Contemporary British Children's Fiction and Cosmopolitanism* (2017), *Cosmopolitanism in Contemporary British Fiction: Imagined Identities* (2012), *Children's Literature in Context* (2011), and *The Fictional Role of Childhood in Victorian and Early Twentieth-Century Children's Literature* (2004).

Sue Walker is professor of Typography at the University of Reading, UK and Co-Director of its Centre for Book Cultures and Publishing. She has a long-standing interest in the history, theory and practice of information design. Her publications include *Book Design for Children's Reading* (2013) and articles on the children's books written and designed by Marie Neurath at the Isotype Institute in London in the mid-twentieth century. Her current research involves interdisciplinary working on health communication for young people.